MACMILLAN DOCUMENTS IN

General Editor: Jeremy Black

Published titles

DOCUMENTS ON THE LATER CRUSADES, 1274–1580
Edited and translated by Norman Housley

DOCUMENTS ON THE CONTINENTAL REFORMATION
Edited and translated by William G. Naphy

DOCUMENTS ON THE FRENCH REVOLUTION OF 1848
Edited by Roger Price

Forthcoming titles

DOCUMENTS ON THE FRENCH WARS OF RELIGION
Edited and translated by David Potter

DOCUMENTS ON THE EUROPEAN UNION
Edited and translated by Anjo G. Harryvan and Jan van der Harst

Further titles in preparation

Documents on the Continental Reformation

Edited and translated by William G. Naphy

First published 1996 by
MACMILLAN PRESS LTD
Houndmills, Basingstoke, Hampshire RG21 6XS
and London
Companies and representatives
throughout the world

ISBN 0–333–62859–4 hardcover
ISBN 0–333–62860–8 paperback

A catalogue record for this book is available
from the British Library.

10 9 8 7 6 5 4 3 2 1
05 04 03 02 01 00 99 98 97 96

Typeset in Adobe Garamond by
Stephen Wright/Rainwater Consultancy
Longworth, Oxfordshire

Printed in Hong Kong

For Arlene Naphy
and Paul and Ruth Naphy

Contents

Chapter Four: The Conflict Intensifies   56

Acknowledgements

I would like to express my thanks to Dr Jeremy Black and the editors of Macmillan Press for allowing me to undertake this project, as well as to Dr Andrew Perregree for recommending me to the Press. The task has proved both rewarding and illuminating. My gratitude is also extended to Dr Penny Roberts who was kind enough to supply a translation of the extracts from Pithou. My thanks are also extended to the Bayerische Staatsbibliothek (Munich), the Zentralbibliothek (Zürich) and the InterDocumentation Company (Leiden) and the editors of their *Flugschriften des frühen 16, Jahrhundert* for permission to reproduce the illustrations. I should also like to thank Christine Gascoigne of the Library of St Andrew's University for her assistance in obtaining artwork for reproduction.

Aberdeen

W. G. Naphy

Preface

One of the greatest difficulties facing anyone trying to teach the history of the Reformation is the almost total inability to get students to appreciate, let alone understand, the depth of feeling and the breadth of emotion accompanying the religious debates of the sixteenth century. It seems almost inconceivable to modern students that issues such as predestination, transubstantiation, Purgatory or church statuary could produce so much violence and animosity. Inevitably, they seek to find explanations for this behaviour which are social, political, economic or ethnic. Such motives are comprehensible to the modern mind; religious sentiment is easily discounted as a convenient excuse masking the real reason(s).

Of course, there are very good reasons for assuming that the Reformation is more than simply a debate or dispute about the finer points of theology or religious practice. The sixteenth century was as complicated and as complex a world as our own. It is as impossible to isolate explanations for specific behaviour − not to mention movements − then as now. What is clear, however, is that religious sentiment and belief were an integral part of the world of the average person during the Reformation. The error made by some students when examining the period nowadays is not the tendency to seek out other issues in addition to religious beliefs but to discuss these issues as totally divorced from the religious element. Belief may be viewed − and used − today as no more than a cynical cipher for other goals or ideas but this was most definitely not the case in the sixteenth century. Religion, its spirituality, beliefs and practices were central to the structure of society and foremost in the minds of most people in the Reformation period.

This desire, therefore, to stress the religious element of the Reformation within the context of the other issues of concern to individuals and societies in the sixteenth century has guided the selection of the texts in this volume. There has been no attempt to focus on beliefs nor to place non-religious issues in the forefront; they are left mingled together. If the result is a series of texts which are complex in their presentation of sixteenth-century concerns then they are successfully representing the reality which was Europe during the Reformation.

One concern which I have been keen to communicate through these texts is the very emotional and emotive nature of the debates, and changes which sprang from them. The religious discussions were of great interest to most people in society and they were concerned to understand the matters under debate and to participate in formulating the conclusions which resulted. People in the Early Modern period took a personal interest in these debates because they touched upon beliefs and issues which were of grave concern to them individually. They were supremely concerned about their relationship to God (who was more than able, in their mind, to punish them and their communities for wrong beliefs and practices), their future and eternal state (Heaven or Hell) and the fate of their ancestors (likewise, Heaven or Hell). In short, the people of the sixteenth century were rarely idle, apathetic bystanders in the process of promoting or resisting the ideas which appeared during the Reformation.

Also, I have tried to show the wide range of avenues available for spreading the new ideas. Because most will be aware of the important role of the printing press in this process I have endeavoured to highlight the crucial part played in this by individuals propagating the reform ideas by word-of-mouth. Thus, the work of ministers, missionaries, and travelling merchants has been given a primary place in the documents selected. Since the majority of people were illiterate this is probably more representative of how most individuals initially encountered Reformation ideas. Moreover, it helps students to understand how the Reformation was able to spread so widely and so quickly amongst communities almost wholly illiterate.

One particular feature of this movement which seemed well worth touching upon in a number of documents was its violence. The degree to which the Reformation ripped Early Modern societies apart is quite important. Admittedly, it is true that those same societies were often put back together again in a very familiar (and similar) pattern. The threat which this violence posed as well as the desire to control it – and also to use it – are highlighted in the extracts. It is this particular aspect which modern students find so difficult to appreciate: religion was an element of European society capable of producing extreme emotions and violent passions.

Thus, one will see iconoclasm (the most obvious example of this tendency towards violence) treated in detail. However, the potential for the new ideas to cause riots, intercommunal fighting, family disruptions will also be touched upon. Thus, one will see street disputes, sermons interrupted, and churches sacked. Also, the most extreme forms of violent reaction to the new ideas – murder, massacre and execution – will be noted. The hope is that this will help students appreciate the authenticity of interest in the Reformation and the liveliness of the debate as well as the disorder accompanying the disputes. The Reformation (that is, the correct form and place of religion in society) was much more than a clinical discussion of esoteric theological issues which, upon occasion, excited some popular interest. It was the central issue for individuals, societies and nations for over a century.

In this context of riot and disorder it seemed essential to allow the chaotic mix of voices to be heard. As a result, the documents have been drawn from memoirs, diaries, court cases, letters and eye-witness accounts. In general, I have attempted to avoid the more 'official' accounts of events, the histories. A warning must be raised at this point. Readers should be aware of the fact that all these documents represent the point of view of an educated élite. Even in court documents where 'common people' are heard giving testimony, their words are being mediated by the secretary or scribe recording the case. However, by using documents which have a journalistic feel to them, one hopes that the emotions and enthusiasm of the events will be communicated to the student.

Also, there has been an attempt to emphasise one other aspect of the violence of the Reformation, namely, the extent to which this is a clash of ideas, a dispute – an argument. Thus, where the voices and ideas of the 'leading men' are presented they will be found in the midst of debate. Just as official histories have been avoided so have the more formal publications and treatises of the leading reformers and their opponents. Hearing them argue in debates and discussion halls allows their activities to fit naturally into the process of debate and argument (in churches, streets and family homes) noted elsewhere. In a very real sense the Reformation is not a pronouncement but an argument, more often a shouting-match than a debate.

Perhaps some specific remarks on the choice of the sources themselves would be useful. The reader and, more importantly, the teacher will immediately notice that there is an almost total lack of documents by the great leaders of the Reformation. This has been intentional. Many of the letters, treatises, and books of these men are already available elsewhere in English translations. There seemed little reason to reduplicate that work. Also, for the reasons given above, there has been an attempt to present the voices, memories, opinions and ideas of individuals who were less central to the great events but who were on the cutting edge of the ebb and flow of the ideas.

One important exception has been made to this general approach. I have included a number of letters by Erasmus. These are meant to serve as commentary, even asides, on the other documents and the events they relate. As the great moderate and universal critic Erasmus seemed ideal for this task. Also, it meant there was less need for interpretation to be provided by the editor. While I have provided information on each document, I have tried to limit that to setting the necessary context. If the documents are meant to provide the reader with access to the events and ideas of the Reformation then it seemed reasonable to allow the interpretation to proceed from a contemporary source as well.

In addition to avoiding the utterances of the best-known reformers, I have also tried to rely less on the more 'official' and impersonal documents produced in the period. Thus, theological works, commentaries, educational materials, catechisms, etc., will be noticeable for their absence. This is not to imply that these documents were not important to the Reformation process (even less for the process of confessionalisation as the century progressed). Instead, these have been omitted for two reasons. First, as with the writings of the leading reformers, they are often already available in English. Second, these have a way of leading the reader to feel that the Reformation was both boring and wholly interested in fine points of doctrine. The emphasis, thus, is on the practical spread of the Reformation rather than the theoretical elements being spread. If students are to understand and appreciate the Reformation as a vibrant, powerful movement capable of shaking nations and re-ordering societies then it would seem reasonable to avoid such documents.

Therefore, the documents which have been selected have been chosen because they give the greatest possible insight into the complexity of the movement which convulsed Europe in the sixteenth century. The documents are intended to give the student access to the widest number of issues which became entangled in the calls for religious reform. Documents which recorded and reported the events in all their complexities seemed best able to do this. They also have the advantage, as noted above, of evidencing the strength of feeling accompanying those very events.

A similar idea lies behind the translations which have been prepared. In most cases the language of the original is much too complex if translated literally. The use of long sentences with innumerable dependent clauses produces a form of English which is both confusing and (often) impenetrable to modern readers. Worse still, literal renderings will often lead readers to wonder how anyone could have ever become enthusiastic about such things. A difference in approach to literary expression should not be allowed to obscure the meaning or to create the impression that the entire movement was, by definition, boring.

The vibrant spirit of these documents, the overwhelming importance (to contemporaries) of their contents, the violent emotions generated by the new ideas, and the enthusiasm of the adherents of both sides should not be lost in translation. As a result, I have tried to translate these as often as possible into contemporary, colloquial English. Obviously, my readers will be left to decide to what extent I have been successful. However, I freely confess that the specialist may find the translations very free indeed. I can only hope that they will accept that I have provided these documents first and foremost for the use of students approaching the Reformation (and perhaps Early Modern history) for the first time. Thus, in choosing between accuracy and accessibility I have erred on the side of the latter.

Specialists may find reason to complain about the small number of illustrations which have been included. It is perhaps possible to argue that in any examination of an age of widespread illiteracy that more emphasis should have been placed on visual forms of communication and propaganda. However, it is widely accepted that most (urban) people had access to the printed word either through basic literacy or knowing someone who could read. Nevertheless, the visual form was still important. It is crucial that the 'reader' of these illustrations avoids the temptation to view them solely, or primarily, as works of art, i.e. beautiful woodcuts. They are, in fact, the Early Modern equivalent of our satirical political cartoons. If one bears this in mind, it should be possible to approach these cartoons and, indeed, read them as contemporaries would have.

Taken together, one hopes that students will have some sense of the scope of involvement and interest in the spreading religious ideas which existed in the sixteenth century. In individuals and nations the Reformation exposed a raw nerve. However, the debate was rarely ever confined, or confinable to religious matters alone. Once the questioning began (of that most important of concerns, religion) nothing remained sacred. Social, ethnic, economic and political groups and concerns all became part of the spreading demands for change and, later, the official attempts to limit that very change. The Reformation was a confused and confusing time; the documents make no attempt to simplify it.

References to Sources and Suggested Readings

Each extract is accompanied by a reference in **bold** type which combines numbers and letters. These refer to the appropriate source for the extract as well as the relevant volume, page, or text number in the original. Also, each chapter (and some documents) are accompanied by 'Suggested Readings' and then a series of numbers. These correspond to the works listed in the 'Suggested Readings' section (pp. 151–169) at the end of the volume. This system, while cumbersome, allowed all the elements of the bibliography to be found in one place.

1 Warning Signs Appear

'I myself, God is my witness, have heard the grumbling, the muttering, and the threats of popular revolt'

[*Suggested readings*: 84, 85, 126, 139, 140, 172, 193, 208, 223, 240, 276, 286, 288, 290, 308, 322, 323, 336, 337, 341, 360, 366, 371, 373, 382, 390, 404, 406, 421, 435, 439, 442, 443, 452, 470, 479]

1   Erasmus to Thomas More, English Humanist, author of Utopia

Erasmus was often attacked for his attacks on abuses within the Church. He used satire to ridicule the behaviour of the leadership and so was seen to be bringing the structure 'into disrepute'. By using satire, he produced a critique which was easily accessible to the average person (even when they were illiterate and had to have the criticism read to them). This made his attacks all the more dangerous and devastating.

Paris (?), June [1511]

[**A2: no. 222.**1–77 – on Erasmus: 9, 47, 65, 66, 98, 100, 117, 180, 195, 198, 199, 267, 298, 318, 365, 376, 377, 378, 379, 394, 456, 472]

There is nothing more ridiculous than treating a serious subject ridiculously. Obviously, therefore, there is nothing funnier than treating nonsense in such a way as to show that one has actually been talking about everything except nonsense. As for me, others can decide. But, unless my conceit has blinded me, I have praised foolishness without being a complete fool.

Next to refute the criticism against criticising. Intelligent men have always been allowed, with wit and without consequence, to mock society's customs as long as the freedom did not descend to ranting. The thin-skins of modern people amaze me; apparently they cannot bear anything except high-flown titles. Moreover, there are some so mixed-up religiously that, rather than tolerate the slightest joke at the expense of the Pope or a ruler, they will overlook outrageous insults to Christ – even more so if their wallets are touched. If the lives of men are criticised by someone, but no one is named specifically, is that person really criticising, or is this actually teaching and admonishing? If not, then how many times can I not criticise myself? Anyway, if someone criticises every category of men leaving none out, then the anger is against all abuses rather than any man. Thus, if someone complains that they have been insulted then they reveal a guilty – or worried – conscience. St Jerome wrote similar satires. He was much more direct and biting and did not always leave out the names. I have never mentioned a name and, what is more, I have controlled my pen so that any intelligent reader can see that I am trying to entertain rather than hurt. I have also avoided Juvenal's example and avoided dredging up sleaze; my aim is fun not filth. If this method still fails to make some happy than they should keep this in mind: being laughed at by [the goddess] Folly is acceptable. Since I made her the speaker, her words had to fit her character.

---

2   Reformation of the Emperor Sigismund (Basel, *c.* 1438)

A widely familiar document which went through eight printings in the period 1476–1522. This document highlights the extent to which many Germans had deep-seated complaints against the Roman Church. In addition, these complaints went well beyond criticism of the morals and behaviour of churchmen to include social, economic, political and even ethnic grievances.

[K6 – on German anti-papalism: 51, 52]

Concerning Justice and Punishment

Nowadays even churchmen own serfs. These men ought to defend God and set an example of righteousness and truthfulness for us all. I'll be blunt: Everyone claiming to be a Christian while holding people in bondage should let them go free or lose all their goods and possessions and be forced to do penance. If a monastery does such, it should be levelled. Such a consequence would not displease God....

Defending their property rights is not enough for monasteries. They exploit women and children and, when a father happens to die, they inherit his children. In which book did they find support for this? Who gave them permission? Certainly not the Emperor! The Popes allow it...but this just sentences them to hell....Monks act and rule just like secular lords. This must not be allowed. We must find our real interest and follow our consciences. This is the godly path.

Concerning Guilds

The imperial cities were the birthplace of the guilds. Neither prayers nor charitable works will be able to save the soul of the person who allowed their establishment because they are a great evil in society. The reasons shall become clear.

To begin. The guilds have become too powerful. It is certainly reasonable that three or four guild members have places on the city councils. However, although they should protect and promote the public good, in fact they strive to better the position of their respective trades. Do the councillors step in to punish bakers' undersized loaves or butchers' overpriced meat? Absolutely not! They think, 'If I punish you today you'll punish me tomorrow. You scratch my back, I'll scratch yours'. Public welfare is left to fend for itself, promises are forgotten, truth suffocated, justice killed, and souls go straight to hell...

_____

3 Erasmus to Servatus Roger

Servatus Roger (d. 1540) lived at a monastery in Steyn, and was a very close friend from Erasmus's youth. Erasmus was especially critical of aspects of the monastic orders. They were often the target of reformers as they often were large landowners and seen as dens of vice. In addition, their image was tarnished by the fierce competition and rivalry between the various orders.

Calais, 8 July 1514

[A2: no. 296. 23–190, passim]

We say that godliness depends on a place, upon a style of clothes, a pattern of living, upon outward activities. We say that changing white clothes for black does someone in, or the exchange of a hood for a cap or even a change of residence. These rituals may have come from a sense of religious zeal but I think that serious harm has been done to Christian godliness by them. From their start they have mushroomed and a million different types have appeared. Because of the leniency and indulgence of the Popes the whole situation has been made worse. There is nothing more vile and ungodly than this sort of loose religious behaviour. I doubt that any one could identify Christ's image – except for a few meaningless Jewish-like practices – in any of these even if you limited your examination to the better kind, even to the best kind. Nevertheless they use these as an excuse to put on airs and look down their noses at everyone else. It is more in keeping with Christ's ideals to consider all Christians to be of one family, one monastery, to treat everyone like a fellow canon or fellow brother, to hold baptism to be the most important religious profession. One should not dwell on where one lives but how one lives.

_____

4 Enea Silvio Piccolomini (later Pope Pius II) on Martin Mair's 'Complaints of the German Nation'

Taken from a famous, published dispute in which Enea Silvio Piccolamini refuted the earlier arguments of Martin Mair, chancellor to the Archbishop of Mainz. In effect, a response to the 'Complaints of the German Nation' raised in 1417 at the Council of Constance. The 'Complaints' only survive in the condensed form produced by Piccolomini for his reply. This document, like the Reformation of Kaiser Sigismund, stresses the complex nature of the relationship between the Germans and the Roman Church, especially its leaders.

Aschaffenburg, 31 August 1457.

[S1, S2:]

Positions in the Church do not go to the best qualified but to the highest bidder. New indulgences are announced every day for only one reason: to enrich Rome.... Law suits are transferred to Rome when it is clear they should be heard in our courts. Every available trickery is used to cheat us – barbarians – of our money.

Our proud nation, famous for its strength and courage which gave it the Imperial power of Rome and made us lord and master of the world, is reduced to begging, burdened by humiliating demands, cowering in the dirt, whimpering miserably. All because of these abuses. Finally, our leaders have begun to wake up and speak out, to consider how to stop these disasters, break the chains, and restore the ancient liberties which they lost.

---

5   Jacob Wimpheling on Piccolomini's Response to Mair

Jacob Wimpheling produced a response to Piccolomini's refutation of the 'Complaints of the German Nation'. The intensity of German feeling against the Church is obvious in this extract. The solutions, as proposed, would have had a far-reaching effect on the entire structure of the Church and, perhaps more importantly, its wealth and patronage.

19 May 1515.

[S1, S2:]

Church money and jobs go to worthless men and Italians.

The more important and valuable jobs are given to people of unproved ability or character.

Few churchmen live where they have their jobs. They have so many parishes that they cannot live in all of them at once. Most do not even recognise their parishioners' faces. Souls are neglected; the churchmen concentrate on worldly rewards.

Worship services are cut back.

Hospitality disappears.

Church laws are meaningless.

Church buildings are falling down.

The churchmen live scandalous lives.

Good, learned, able priests whose abilities might raise the moral and professional level of the clergy abandon their education because they have no hope of success.

The religious profession is divided by competition and hate. Even death is wished on others as well as hate and jealousy.

People are encouraged to get more than one job.

People use crooked lawsuits to collect multiple posts.

Some get positions by bribery.

Some posts just remain empty.

Qualified youths are left unemployed and to live like vagrants.

Leading churchmen lose their power and authority.

The structure of the Church is destroyed....

[The Pope] should ensure that the pure Gospel is preached. False beliefs, blasphemy, and unchristian teachings should be eliminated. The enemies of the faith should be driven off Christian land....

Would not [the Pope] be better off with advisors trained in the Bible and Church laws? By men who can preach? By men who can ease troubled minds in the confessional? Undoubtedly it was inspiration when the Council of Basel was led to order that a third of all Church posts go to men trained in the Bible....

Rome and our gracious Mother Church must reduce the worst of the tax burden placed on our country. She should be gentle and considerate to those men who replace our present Church leaders. The money they have to send to Rome comes from the pockets of poor tradesmen, country pastors, destitute peasants. Many men cannot adequately care for their families because of these taxes. A reduction might prevent a revolution of our fellow countrymen against the Church. I myself, God is my witness, have heard the grumbling, the muttering and the threats of popular revolt.

---

6   Erasmus on the Vernacular Bibles and Lay Interpretations of Scripture

While it is true that the overwhelming majority of people could not read, the importance of a Bible in everyday language should not be underestimated. Most people would have been within range of someone who could read and therefore able to hear the Bible being read in their own language.

1516.

[O1: 96–8 – 70, 76]

In fact, I strongly disagree with the people who do not want the Bible, after it has been translated into everyday language, to be read by the uneducated. Did Christ teach such complex doctrines that only a handful of theologians can understand them? Is Christianity strong in proportion to how ignorant men are of it? Royal secrets may well be best concealed but Christ wants his mysteries told to as many as possible. I want the lowliest woman to read the Gospels and Paul's letters. I want them translated into every language so that not only will the Scots and Irish be able to read and understand them but even the Turk and Saracen. Clearly the first point is that people understand somehow. Some may mock the Bible but a few may be captured by it. I would like to hear a farmer sing scripture as he ploughs, a weaver to keep time to his moving shuttle by humming the Bible, the traveller to make his journey better by such stories. Let all Christian conversation spring from the Bible. Our daily talk shows what sort of person we are. Each man should understand whatever he can and then share whatever he can. Those people who are a bit slow should not be jealous of those ahead and those ahead, in turn, should encourage the rest so that they do not give up. Why must we limit this duty, which is placed on everyone, to only a few? This makes sense. Baptism is given to everyone – and here one sees the first confession of Christian belief – also the other Sacraments and (in the end) immortality as well, without distinction. Why then are doctrines kept only for a few whom most people call theologians or monks. They make up only a tiny section of the Christian population – and I wish they lived more like their names! I am afraid that some theologians are very unlike what their name implies for they are concerned with earthly rather than heavenly matters. The monks, too, claim to embrace Christ's poverty and despise the world and yet they are often very worldly. The true theologian, in my opinion, teaches (by a quality of mind, the expression, the eyes, by a life that has no use for wealth, not by complicated arguments) that Christians should not trust in the things of this world but rely on spiritual supports. For example, that wrongs should not be avenged, that those who wish ill should be wished well, those who deserve ill should get better, that all good men – all part of the same body – should be loved and valued the same. Evil, if it cannot be removed, should be tolerated. Also, people who have lost every possession, or who have given up possessions, or who grieve are blessed and should not be despised. Even death should be welcomed by the true believer since it is really the gateway to eternal life. If anyone, led by the Holy Spirit, preaches or teaches, or exhorts, or spreads or encourages others in such beliefs then that person is a true theologian even if only a manual worker or a weaver. And, if someone's life shows these beliefs then that person is a great teacher of the Church. Some people, even non-Christians, may argue better about angelic knowledge but the duty of a true Christian theologian is to convince us to live like angels without sin's stains.

---

7 Ulrich Wiest (Master Singer, Augsburg, *c.* 1450) on Warmongering German Bishops

In Summer 1449, the Archbishop-Elector of Mainz, Dieter von Erbach, along with eighty-six other princes and lords declared war on the town of Hall in Swabia. The high number of clerics in Germany who were also secular lords, the fragmentation of the German political landscape, and the inevitable in-fighting which this produced was a particular problem in the German Church.

[K1: 366–72, passim]

The poor naïve Christians are innocent even as their blood flows in this war, confessing sins they cannot name. But the Church leaders who should lead the Church, whose godliness should be an ornament for the faith are at the front of the battle in word and deed. The Prince-Bishop of Mainz loves sword and fire. He should stay at home and sing in the choir and beg that he himself be spared the rack and the fire. The Bishop of Eichstätt is there beside him. Babenberg relishes war's games. This is the thanks we get for our donations! The faith built up by the churchmen of old which has stood the test of time is frittered away by these profligate churchmen. We cry out to you, O Lord, in our pain. The outcome is all too clear. Revenge will see all the priests killed. All prophets agree that when God's patience is exhausted He will step in and snap the bishops' pride and lust. He will whip up a whirlwind of anger which will blow the Church away like so much dust. Christians do not give donations to see them wasted on unchristian pomp and partying, on lives that offend God and Christ. Charity pays for tournaments and pageants....With donations they gamble and give parties, with donations they buy, invest and sell for profit, with donations they hire mercenaries for war, with donations they finance a splendid court-life, donations give them money to waste on games and sports, to engage in every silly thing, to supply the bishops' free-time with amusements, to allow them to taste every evil pleasure, to fill their pockets with unneeded wealth....Donations are used to produce contempt for truth and good. Donations become tools of greed, pride, gluttony, apathy, abuse of power. O lord our God, hear our plea. Why do Your servants have to suffer while these greedy bishops just get more arrogant? I beg You, O Lord, bend their stiff and proud hearts, turn their minds from pride and teach them humility.

---

8 The Reformation of the Emperor Sigismund (Basel, *c.* 1438)

Many Germans saw the evils which came from combining clerical and secular power. However, one should be aware of the extent to which leading nobles were also aware that any reduction of the Church's secular power would inevitably benefit them.

[K6]

Concerning the Bishops

Just look at the behaviour of today's bishops. They start wars and cause general unrest. They act just like regular princes which, of course, is what they really are. Instead of being used for honest work in the parish they use the godly donations for this sort of activity – it should not go to finance wars. I think Duke Frederick was absolutely right when he told Emperor Sigismund at Basel that the bishops were blind and it was up to [the princes] to open their eyes....

Bishops should not own castles. They should live in the main church in their diocese and live there like a Christian should. They should be an example to the priests in their diocese. Instead all they do today is ride about like princes. Peace would stand a better chance if this sort of behaviour were abolished....

No priest should be given a church by a bishop unless he can prove his learning by presenting a university diploma. This alone should be the required qualification. The minimum standard for a priest should be a B.A.; cardinals should hold doctorates in Law and Scripture; bishops, doctorates of Scripture and training in Theology and Canon Law....

Everyone knows the harm and suffering caused by giving churches to ignorant, unqualified priests. They cannot preach the Gospel, nor administer the Sacraments. We call them 'blind guides'. If you follow them you just end up in a ditch....

Henceforth, bishops must hold a yearly meeting with the church leaders and priests of their diocese. There, the bishop should read out all the regulations and check to see that everyone is obeying them. He should try to eliminate any fighting amongst his workers....Those who disobey should be warned, then exiled from the diocese. The secular courts should be informed of serious crimes....There should be an organised rule for every church so that there are not a lot of different customs and practices from one to the next. The worship service should follow a uniform pattern, too, which it does not do at the moment. In fact, no two dioceses have the same rules or set prayers....

There should be a yearly inspection, at the bishop's direction, of the diocese by the bishop's assistant and his legal officer. The legal officer should be a priest; such a task should not be entrusted to a layman. Whenever possible the bishop should go on the inspection himself. The costs of these visitations should be paid by the local churches and the bishop....

The local church is the most important part of the Church after the bishop. This is how to restore order to them. There should be two priests in each local church. If the church cannot afford two priests it should be merged with a nearby church. There should be the same salary for every priest and the same responsibilities.

The bishops have been extorting money from the priests and threatening them with lawsuits. This has been one of the causes of the ill-will between the bishops and the priests. For example, they blackmail the priests who have mistresses; they are afraid of being fired and excommunicated and so they pay money to keep the bishop quiet. The bishop gets the money he wants and turns a blind eye to immorality....All of this deceit could be stopped if priests could marry as they do in the Eastern Church and in Spain. Christ never prohibited marriage. In my opinion, ever since Pope Calixtus forced celibacy on the Western Church much evil has sprung up. Just look at the immorality in the Church today, no matter how good clerical purity might be as an ideal. Look at how many priests have been fired for having mistresses. Some are even secret homosexuals. This is the root cause of the hatred between parishioners and the priests. Thus, local parish priests should be allowed to marry. They will lead a more godly and honest life this way and the troubles with the parishioners will disappear. However, no priest should be forced to marry. As long as he is honest he can stay celibate if he wants. But, if he is then caught fornicating he should be suspended for three months while he is in jail on bread and water. If it happens a second time he should be fired, thrown out of the priesthood, and spend the rest of his life as a layperson....

Priests who commit adultery should be thrown into a dungeon for the rest of their lives....

---

9 Thomas More to Martin Dorp (1485–1525)

More ridicules that lack of religious knowledge among the clergy while praising the interest in religion shown by many lay people. One feature of the Reformation (if not all early modern periods) which is most often difficult for the modern observer is the great popular interest in religion – indeed, in the finer points of religious belief. Here is an excellent example of what would have been a typical topic of dinner conversation.

21 October [1515].

[M3]

Once I was at a dinner and there was an Italian merchant there. His education was as vast as his wealth – and he had a lot of money. There was also a monk at the dinner who was trained in theology and a great debater....No matter what anyone said, no matter how carefully and cautiously qualified or thought out, it was no sooner said than [the monk] would tear it to pieces with a syllogism. It did not matter at all that the topic had nothing to do with theology or philosophy and was totally unconnected to his entire profession. When dinner started he had assured everyone that nothing was beyond him when he said that he could argue both sides of any issue. In time the merchant turned the conversation to topics more related to theology....Finally, to get a laugh, the merchant said that it was better, that is, less sinful, to keep a mistress than to chase around town after lots of women. This brought forth a strong rebuttal from the theologian....[The monk] said that it was the famous opinion of the excellent author of that marvellous book, *A Direction for Men Who Keep Mistresses* that keeping a mistress at home was worse than bedding ten prostitutes somewhere else. This was because, firstly, the kept woman was a bad example and secondly, she was more convenient and therefore the chance for sinning greater....When [the merchant] realised that the theologian did not know his Bible as well as he knew trivial things, he started to argue with him and based his statements on authority. As they were needed, he made up brief 'biblical' quotations to back up his opinions. After he had made up the quotations (which were totally unknown) he proceeded to give chapter and verse for them: one from Paul, one from Peter and a third from a Gospel. He was very careful to give even the chapter numbers but, if a book had only sixteen chapters, he deliberately placed his quotation in the twentieth. What was the theologian left to do? Before he had been unbeatable, like a curled-up porcupine defended by its quills. These made-up quotations were more difficult for him. It took some fancy footwork but he did manage to get around them. He knew nothing about the Bible and not once did he doubt that the quotations were real. He thought it was a serious sin to refuse to accept the Bible but a greater disgrace to be defeated. This in spite of being surrounded on all sides! Do you know how this clever Proteus finally got out of the trap? Whenever some fake view was put to him, supposedly drawn from the Bible, he said: 'An excellent quotation indeed, sir, but I understand that passage this way'. Then he would give a view based on alternative interpretations. He admitted that in one sense the passage supported his opponent but that the other meaning was his escape route.

---

10   Erasmus to Marcus Laurinus

Erasmus defends his new (Greek) text of the New Testament against his critics who, in his opinion, are more concerned about protecting their monopoly over religious knowledge than promoting truth. The very conservative nature of many leading churchmen, especially in the universities, is highlighted here. The late middle ages were marked by entrenched philosophical debates which centred, to a large degree, on ideas and issues formulated centuries before. The room for truly new ideas and approaches was, therefore, greatly restricted.

Louvain, April 1518

[A2: no. 3. 263–8, passim]

No one needs my assistance more than those who yap like dogs about my work and their comfort. And none bark louder than those who have never even seen the cover of one of my books. My dear Mark, you try it and see that I am being truthful. Whenever you meet someone like this, let him rant on about my New Testament and when he has made himself hoarse ask if he has read any of it. If he can say he has (without blushing) then ask him to show you one passage he dislikes. You will not find any one of them who can do it. Just look at how Christian this sort of behaviour is. These monks (do they deserve their name) stand up before an uneducated crowd and destroy someone else's reputation. Even if they later tried, they could not undo the damage caused. And yet, they know nothing about the thing they are attacking. Moreover, they forget Paul's warning that slanderers will not inherit God's Kingdom.

There is no charge worse than heresy and yet this charge they level – by a mere nod – at men with whom they disagree. This is like the story about the Swiss. If someone there in a crowd points his finger at someone else everyone else does the same thing. Everyone rushes to get in on it. As soon as anyone in the herd grunts everyone joins in and soon, all grunting together, they incite people to throw stones. They forget whatever they ought to be doing and act as though their calling in life is to slander the character of other men by the violence of their tongue. As the Psalms say: 'they have sharpened their tongues like a serpent; adder's poison is under their lips'. Those who ought to teach Christian piety prefer to attack it in others.

---

11 Tetzel's 'Sample Sermon for Priests Selling Indulgences'

The various practical abuses which so annoyed Germans were encapsulated in the work of Tetzel (and others) to raise money for the building of the (present-day) basilica church of St Peter in Rome which replaced the building provided by the Emperor Constantine. Here is part of a 'sample' sermon for parish priests given by Tetzel to help them promote and sell indulgences to their parishioners. The sheer brazenness of the sale of indulgences as a form of revenue raising was galling to many thoughtful observers. There is little doubt that there was significant popular opinion against these sales amongst decision-making and decision-shaping Germans.

[**K3**: 18–19]

Second Sermon:

Most worthy Lord. I beseech [you] that the people don't fail to take advantage of the great grace offered to them which can save their souls....Listen to the cries of your parents and the pleading of the lost. 'Have mercy, have mercy on me. You, my friends will surely help me. The Lord's hand is heavy upon me. We are in great pain and torment. You have the power to ease our anguish a little and yet you do nothing'. Open your ears. A father cries out to his son, a mother to her daughter: 'Why is the Lord tormenting me?'

Third Sermon:

Listen! Every mortal sin requires seven years of penance even after confession and contrition. The debt must be paid in this life or the next. How many mortal sins do you commit each day? How many every week? Per month? Yearly? Throughout your life? The total is infinite and infinite is the penance which must be suffered.... Won't you part with even a farthing to buy this letter? It won't bring you money but rather a divine and immortal soul, whole and secure in the Kingdom of Heaven.

---

12 Account of Tetzel's Preaching

The above, theoretical model for Tetzel's sermon is given reality in a contemporary account of his preaching. Even average church members were able to grasp the inappropriateness of this behaviour. However, there was also a great understandable concern to 'do the right thing' for themselves and, especially, their deceased relatives. These indulgences played on the best (and worst) aspects of people's concern for themselves and others. There was always the grave danger that the common people might come to the conclusion that they were being both frightened and fleeced.

[M4: 5.362]

[Tetzel] got an immense amount of money while preaching in Germany, especially at the new [silver] mines at St Annaberg which is where I, Frederick Mecum, heard him two years ago. There a large sum was collected. All the money was sent to Rome. What this stupid and brazen monk said was incredible. He claimed that if a Christian had sex with his mother and then put some money in the Pope's indulgence chest that the Pope had the power in heaven and earth to forgive the incest and that, if the Pope forgave it, God would have to as well. Also, if they gave happily, buying grace and pardon, then the hills of St Annaberg would turn to solid silver. Also, as soon as a coin rang in the chest the soul, for whom it was paid, would spring up to heaven. This indulgence was so valuable that when the commissioner [Tetzel] came into a city the official letter announcing it was carried on a satin pillow or one embroidered with gold. All the priests, monks, city councillors, scholars, men, women (married and unmarried) and the children met him with banners, candles, songs and a parade. All the bells rang out, the organs played, he was led into the church, a red cross was put up in the middle of the church and the Pope's flag was displayed. Basically, even God Himself could not have got a better reception or been entertained with greater honour.

---

13   Luther's 'Complaints to Charles V' (Diet of Worms, 1521)

The previous complaints and problems are summed up in this last extract which is part of a series of 102 complaints laid before Charles V by Luther at the Diet of Worms, 1521. One can easily see how the sale of indulgences could be viewed as yet one more proof – in fact, the clearest proof – of the anti-German attitude of the Roman Church, its blatant avarice, and its overweening power inside Germany.

[W2: 670–704, passim]

14   The Pope is insatiable. Every day he comes up with some new way to squeeze money out of the Germans....

18   He strives...to stop the free election of churchmen in our cathedral churches. Instead he appoints whomever he wants and ignores a lawfully elected bishop....

19   Popes and bishops say that there are certain sins which only they can remove. When someone commits such a sin he quickly sees that only money will

take care of it. Rome gives out no dispensations except for payment in gold. A poor man will see his case ignored because he has no money. On the other hand, a rich man can get a note from Rome granting absolution for sins he might commit in the future: for example, murder and perjury. This proves that Rome's greediness actually increases the number of sins and vices in the world.

22 We think it is disgusting that the Pope allows so many indulgences to be sold in Germany. This practice confuses and cheats the simple people out of their money. The Pope sends special men to sell these indulgences and allows them to keep part of the proceeds for their expenses....The local bishops and lords also get a 'cut' for helping to arrange the sales. This money comes from the poor who cannot see the Papal court's con-job.

39 There should only be one reason for people being required to do spiritual penance, that is, to save their souls. But, these days, Church judges make the penalties so difficult that most people are forced to pay a fine as an alternative. This allows an immense amount of money to flow into Rome's pockets.

2 The Church is Challenged
'Right now Germany is seething'

[Suggested readings: 97, 119, 120, 150, 170, 174, 175, 182, 187, 188, 189, 204, 209, 212, 213, 214, 221, 224, 225, 234, 235, 237, 246, 257, 259, 260, 263, 264, 280, 289, 301, 309, 310, 311, 312, 313, 315, 316, 331, 333, 348, 354, 363, 367, 374, 375, 381, 393, 395, 397, 400, 401, 408, 409, 416, 418, 419, 426, 427, 429, 434, 441, 446, 447, 451, 454, 466, 474, 478, 484, 485, 486, 414].

1 Erasmus to Henry Guilford

Erasmus thinks that the initial reforms are positive and will bring about the necessary corrections within the Roman Church. It is interesting to note, however, that he thinks real change will have to come from the secular nobility rather than from within the leadership (the hierarchy) of the Church itself. This reliance upon political powers for change would have dramatic consequences for the position of the Church which was so heavily involved in power-politics itself.

Antwerp, 15 May 1519.

[A2: no. 966.10–33, passim – 64]

It is as though the world is coming out of a coma and returning to its senses. Some people are still fighting against it and fighting for their old ignorance, tooth and nail. Such people will be ashamed of their stupidity when they see that great kings and nobles love and encourage good education.

Oh, the peculiar changes in life! Once upon a time religious people had enthusiasm for improving their minds. Nowadays they are mostly concerned about filling their bellies, satisfying their lusts, growing rich. Kings and nobles have inherited the love of knowledge. Does any monastery or religious school have anyone equal in scholarship or character like those at your court? We really ought to be ashamed of ourselves. The dinner-parties of the priests and monks drown in drink, ring with dirty jokes, echo with drunken riot, and reek of poisonous lies while the tables of the princes resound with quiet, sober discussion.

2 Luther's 95 Theses (1517)

The narrow focus and lack of an overt desire to effect a break with the Roman Church is apparent in what is considered to be the opening salvo of the Reformation. One can see, though, numerous echoes of the complaints which Germans had been making for nearly a century. It is perhaps easy, therefore, to see how and why these points would have found such a receptive audience once they were translated into German and widely published. It is worth saying that Luther intended neither the translation nor the publication of his theses. Once publicised these complaints became a rallying point for protests against the perceived evils and ills of the Roman Church within Germany.

[K3: 21–6, passim – 8, 45, 48, 49, 53, 54, 55, 56, 58, 59]

Debate about the power and usefulness of indulgences.

> The following points are to be debated at Wittenberg. Martin Luther, who is a lecturer there and has a Master's degree in Arts and Sacred Theology will be the chairman of the debate. He asks that anyone who cannot be there to debate in person should submit their ideas in writing.
>
> 2   [Repentance] should not be seen to mean the sacrament of penance, that is, confession and repayment which is given by the clergy.
>
> 5   The Pope doesn't want, nor can he, remove penalties except ones that he has imposed.
>
> 6   The Pope cannot remove guilt. He can say and prove that God has removed guilt....
>
> 8   Church rules only apply to the living. Even the rules state that they don't apply to the dying.
>
> 10   It is stupid and evil for a priest to apply Church sanctions to the dying and reserve their punishment until Purgatory.
>
> 19   It doesn't seem certain that every soul in Purgatory is sure of his salvation....
>
> 21   Those who preach indulgences are wrong when they say that a papal indulgence can remove every penalty.
>
> 24   Most people have been deceived by this meaningless and over-blown claim to be able to remove all penalties.
>
> 27   It is a human [not divine] teaching to say that a soul springs out of Purgatory the moment a coin rings in the [indulgence] till.
>
> 32   Anyone who thinks that owning an indulgence certificate can guarantee their salvation will end up in Hell along with those who taught them to think this way.
>
> 36   Every Christian, who truly repents, has a right to have every penalty and all guilt removed. They don't need an indulgence certificate for that.
>
> 41   Papal indulgences should only be provided with extreme caution. People must not be misled into thinking that these certificates are better than other good works.

45   Christians should be taught that they shouldn't pass by a man in need and then buy a certificate. This doesn't get them a papal indulgence but a share in God's wrath.

50   Christians should be told that were the Pope to realise how the indulgence preachers were tricking the people, then he would prefer St Peter's basilica to burn to the ground rather than have it built with the blood, sweat and tears of his sheep.

52. Even if the indulgence preachers, or for that matter, the Pope were to offer a man eternal security it would be useless to rely on an indulgence certificate.

62. The Church's treasure is actually the most holy Gospel of God's word and grace.

63. This treasure is usually disliked because it says the first will be last.

64. The treasure of indulgences is well-liked because it makes the last first.

65. One used to use the treasures of the Gospel to catch men of wealth.

66. Now one uses the treasures of the indulgences to catch the wealth of men.

75. It is insane to claim that a papal indulgence could remove the penalty from someone even if they had raped the Virgin Mary.

79. It is blasphemy to say that a cross with the papal coat of arms is as valuable as the cross with Christ [hanging on it].

81. The misleading preaching of indulgences makes it very difficult for educated men to protect the Pope from the slander and crafty views of the common people.

82. For example: 'Why won't the Pope let everyone out of Purgatory for the sake of love. He seems more than willing to do it for the love of money. The first would be just, the latter worthless'.

86. Also: 'The Pope is wealthier than Crassus [a Roman fabled for his wealth]. Why doesn't he use his own money to build St Peter's basilica rather than the money of poor believers?'

94. Christians should be encouraged to be concerned about following Christ, their leader, through punishment, death and Hell.

95. If they do that they can be sure that they will enter Heaven through trials rather than the fake assurance of peace.

---

3   Duke George of Saxony to the Chancellor of Leipzig (17 January 1519)

Letter to arrange the Leipzig Disputation which was one of many attempts to settle the areas of dispute and restore unity to the Church. Many leading political figures were determined to avoid open splits within the German political structure. They were well aware that civil strife would only allow for even greater advances by the Turks to the East who had recently made significant inroads into Hungary and were threatening the eastern borders of the Holy Roman Empire. However, there was an equally strong temptation to exploit this religious dispute to weaken the power of the newly elected Emperor, Charles V (who was also King of Spain).

[S4: App. 11, 119ff.]

We got your esteemed letter and we are now assured that Your Grace will not allow the debate which Dr Eck wants to have with us and our university's theologians, that you intend to stop it because, as you wrote, you have been warned against it in blunt letters from Rome although no formal orders or prohibitions have come from the Pope.

This has not really come as a surprise to us. In our opinion, our university has always been a place for all kinds of learning, where one could debate or propose whatever he liked, in conformity with the Catholic faith, against which nothing overly blasphemous should be disputed. Thus, Leipzig has had many debates on the Trinity, the Sacrament of the Eucharist, and other religious matters. No one has been turned away. No conclusion has ever been given against the Christian faith (thank God) and (God willing) never will be.

We were of the opinion that a debate should be held about whether or not a soul springs to heaven as soon as a penny rings in the [indulgence] plate. To stop poor ignorant people from being deceived it seemed good to have some conclusion reached on the matter. It did not seem wrong to give in to the wishes of those for whom this was so important. However, we would not think that present actions came on your initiative...though we feel that Your Grace has been got at by some who are perhaps afraid that their leisure and drinking-parties might be disturbed. For example, the sort of lazy and wasteful men we have reported. We think that they would consider the proposed debate an excellent idea and one not to be missed if a good meal were provided and if they got a nice fee for little work. But since their free-time would be disturbed they insist that Your Grace and everyone else let them have their way – just like bad soldiers who hear a shot and think they have been hit. Dr Eck has not written about what he wants to debate. They are afraid he will propose a topic they cannot explain....

It seems contrary to their vocations for our theologians to decline such debates. As Bible teachers, they should delight in shining light on the matters which they have chewed over so often, after all, they have the best places in lectureships and feasts. However, if they know the truth and do not do it or refuse to provide it on the day then I would be just as happy to have an infant do their job. Eventually, it might do our bidding and tell us what it knew. Until then we could feed it milk and plain food. Your Grace should ask your shepherd what he thinks of dogs which will not bark at, or attack a wolf. If they cannot take these debates and are afraid of losing then we would rather they be replaced by old women who could be paid to sing songs and make cloth for us.

This is our friendly request, then: Your Grace should not give in to such people who call themselves theologians but are ashamed of displaying their knowledge. Moreover, that you would use your power to persuade them to permit the debate unless Rome officially forbids it.

---

4 Leipzig Disputation (5–7 July 1519)

One major issue was Luther's views on previous groups which were separated from Rome. Contemporaries seem to have had a very strong sense of the continuity between those views and ideas which led to what historians call 'the' Reformation and those of the previous reformations – exemplified by men like Hus and Wycliffe.

[S5: 55–139, passim – 13]

Luther [says]: The excellent doctor [Eck], at the end of the last session, mentioned the views of Wycliffe and Hus which were condemned along with Pope Boniface VIII who rejected them. As I have already said I cannot and will not support the Bohemian break-away Church. I do, however, defend the fourteen centuries – old position of the Greek Church. I do not care if the Bohemians agree or not. I am certain that the Pope and all his flatterers do not have the power to throw that many [Greek] saints – who were never under their control – out of heaven.

Secondly, and I am sure on this, that many of Hus' beliefs were completely evangelical and Christian. The Universal Church cannot condemn him, for example, when he said that there is only one Universal Church. Irreligious flatterers have condemned even this in spite of the fact that the whole Church says, 'I believe in the Holy Spirit, the holy catholic church, the communion of saints'. The beliefs of Hus include this most worthy belief.

And this point: it is not necessary for salvation to believe that the Roman Church is supreme. I do not care if this was said by Wycliffe or Hus. I know full well that Basil the Great...and a host of other Greek bishops were saved. They still said the same thing. New beliefs cannot be created by the Pope or the Inquisitors. They should judge by the ones already there. Also, no Christian – unless there is some new, approved revelation – can be forced to exceed the Bible which is quite correctly, divine law.

Nothing can be accepted by us unless it can be proven by the Bible or an obvious revelation....

As long as the excellent doctor insists on throwing the Hussites, who have only been around a century, in my face I will respond with the Eastern Church – the better part of the Universal Church – and its fourteen centuries. If their refusal to accept the Pope makes them heretics then I call my opponent an heretic for saying that all these saints, famous throughout the universal church, are damned. The same is true of Pope Boniface VIII – time has shown just what sort of Pope he was and how reliable his actions were.

In conclusion, therefore, I ask the renowned doctor if he will admit that the Popes were men and should not be treated like gods....

___

5 'To the Christian Nobility of the German Nation on the Reform of the Christian Estate' (August 1520)

Luther addressed his views to a wider audience as well. His discussions – to the disgust and annoyance of his opponents – were not confined to disputation halls. Nor were his views limited to the 'purely' theological. In time, his spreading ideas led many well beyond his intended goals. One must remember that the Church leadership and structure which was being attacked was an integral part of Germany's political, economic, and legal framework. Freedom to attack the Church, therefore, could easily be translated into license to attack every perceived social ill and injustice.

[L5 – on economic issues: 153, 243, 247, 250, 252, 253, 319, 420, 462]

21 The abolition of begging in Christendom is one of our greatest needs. There should be no begging among Christians. If we were brave and determined it would be easy to make a law forcing every city to provide for its own poor and to forbid entry to every foreign beggar whether a pilgrim or a begging monk. Every city should support its poor and should be helped by neighbouring villages when the city is too small. Anyway the villages have to feed so many vagrants and liars disguised as begging monks. This would, also, allow them to know who was really poor and who was not.

___

6 Luther, 'Babylonian Captivity of the Church' (October 1520)

The following passage highlights the areas where misunderstanding could take place. One could easily read this as a general call for individual liberty. As almost every issue was, or could be, perceived as religious then this could become a licence for each and every individual to sit in judgement of each and every aspect of society and its structure.

[L5 – 22]

On the Sacrament of Baptism

Therefore, I say that no Pope or bishop or anyone else has the right to impose one letter of law on a Christian man without his consent. If this is done it is tyranny. Thus, the prayers, fasts, donations, etc., decreed and demanded by the Pope in his decretals (whose number matches their evil) are decreed and demanded without any right whatsoever. Whenever he tries to do this he sins against the Church's liberty.... To be subject to their rules and dictatorial laws is to be made a slave of men.

This ungodly and desperate tyranny springs from the Pope's followers who trot out and misuse Christ's words: 'He that heareth you heareth me'.... Therefore, the Pope's traditions bind no one. No one needs to listen to [the Pope] except when he teaches the Gospel and Christ.... It is blindness, pure blindness which rules the Pope.

On Ordination

All people who know they are Christians, therefore, must be certain of this and apply it: we are all priests and there is no difference between us. Thus, we have the same power as regards the Bible and the sacraments. However, this power cannot be used by anyone without the consent of the community or a superior. What belongs to everyone in common cannot be claimed by one person unless he is called. Thus, the sacrament of ordination, if it is to have any meaning at all, has to be the ritual by which a person is called to the Church's service. Moreover, priesthood is the ministry of the Word – listen – not just of any word but of the Gospel. Being a deacon is not reading the Gospel and the Epistle, as it now is, but the job of distributing the Church's donations to the poor. This frees the priest of worldly matters so he can concentrate on praying and the Word. This is why deacons were appointed originally (see Acts 6). Thus, those who do not know or preach the Word are more than just not priests and bishops, they are actually a plague on the Church, calling themselves priests and bishops – in sheep's clothing no less – they abuse the Gospel and prey on the Church like wolves. Unless these false churchmen who fill the Church at the moment find some way to work out their salvation (i.e. realise their false professions and grieve that they claim an office they do not know and cannot fulfil) with tears and prayers, lamenting their miserable, hypocritical lives – unless they do that, they are truly people destined for eternal damnation.

---

7   Luther on Indulgences and Grace

Despite the wide-ranging aspects of Luther's complaints, and their subsequent openness to misinterpretation, it is clear that he remained concerned with the theological elements of the argument. His complaint was essentially against the abuses, whether structural or theological, within the Church rather than a wider critique of the general society.

[L3: no. 1.469ff.]

My sixth point is that no one can prove from the Bible that any other punishment or satisfaction is required from the sinner for divine justice except a sincere and real repentance and conversion; this, accompanied by a determination to bear Christ's cross and do the sort of good works mentioned above. The latter can be imposed by no one....

My fourteenth point is that sinful and lazy Christians, who refuse to set themselves to doing good works or who lack patience, have been granted indulgences. These improve no one, rather they tolerate and permit imperfection. Thus, no one should speak against indulgences nor should anyone persuade people to take them.

---

8   Luther, 'To the Christian Nobility of the German Nation on the Reform of the Christian Estate' (August 1520)

One can again see, in the following, that, if one failed to share Luther's rather narrow focus on religious issues, how his statements could be seen to be calling for radical change throughout society.

[L5]

The Three Walls of the Romanists

In any case, as I have said elsewhere, if we are all priests having one faith, one Gospel, one sacrament, why should we not also have the power to examine and decide what is right or wrong in religious matters? What is the point of Paul in I Corinthians 2, 'He that is spiritual judgeth all things, yet he himself is judged of no man', and II Corinthians 4, 'We have all the same Spirit of faith'? Why should we not have the same power to decide what agrees with faith and what does not, just like a faithless Pope?

These Scriptures and many others should make us free and bold and the spirit of freedom (as Paul calls Him) should not be chased away by the inventions of the Popes. We should march forward boldly to test what they do and do not do using as a ruler our interpretation of the Bible which relies on faith. We should force them to follow the better interpretation and not theirs. Once upon a time Abraham had to listen to Sarah though she was more his subject than we ever have been to any man. Balaam's ass was wiser than the prophet as well. If God could speak against a prophet through an ass why should He not speak against the Pope through righteous men? Paul pointed out Peter's error in the same way. Therefore it is the duty of every Christian to side with the faith, to understand it and defend it and to condemn every error.

---

9   Articles of the Peasants of Stühlingen and Lupfen (Spring 1524)

Increasingly, many (common) people began to apply some of Luther's ideas to other (nontheological/religious) issues. A blend of religious, social, economic and political complaints became apparent. Here, then, is a perfect example of how these complaints could combine into calls for truly radical, indeed revolutionary change.

Articles of the Peasants of Stühlingen and Lupfen, Spring 1524. Complaints which immediately preceded the outbreak of full-scale revolt among the peasants (The Peasants' War).

[G3: 101–23, passim – 35, 67]

20   In the past there was a fine of three or five shillings for assault; now it is a felony....

22   We have to grind our grain in mills that are located inconveniently far away....

23   We have no idea where the interest and rents we are told we owe the counts have come from....

24   We are burdened and oppressed by many obligatory services....

41   Wild game should be totally free....God and common law say that wild game was created to meet the needs of the common man and can be trapped and hunted by everyone. Nevertheless, our lords make severe restrictions and impose heavy penalties on hunting...game.

59   Bondage and freedom. By right every man is born free. Neither we nor our forebears have committed any crime for which we should be made serfs. Nevertheless, our lords say we are and should be bound to them and are compelled to do what they command just like slaves. Who knows, eventually we may be sold like slaves as well. Our basic plea is that the counts should be forced to admit that we should be released from serfdom and that they should never bind any other man. Otherwise, we swear to remain loyal subjects, and to fulfil all our ancient and traditional obligations owed to our lords.

---

10   Twelve Articles of the Peasants (March 1525)

Complaints raised during the Peasants' War. The Peasants' War deeply shocked Luther and other leading Germans on both sides of the religious disputes. Luther retreated into a conservative attitude towards society, and a reliance on political support for his religious changes. Change, when it came, was to be within the context of law and order and directed from above.

[L2: 151, no. 50 – 6, 14, 32, 33, 50]

Article 1: To begin, we humbly beg and desire, and are determined and resolved that power and authority should be given to us in the future to allow each community to nominate and appoint its own pastor. Also, if he acts inappropriately, that we can fire him. The appointed pastor should teach only the pure and simple Gospel without alteration, doctrine or human rules....

Article 2: We are ready and willing to pay a fair tenth of grain as this is based on the Old Testament and fulfilled in the New. God's Word clearly teaches that a pastor is necessary for giving to God and distributing to the people. In future we want our church provost (appointed by the community) to collect the tenth. This will then be used by him to support the pastor (elected by the community) with a decent and fair salary set by the community. Whatever is left will go to the poor on the basis of need and the community's decision. If there is a surplus it should be saved so that no one needs go away poor. Also, this surplus should be used to avoid the need for a land tax on the poor. If some villagers have sold their tenth because of poverty and the village as a whole decides to use it, the original buyer should not lose out. Some fair agreement should be reached with him so that he can be repaid with a fair amount of interest. But if someone has a tenth which is theirs because their ancestors gained it (and they did not buy it directly) then they should get nothing; the tenth should be used to support the pastor (elected, as above) and help the poor (as taught by the Bible). We refuse to pay any of the 'small tenth' – God provided men with cattle for their free use. Thus, we refuse to pay some additional tax dreamed up by men.

Article 3: Traditionally, men have controlled us like property. This is deplorable since Christ has delivered and redeemed all of us, without exception, by His shed blood – the great and lowly equally. Thus, the Bible agrees that we ought to be free and this is our wish. We have no desire to escape proper authority. God has not taught us to give ourselves over to immorality, guided by the lusts of the flesh rather that we should love Him and our neighbour. As these are commanded in the Lord's Supper we are happy to obey. Disobedience to authority was never taught by God instead He says that we should be humble to those above us and to every one. We are fully prepared to obey our elected and natural superiors in any way appropriate with our religion in obedience to God's Law. We assume, therefore, that you will release us from serfdom unless someone can prove to us from the Bible that we, true Christians, are serfs....

Article 5: We are upset about wood-collecting. The nobles have taken over all the woods for their use alone....

Article 6: Our sixth complaint is about the great burdens of work in kind imposed on us; the demands are increased every day....

Article 8: We are crushed by the tenant farms we have which cannot produce enough to pay the rents owed on them....

Article 10: We are also upset by the seizing of meadows and fields – which used to be held by the community in common – by certain individuals.

We intend to take these back into common ownership.

---

11   Erasmus to Albert of Brandenburg, Archbishop-Elector of Mainz

Luther's views, in addition to misleading some into radicalism, led to splits with more cautious reformers, like Erasmus. Erasmus advised against rash action against Luther while being careful to distance himself from Luther.

Erasmus to Albert of Brandenburg, Archbishop-Elector of Mainz. Erasmus was very aware of the dangers posed by taking a harsh line against Luther.

Louvain, 19 October 1519.

[A2: no. 1033. 46 – 179, passim]

A heart which has some brilliant sparks of Gospel learning should not be crushed, I think, but should be shaped and given to preaching Christ's glory. But, at the moment, the theologians I know are not advising or teaching Luther. They only ridicule him in public with their crazed howling; they tear him limb from limb with their vicious, venomous lies. All they can say is 'heresies' or 'heretics'. The most disgusting displays have occurred even here and there by people who have never read a word Luther has written. Everyone knows they are attacking things they cannot even understand.... These people condemn Luther's ideas when everyone knows that the same views can be found in St Bernard and St Augustine – they are considered orthodox, even godly.

I have always advised that such public shouting should be avoided and the debate conducted by writing and discussing. Also, at the very start I urged that nothing be condemned before it had been read let alone studied – I avoided adding, what they did not understand – especially not in public.

Every sane person agreed with this advice but some just assumed that my suggestions meant I had helped write some of Luther's books and had had them printed here in Louvain. Not one single letter came from mine and they were published without my knowledge or approval. But some men have chosen to ignore the evidence and, relying on their false suspicions, have caused a number of tragedies here. I have never witnessed anything so wildly violent in my whole life. Some, whose calling as theologians should lead them to teach, have devoted themselves to confining, smashing and crushing instead. Using coercion rather than argument was rejected by St Augustine even against the Donatist and they were not just heretics but bloodthirsty thieves. People who should have a duty to kindliness are wild to drink human blood. Luther caught and crushed is their one great desire. The hangman's work rather than the theologian's vocation. If they are so keen to prove their religious zeal let them convert Jews, let them unite to Christ those separated from Him. Even better, let them improve the public morality of

Christians. They are the very epitome of decay – worse than Turks. What justice is there in deciding now to charge someone who has suggested a debate about issues which have always been open to debate in the theology schools? Why punish someone who wants to learn and is willing to accept the judgement of the universities? No wonder he is unwilling to accept the verdict of people who would clearly prefer him to be a dead man than a good man.

Let us look at the root of this evil. The world is under the heavy yoke of human rules, opinions and beliefs taught by scholastics, the tyranny of the 'poor' friars. The friars are servants of Rome but they are so numerous and powerful that they can terrorise kings and even the Pope himself. When the Pope supports them they praise him like he were God but when he tries to do something they do not like his power becomes a mirage. They are not all bad, I would never say that, but many would trap the souls of men to get wealth and absolute power. Lately they preach only their own new and shameless ideas, brazenly ignoring Christ. As, for example, even the illiterate reject their views on indulgences. Because of all these reasons, and more, Gospel truth has become powerless. As things have got worse and worse it was bound to happen. The last dying ember of Christian godliness which could have set the world aflame again has been snuffed out. In this decayed environment the fundamentals of religion have become a set of rules even more complicated than the old Jewish ones. Good men weep and deplore this state of affairs. Theologians (in private) who are not monks, and even some who are, admit that this is the case.

It was this mess which made Luther dare to fight the unbearable arrogance of these people. What other explanation is there for the actions of someone who clearly is not after fame or money? I am not talking about Luther's specific ideas which some attack, only the reason for his ideas in the first place. Certainly, Luther questioned indulgences but only because of the way they were being abused. Yes, Luther talked about, in great restraint, the Pope's power but only after some had made outrageous claims about it, especially those three Dominicans: Pelagius, Mazolini, and Cajetan. Undoubtedly Luther was less than respectful about the teachings of St Thomas Aquinas but the Dominicans had been treating them as better than the Gospels....

Godly minds were troubled that the theological schools seemed to never mention Gospel truths. The holy writers of the past, admired for so long by the Church, were said to be out of date. Christ was rarely mentioned in sermons; they were all about the Pope's power and the fashionable views of recent men. All the talking was for profit, flattery, promotion, and deceit. Luther may have spoken too forcefully but I am sure that the real blame must be placed here.

12 Erasmus to Luther

Erasmus was also concerned to distance himself from Luther. He found some of his views disturbing and was increasingly forced to voice his support for the unity of the Church. He continued to hope for a reconciliation between Luther and the Roman Church hierarchy. Continued bitterness and recrimination would only damage the prospects for compromise. At the same time, he realised that he had to maintain a distance from Luther if he was to serve as a mediating voice in the disputes.

Louvain, 30 May 1519.

[A2: no. 3. 605ff. – 44]

I was pleased by your letter because it showed how sharp your mind is and evidenced your Christian spirit. I cannot begin to describe the problems your writings have caused here. Thus far I have not been able to get rid of the idea (fixed in some minds) that I helped produce some of your writings or that I am the ringleader of, as they say, your faction. They used this as an excuse to smother good writings which they already hated because they felt it undermined the high standing of theology. They think no more of the latter than they do of Christ but it was a good excuse to attack me since they think I am important in promoting education. The whole lot are carried along by shouting, arrogance, deceit, slander, and lies. If I had not seen this with my own eyes I would never have believed that theologians could be so crazy. It is like some horrible disease. This poison, which started with a few, has spread far, and thus a large section of the university is infected with this plague of madness.

I have said that you are a perfect stranger to me, that I have not read any of your books, and that as a result I have not decided to approve or disapprove of what you have written. I have said that people ought not to be so vicious in public about books they have not even read, rather, that they should leave such things to those of better discernment. Also, I have questioned whether it was wise to discuss these matters, which might better be left to books or scholarly discussion, in front of wider audiences. This was especially important as everyone spoke well of the author's character. None of this did any good. Still they rant and rave with their one-sided and scandalous arguments. How many times have we restored peace! How many times have they started another quarrel on the basis of nothing! And they call themselves theologians. The people at the court hate the theologians – and I get the blame even for that! The bishops at least are favourable to me. The theologians have no use for books; they plan to win by slanderous lies. These I ignore, assured of my own uprightness. They are becoming nicer to you. They are afraid of what I might write which shows they have a guilty conscience. They know I could show them in their true colours (and they deserve it, too). But Christ's example and words hold me back. Wild animals are calmed by kindness but goodness turns these men into savages.

13   Erasmus to Duke John, Elector of Saxony

Eventually the relationship between Luther and Erasmus became very strained. Not only did Erasmus refuse to accept the need to break with Rome but he began to have serious theological disputes with Luther as well. The most notable was their conflict over the power and place of the human will in salvation.

Basel, 2 March 1526.

[A2: no. 1670. 9–80, passim]

I published a book, *On Free Will*, about a year ago. In it I was very careful not to attack anyone by name. I even gave the book the modest description of a discussion or conference. I was only trying to question and spark discussion on the sole basis of the Bible; I was in no way judging. Luther could not have asked for a more courteous opponent for a debate. He had the chance to prove his view, if it were true. If not, he was being corrected as courteously as possible. No matter how thin-skinned a person might be there was nothing offensive in my book. In spite of this, my book caused some princes and theologians to develop a violent dislike of me. They decided that instead of fighting Luther I was in fact secretly working with him. No matter how hard I have tried to stay out of this dispute I have been forced into the ring by powerful rulers. I can swear by God that I wrote nothing in this book which was against my actual beliefs. Moreover, I have not been paid one single penny by anyone to attack Luther. His book [*On the Bondage of the Will*] in response to mine went well beyond the bounds of a fair reply. It was full of sneers, witty comments, insults, threats and accusations. Indeed, this book has more libellous remarks in it than all his previous books put together.

I can tolerate being called stupid, ignorant, a drunk, a moron, retarded, an idiot. These are human insults and I am human. But these were not enough for him. He went on to say I was like Lucian because he said I do not believe in God. That I was like a pig from some Epicurean herd because I do not believe God is involved in human affairs. He makes me out to despise the Bible, wreck the Christian faith, an enemy of Christianity, a despicable hypocrite saying I am insincere – all I have written has been written in a godly spirit. He said that I was only trying to divert attention from worse ungodliness. He said other things which a person would not even say about a Turk or a Muslim. He was encouraged to do this by certain traitors and he cannot see what sort of mask he has on. If Christianity is really the sort of faith he has described then he has no idea how many people have been revolted by his rude pen. Are his teasing jibes, his foolish mocks, his vicious laughs, his slanders, threats, deceits really appropriate for such an important matter – a matter so serious and important that it has almost ripped apart the whole world? If he had managed to destroy my views boldly and strongly by using the Bible and his own views he could have done his side a great service. Not only that but he could have convinced a lot of people who were offended by him in this matter – and also by the rest of his beliefs as well. He brags about having the Spirit. Can anyone really believe that Christ's Spirit could live in the heart of any person capable of saying such arrogant and bitter, such violent, lying and scurrilous things? Despite repeated warnings he refuses to change his behaviour. In fact, he is getting worse.

On my side, I have done everything I can, wholeheartedly, to help good education and theology. God gives every person separate gifts and every person helps His Kingdom in a different way. Thus, while Luther may not allow anyone to disagree with him the fact is that there are a lot of people who do disagree with him in their books and they do not argue against him politely as I have done. No, they use outrageous insults as they rant against him. These are the sort of people he should have drawn his pen against. Some people in his own party have written extremely impressive books on Communion which oppose his ideas. Nevertheless, he will not permit me – I have never even been in his camp – to disagree even modestly. What sort of good can come of his sneering comments, his ridiculing laughter, the malice? All it can do is stir up rebellion everywhere and bring the Gospel into disrepute (as well as learning). This will happen even if it causes no immediate problems for Your Excellency. If he is trying to teach the Gospel then we should remember that the purpose of the Gospel is to stop us from sinning not to give us more freedom to sin regardless of whether or not there is punishment. Nor does the Gospel undermine civil law; in fact it sustains it. The law punishes people for falsely accusing someone of theft or lying or perjury. In fact, the law executes people who publish libellous books.

In Luther's book (and twelve thousand copies have already been printed), he says that I do not believe in God and that I ridicule the Bible. He is thus judging someone else's conscience. His supporters are copying this damned example. Despite this, I am sure that the law has not totally died in your country. If you punish thieves and perjurers then all I can say is that attacking someone else's reputation is worse than theft because good people think their reputation is more valuable than their own lives.

I am writing, famous Prince, not because I want revenge. Rather it is in the public interest that someone remind Luther, by the use of the law and authority, that he cannot be allowed to rant so rudely against anyone. This sort of behaviour does not help anyone, instead it just tends to destroy everything that is good.

---

14   Declaration of the Cities (4 August 1526)

Divisions also began to appear at the level of high politics. Imperial politics became increasingly complicated, if not well nigh impossible, as territorial princes and independent Imperial cities lined up for or against Luther. Just as the peasants had used Luther's words to justify and underpin their calls for radical reform, elements within the German political structure were quick to use the religious split to further their political goals.

[F1: App. 11, 552ff.]

We would point out that these requests can be summed up with this: this Diet should neither do nor conclude anything which would injure our Holy Christian faith, its beliefs, structure, ceremonies, or practices. Indeed, as His Majesty the Emperor ordered at [the Diet of] Worms, these should be kept, done and (by command) used everywhere in the Empire. This to continue until the Emperor can go to Rome to see the Pope and then together they will announce and proclaim, as is proper, a General Council and assembly of all Christendom.

We, the representatives of the Empire's Free Cities, who freely obey as subjects His Majesty – our proper, only Lord by nature – declare that we are bound to him in everything which will secure the peace and unity of the Empire. However, the Electors and Princes of your Empire are well aware of how badly and seriously the mistakes, disputes and arguments over these articles (especially about practices and abuses) have increased in number in the last few years. Also, how impossible it has been and, one presumes, will continue to be, to enforce the Imperial Edict of Worms even though its enforcement was ordered in the Princes' reply to the papal ambassador at the Nürnberg Diet.

We, the representatives of the Empire's Free Cities, are certain that...His Imperial Majesty will realise that continuing to try to enforce the Worms Edict about practices and abuses would be very damaging.

---

15 Account of Carlstadt's Alterations to the Mass (16 December 1521)

Even amongst Luther's theological supporters, splits began to appear. Alterations to the Mass were made by Dr Carlstadt while Luther was in hiding after the Diet of Worms. For many thoughtful observers, this tendency to split became the least attractive and most potentially dangerous feature of the reforming movement.

16/27 December 1521

[S7: 5.121]

Last Sunday Dr Carlstadt announced in the Wittenberg parish church that on the next Feast of the Circumcision....He would give out Communion in both kinds, bread and wine. He said he would preach a short sermon, say the words of consecration and leave out everything else. Also, he would not wear the normal clothes of a priest at the Mass.

On Christmas Day, [Carlstadt] preached about the Sacrament and encouraged everyone to take the wine as well as the bread. After the sermon, he went straight to the altar, said the 'I confess' and read the service up to the Gospel reading. Then he omitted all the bowings, gestures, crossings, the offering of the cup and the bread and the part after called the little Canon. The section from the great Canon to the

Consecration he performed without using a cross. He left out the elevation, he then immediately passed the bread around and then the cup of Christ's Blood and said to every single person: 'This is the cup of my blood of the new and everlasting testament, the spirit and mystery of faith, which is shed for you and for many for the remission of sins'....As soon as the bread and wine were distributed he left, as did most of the people.

16 Melanchthon on the Zwickau Prophets (27 December 1521)

Even more radical religious activities began to appear. Melanchthon gave his impressions of the Zwickau prophets, 27 December 1521, to the Duke-Elector of Saxony. Although radical social goals were crushed with the defeat of the peasants there was still plenty of scope for radical change. This is just one more example of the inability to stop fragmentation within the reforming movement once the process of change got underway.

[K3: 100f. – 11]

Your Highness has no idea how diverse and dangerous were the divisions which were stirred up about God's Word in Zwickau. Some people I did not know were arrested there and investigated. There were three men, two of whom were illiterate weavers, the third was educated....I heard them. It was truly amazing how they spoke about themselves. They claimed they were sent to teach by the clear voice of God. They had regular chats with God. They could see the future. In short, they were prophets and apostles. I can't really explain how they affected me. I came to the conclusion that I didn't want to reject them. For various reasons it seemed as though the Spirit might be moving them. None could judge this matter fully except [Luther].

17 Bishop Brask of Linköping to Johannes Magni, Legate of Pope Adrian VI and Archbishop-Elect of Uppsala (23 November 1523)

Despite these divisions and the various political troubles, Luther's views quickly spread beyond Germany with equally serious consequences for the Catholic faith in other lands. Political change (the removal of bishops who held lands and secular power), as well as violence, were a regular feature of the spread of the new ideas.

20 June 1524.

[K3: 152f. – on Protestantism on Europe's fringe: 86, 87, 88, 167, 168, 266, 283, 359, 453, 477]

Moreover, reverend father, the host of foreigners who agitate for the Lutheran schism keep increasing. They are helped by the sale of [Luther's] writings. This is in spite of our prohibition and threats of punishment. I'm afraid that the medicine will arrive too late unless it can be applied to this fatal plague quickly by your wise council and authority.

---

18 Bishop Brask to the King of Sweden

21 May 1524.

[H1: 18.236]

It is my solemn duty to advise you to ban the sale of Luther's books in the Kingdom and to refuse any aid or comfort to his students until the scheduled Council has made an official ruling....I know of no better way for Your Grace to win the love of God and that of Christian Kings and Princes than if you were to restore Christ's Church to the harmony it used to enjoy.

---

19 The King of Sweden to Bishop Brask

King of Sweden determined to have Protestant Reformation

8 June 1524.

[H1: 18.236]

In answer to your request that we ban the sale of Luther's books we cannot imagine how this could be done. We are told that, as yet, his views have not been condemned by impartial judges. Also, since anti-Luther writings have been allowed to circulate it seems fair that his should be kept available to the public. Thus, you and other scholars can examine them for error and point this out to the people. Then his books can be condemned. As to your accusation that his students have found shelter at the court we can only respond that none have requested it. If they should , you are fully aware of our duty to protect them to the best of our ability. If there are some in our protection whom you wish to accuse then lay a charge against them and give their names.

---

20 An Account of the Arrest of Magnus Lauritssen, Bishop of Hamar

23 June 1537. *↓ last Catholic Bishop of Sweden*

[W1: 347]

The bishop, on his way to Strandbakken with Truid, knelt and thanked God for his entire life. He said goodnight to the canons and priests and farewell to the cathedral and cloister, to his officials, the common people (free townsmen and serfs). He begged that they all pray for him and he said that he hoped he would return soon. He closed with: 'O God our heavenly Father, grant that we may meet again in heaven if not before'. He wept as he prayed and said: 'Farewell, farewell, farewell'.

---

21 Archbishop-Elector of Mainz to Pope Leo X (July 1521)

Supporters of the Roman Church were well aware of the threat posed by Luther and his teachings but were not always able to do more than report on the rapidly deteriorating situation. Catholic observers and Papal advisors were very concerned to alert the Pope to the deteriorating position of the Church in Germany.

[K3: 89]

Most blessed father.... Today, in spite of all the efforts of good men, in spite of your blessed decree and the Imperial edict against [Luther] and his accomplices, the horde of Lutherans is still growing. Lay people who support the clergy simply and honestly are an endangered species. Even a large number of the priests are for Luther. Even more of them are too ashamed to stand up for the Roman Church.

---

22 Aleander, Papal Ambassador, on Anti-papal Sentiment in Germany (8 February 1521)

[B11: 48]

Right now Germany is seething. 'Luther' is the cry of nine of every ten. The tenth, even if he does not like Luther still shouts, 'Death to Rome's Court!' Everyone cries and shrieks, 'Council! Council!' and are determined to have it meet in Germany.

---

23 Dispatches of Gaspar Contarini, Venetian Ambassador to the Venetian Government (25/6 April 1521)

Contarini is reporting on the religious and political situation in Germany during the Diet of Worms.

[B1: 1.268]

25 April: I cannot tell you how well thought of [Luther] is at [Worms]. It is so strong that I think that something bad will happen when the Emperor leaves and the Diet is dissolved – especially against the leading churchmen of Germany. In actual fact had [Luther] wisely confined himself to his first statements and not

become tangled up in obvious religious errors not only would he be well thought of but he would be the darling of Germany. This was said to me at Augsburg by many, including the Duke of Bavaria. My own observations have confirmed it.

26 April: Luther is the sort of person who will not give ground on an opinion even in the face of argument, threats or pleas....He has many powerful supporters who encourage him. No one dares to attack them....Although his books have been banned by the Pope and the Emperor – who is right here! – they are openly available here in Worms.

---

24 Erasmus to Philip Melanchthon

The break between Erasmus (the leading exponent of reform within the Catholic Church) and Luther (who was increasingly led to create a Church structure separate from Rome) became permanent. Nevertheless, this split failed to dampen Erasmus's determination to introduce reform from within the old faith. Erasmus was also quick to point out that the extremist positions being adopted by adherents on both sides would only lead to worse exchanges and further hinder all attempts at reconciliation.

Basel, 10 December 1524.

[A2: 5. 593–98, passim]

The Pope's supporters are his own worst enemies and the most zealous of Luther's supporters are his. If possible I would have stayed out of it. I am not a judge of what other people believe. There are more than enough people willing to fill that part and one cannot imagine how it will all end. In general I do not object to the evangelical teachings but there are many things taught by Luther that I dislike. He goes overboard on everything he turns to. I agree, Christendom is corrupt and needs a good beating but I think it would be better if we had the support of the Princes and the Pope....[Pope] Clement was not against reform but no one would listen when I suggested that he be met half-way. The advocates of violence run the show. They rip the habits off of monks who could easily have been left in their monasteries. Priests marry, images are destroyed. I favour cleaning religion up but I do not want to see authority obliterated. Freedom does not have to be to sin. It is not necessary to overturn everything when practices which have been abused could have been corrected over time. Some things Luther sees as wrong. But when he tears away at them he does more harm than good. No matter how hard you try humans will always make mistakes; one should realise that some cures are worse than the disease. Is it really a great accomplishment to have removed the statues and changed the worship service? What is the point of telling ignorant youths that the Pope is the Antichrist? That confession causes plague? That they cannot do right even if they try? That good works and merit are a meaningless fantasy? That free will is a mirage? That necessity makes everything happen in a set pattern and that people cannot do anything for themselves? These sort of things have been said. You can say that Luther has never said this, only a fool would. True, but Luther encourages the people who do say them. Moreover, if I had to have a business partner I would prefer a papist to some of the evangelicals I have known.

---

25 Erasmus to Cranevelt (1485–1564), the Belgian Humanist, on the Marriage of Martin Luther and the Former Nun Catherine von Bora

Despite his pleas for toleration and reconciliation Erasmus was as willing as the next person to listen to and pass along the worst of the gossip about the leading figures in the religious debate. He was forced to acknowledge and apologise for spreading this false rumour that Catherine was pregnant at the time of the marriage.

Basel, 24 December 1525.

[A2: no. 1655. 1–6, passim – on family issues: 38, 115, 215, 220, 328, 342, 392, 402, 405, 431, 440]

To Francis Cranevelt,

All the best comedies, after all the chaos has ended, end with a wedding. It looks like Luther's play will also end that way. He has married a former vestal virgin. Just so you will know that the wedding was blessed from the start I should say that just a few days after the wedding songs were sung the young bride had a baby. If you have a moment to spare, Charles will show you an engraving of the husband and wife..

3   Divisions and Disorder Spread
'The rope has reached breaking-point'

[*Suggested readings*: 143, 156, 192, 412, 425, 430, 457, 463, 469, 481, 256]

1   Erasmus to J. Botzheim

Erasmus gives a very gloomy assessment of the Church's predicament after a decade of reforming. He is particularly concerned about the levels of violence accompanying the disagreements between the Catholics and the Protestants as well as the unwillingness by either side (but, in his view, especially by the Catholics) to consider any moderate course which might heal the widening rift.

Freiburg, 13 August 1529.

[A2: 8.253ff.]

It is better to rely on God than princes and armies in days like these. We must ask God to shorten these days. Alas! Christianity has sunk so low that few men even know what it means to call on the Lord. Some rely on cardinals and bishops, some on kings, some look to the black squads of monks and theologians. What do they want? What will they get from protectors who do not care about Catholic piety but only want to get their old power and pleasures back? Either we were drunk or asleep but God has surely sent these harsh teachers to wake us up. The rope has reached breaking-point. If the tension were let off a bit it might make it but they would rather see it snap than give any ground. As head of the Church the Pope deserves honour. But he overstretched his authority and this broke the first strand. Monks and commissioners sold indulgences and pardons – acceptable within bounds – everywhere just to get rich. They were sold in every church (the red boxes, the crosses, the papal coat of arms were everywhere) and the people had no choice but to buy. This broke the second strand. Then came praying to the saints. Originally the statues in the church were for decoration and edification. But eventually the walls were painted over with scandalous pictures. The practice turned into idolatry. The third strand gave way. It was an ancient and godly practice to sing hymns but then music came in more suited to weddings and parties than God's worship, the holy words got lost in complex patterns and none of the Liturgy's words could be heard plainly. There went another strand. Is anything more solemn than the Mass? What of stupid, migrant priests who learn a couple of Masses by rote and repeat them over and over again like some shoemaker making shoes! What of well-known sinners officiating at God's table! What of the most holy of mysteries sold for money! This strand begins to unravel as well. Privately confessing can be useful. But when fools in terror are blackmailed, when something meant to cure troubled souls becomes a tool of priestly evil, then this cord will not last long.

Priests, who demand to be respected as though they were special people, have brought their profession into disrepute by their loose lives. The monks have become unconcerned about purity, unconcerned about what they do or how they live. The people they can no longer deceive are crushed by the monks' wealth and sheer numbers. They claim that their clothes will work miracles, that they can bring good luck into a house and keep the Devil out. But look at the current situation. People used to think they were almost gods. Some still might admit that they are honest.

Customs which are basically good should not be thrown out because they have been abused. I am not saying that. I do say that we have brought this on ourselves. There is no cause for us to be surprised or upset, instead we should concentrate on discovering how to survive the calamity. It seems as though there will be no improvement; the dice can fall as they will. The Evangelicals chose anarchy; the Catholics, instead of repenting of their sins, layer superstition atop superstition. Luther's disciples, if that is what they are, do not pray, do not fast, in fact they eat more on fast days than any other day. Papal ordinances, the clergy's privileges are laughed at and ground underfoot. Our glorious defenders of the Church bring more disrepute on the papacy than anyone else. Peace is rumoured. God let it be so. If the [Holy Roman] Emperor, the Pope, the French and English kings could settle their differences and decide on one course of action then the Gospel religion might be restored. But if we are to enjoy [God's] good gifts we must first deserve them. When princes go insane we are usually to blame.

2 Bullinger (1504–75) on the Initial Opposition to Zwingli in Zürich

The Reformation also began to appear in Switzerland under the direction of Zwingli. Although springing from similar roots, the Zwinglian movement was, in fact, separate from German Lutheranism. Zwingli was much more influenced by the Humanist movement. The city leaders were very concerned to prevent the spread of the sort of disorders which had occurred in Germany. There was always, in the minds of many officials, the threat that there might be another outbreak such as the Peasants' Revolt.

[K3: 384]

Our leader...requested letters to be written to me. In them he ordered that there be restraint...for the tenth time. I answered them in public though I spoke in Latin not German. He said that the truth didn't always need to be said. He thought, at least, that nothing bad should be said about the priests...This little sweet manikin wrote all of this as a friendly warning. I met him myself. Later, despite Utinger's reminder, I couldn't keep quiet. I explained the matter and all the problems...he ordered these letters...which were lifeless. He used the Canons mostly and sacred letters though these were so twisted that their authors would not even recognise them.

3 Bullinger on Zwingli's Preaching (1521)

Zwingli's calls for reform were often very specifically tied to the Swiss situation. For example, he was very harsh in his condemnation of the mercenary trade. Switzerland had supplied some of the best soldiers for most European armies for centuries. In Zwingli's mind though the treaty obligations to supply troops were destroying the Swiss. His views were not helped by the fact that one of the largest sources of money in Switzerland were the remittance payments and pensions of mercenaries.

[E1: 2. 350]

Zwingli preached very strongly at this time about the evil of taking mercenary money, arguing that it would destroy the Confederation. Also, he preached against unions with princes and lords. If they were made then honest men would have to keep a close eye on them. What had been promised should be kept. Unions should be avoided. If God delivered a people from one they should not join another one because they cost blood. He said: 'I wish they had made a hole in the union with the Pope and given that messenger something to take home in his ear'. He said that people might be concerned about a rampaging wolf but that these were no good against the wolves which destroy men. They wear red hats and cloaks and if a man shakes them money pours out, if he wring them they will run with the blood of his brother, his son, his father and his best friend.

4 Accounts of the Reformation Continuing to Gain Ground in Zürich

[E1: no. 213]

[Details on those breaking the fast of Ash Wednesday, 5 March 1522, when meat was not to be eaten. The eating of forbidden foods on fast days was one of the most obvious and visible ways to express support for, and adherence to the new ideas. It was also an activity which struck many people as scandalous. Opposition to fast obligations often combined protests from meat producers, workers and those who disagreed with the regulations on religious grounds. In some cases such diverse complaints could come from the same individual.]

Investigation into who has been eating meat and eggs during Lent: Elsi Flammer, maid to the printer in Niederdorf quarter reported that her boss had ordered her to cook some sausages on Ash Wednesday. These were then eaten by the people's priest [Leo Jud], of Einsiedlen, Bartholemew Pur, and Michael Hurt. Later some of her boss's vineyard workers had also eaten some of the meat

The baker reported Bartholemew Pur: On Ash Wednesday [Pur] and Master Ulrich [Zwingli], the people's priest at the Great Minster, Master Leo Jud, people's priest at Einsiedeln, Master Laurence [Keller], parson at Egg, Henry Aberli, Michael Hirt (the baker), Conrad Luchsinger, and Conrad Escher, were in the printer's [Froschauer's] kitchen. The printer put out two dried sausages. They cut these up and each ate a bit. Everyone had some except Master Ulrich Zwingli, the Great Minster's people's priest.

[Street-fighting breaks out in the city between the supporters of the old faith and the proponents of the new teachings. The very violence that the city magistrates feared began to appear. It is worth noting that violence, especially inter-personal, undirected violence was a feature of the spread of the new ideas and one which normally concerned leaders on both sides of the religious dispute. The problem, however, was that members of the opposition were increasingly demonised.]

A journeyman shoemaker from Würzburg, Michael Ferrich, had a fist fight with James Schmidt of Meilen about the appropriate time for meat-eating. One said: 'March is when some eat meat'. The other said: 'They do not'. The stranger said: 'Well, I think people in this country seem to be better off with cheese than the Bible'. He then ridiculed the other about his 'old cow-country', etc. They then started throwing punches; peace was restored when the neighbours separated them.

[The city government begins to involve itself in the religious debate as the issue starts to effect social control and becomes a law-and-order issue. Christopher Froschauer, an advocate of reform, is called to defend his actions before the council, April 1522. The concern and determination of the magistracy to maintain good order was not helped by the individual nature of the adherence to the new ideas. Being lectured on the Bible by people brought before the courts for public disorder was not a situation city officials found enjoyable.]

The printer, Christopher Froschauer responds to the Council:

Wise, gracious, godly and dear Lords, I plead guilty to the charge of eating meat in my house as you were told. For this reason: I have a lot of work to do, and it is so costly in every sense that I have to work night and day, on holy days and work days. I have to meet the deadline of the Frankfurt Book Fair. This time-consuming work is printing the Epistles of St Paul....Also, it seems to me, that God has shown Himself to us and revealed the Truth through His Word. This we must accept if we are to be blessed. There is nothing on earth given by God for us to rely on except His Holy Gospel which is His Word. This we must believe, rely on and obey. Moreover, our lives must be ruled and directed by this Gospel otherwise we are not

Christians. In addition, it seems to me, that God has faithfully given Zürich a better preacher [Zwingli] than can be found in all of Germany; he is the praise and glory of our town...I am so confident in your wisdom, my Lords, that I can say that should the church rulers punish us for things which are not against God or the Bible that you will come to our defence and protect our godly rights.

[In an effort to restore order the council increasingly sides with the advocates of reform. The council even began to involve itself in the internal affairs of monastic orders, 1 December 1522. This highlights one of the most serious problems facing those areas which wished to embrace the reforming ideas: what is to be done with the monks and nuns? Their lands and houses could be seized and sold which was of obvious benefit to the government. However, this then left any number of former monks and nuns destitute. As these people were usually members of local families it fell to their families and the community to find a place for them and care for their needs should they be too old or unskilled to find gainful employment.]

Burgomaster Röist and the Council:

There has arisen a dispute among the nuns of Oetenbach about a number of things but, in particular, whether the souls are better served by staying in the nunnery or leaving it. The majority think it is better to stay in the nunnery and do not want the others to leave preferring them to remain inside as well. Because of this we have decided that until next Pentecost [Whitsunday] all the ladies should stay in the nunnery living in friendship and love in God's name until some decision can be taken by the state or Church authorities about a more permanent settlement of the dispute. Also, every lady can have whichever confessor she prefers, whether a member of the parish clergy or a monk, and then have her confession heard at the grill as in the past. In addition, parish clergy and monks can continue to say Mass and preach in the church. The parish clergy and the monks must limit their preaching to that which can be supported by God's Word and the Gospel. This will put an end to all other nonsense as previously agreed. This is all allowed on the condition that, after the confessions, Masses and sermons that all clerics leave the nunnery and that none return unless it is to give a sick nun confession or the Sacraments.

5 Second Zürich Disputation (1523)

In an effort to settle the outstanding differences and to avert further violence and civic unrest, the council orders the opposing sides to confront one another in a disputation. This extract is taken from the second such disputation held in Zürich, 1523. This was a very successful method for adopting the reform. Once the city government could claim that it had given both sides a fair hearing it often felt freer to move against the Catholic structure. Also, it was often possible that the old Church would discredit itself in the course of the debate. This was highly likely as leading churchmen were inclined to refuse to participate in these debates. This denied the authority of the magistrates to hold such debates or to sit in judgment on such issues. Thus, the Catholics were in many cases represented by very poor advocates indeed.

[E1: 2. 731–803, passim]

Martin Stanly, pastor at Schaffhausen: Therefore, the Mass is a sacrifice. Psalm 109 is clear on this: 'The Lord has sworn and will not change his mind, "You are a priest forever after the order of Melchizedek"'. Also, Genesis 14 says, 'Melchizedek, King of Salem, offered up bread and wine', etc. [He] offered up bread and wine because he was a priest of the Most High and he blessed Abram....

These Bible quotations prove, first, that the Holy Spirit lives in the true Christian Church which teaches the truth and cannot be mistaken.

Second, all shepherds who have entered the sheep pen by the correct door have taught the truth and not mistakes. These shepherds have been listened to by the sheep. Third, the sheep would not have listened if the shepherds were teaching lies because the elect sheep cannot be led astray by false teaching.

For the past five centuries the shepherds have been saying that the Mass is a sacrifice. All of them could not have been lying, evil shepherds all that time. No, in fact, they have been good, faithful shepherds. The sheep would never have followed or believed them if they were all lying shepherds teaching lies. The priests would have all been from the Devil. I think this possibility is ridiculous. For the past nine centuries the shepherds have said, and the sheep accepted, that the Mass is a sacrifice and that makes it so.

Leo Jud: I answer this way. I agree that Christ is a priest like Melchizedek, as David said. I refuse to agree, though, that he 'offered' up bread and wine. Genesis 14 says 'proffer' not 'offer' which is what you claim.

Martin: I think it means 'offer'.

Jud: Listen dear Pastor, it says 'proffer' not 'offer'. Can you not understand the difference between the two words? 'Proffer' means to 'bring out' while 'offer' means 'offer up', in Hebrew, hozia. The passage means that after battling the kings Abram was tired and he went to Salem. Salem's King, Melchizedek, came out to meet him with bread and wine which refreshed Abram and his companions....[Melchizedek] was not just a priest he was also head of the state, a prefect. In other words he was a state official. At that time it was customary for the head of state to bring out bread and wine – food – to those coming home from a battle. It is clear from this that the story of Melchizedek cannot be used to support the idea that the Mass is a sacrifice.

Ullrich Zwingli: This story is like our behaviour at the arrival of other Swiss confederates. As a token of friendship we bring out bread or wine or something to eat.

Martin: The text says exactly what I said: 'offer'.

Zwingli: Dear Pastor, that is not true. It says 'proffer' not 'offer'. You know what 'proffer' means, surely? Schoolchildren understand it! Those of us who understand the Bible have a duty to correct mistakes.

[The Bible was consulted and it was shown that the passage said 'proffer' as Zwingli said, not 'offer' as the pastor believed.]

Zwingli: Dear Schoolmaster, you have said that it is too early for us to discuss such important matters. I disagree. It is totally, and always, appropriate for Christians to discuss God's Word in spite of whether some council agrees or not – as has been done many times in the past. I really do not care for these councils anyway. The majority of them are not real councils; they are fake, merely congregations of the Devil...

The Council of Constance is a perfect example of this. This council burned Hus and called him an heretic because they said he wanted the common church-goer to get both the bread and the wine in Communion. He was teaching the truth if this is what he said. I say and teach the same thing! This belief is correct and Christian. He was a pitiful martyr to God and killed innocent if he was burned for this.

As far as my beliefs go, dear Schoolmaster, you can translate them into Latin and ship them off to your god, the Pope. You can fill in the one side of the argument, I have already given the other. I have sent them to the church as well, to all godly Christians. I am waiting to read what the opposition will write and wait for simple Christians to judge them. The city rulers will decide what is the correct way to celebrate the Mass in the future.

Simon Stumpff: Master Ulrich! You have no power to give this decision to the city's rulers. The matter has already been settled. God's Spirit decides. If the city rulers decide something which goes against God I would beg Christ for guidance from His Spirit and would oppose it in word and deed.

Zwingli: True enough! I would also oppose them if they were to oppose God. I have not left it up to them to decide. God's Word should not be judged by them. They should not, nor should anyone else. This meeting is not here to judge but to try to discover and understand from the Bible whether or not the Mass is a sacrifice. Thus, the rulers will advise what is the best, most appropriate way to celebrate the Mass.

---

6 The Removal of Organs and Relics in Zürich (June 1524)

The city council, advised by Zwingli, began to make extensive changes to religious practice in the city. This was not confined to theological or moral issues but extended to the very practical as well. Hence, the removal of organs and relics, June 1524. One feature very clearly obvious in the Swiss reformation is the reliance of the reformers on the power of the state and the acceptance (in practice if not necessarily in theory) of the state's competence to settle religious debates. To a certain extent the new ideas became captives to the will of the state.

[E1: no. 547]

There were shrines at the Great Minster to the blessed martyrs Felix and Regula. At the insistence of the common people the bodies of the martyrs were kept and buried there. However, in June, the council and the citizenry decided that they should be removed from the church and that the corpses inside should be honourably and quietly buried or secretly spread out in the charnel house....At the same time, the Zürich magistrates ordered that organ playing should cease in the city and the churches. The bells were not to be rung for the dead or for good or bad weather. Psalms, salt, water and candles were no longer to be blessed. Finally, baptisms and extreme unction were to stop, too. All such superstitions were to stop and be put away because they are all opposed to God's Word.

---

7   The Dissolution of Religious Houses in Zürich (5 December 1524)

The city council of Zürich began to take over various pieces of church property and began the dissolution of religious houses, 5 December 1524. Pragmatic solutions were frequently the only way to deal with the vexing question of the need to care for former monks and nuns. This was all the more important when facing the rulers of the monasteries and convents who were, by virtue of their position and landholdings, local lords and legal officers.

[B14: 1. 129f.]

[The Council] accepted with thanks the offer from the Abbess of our Lady's Minster to dissolve her convent by legal contract and oath. The agreement was put into effect immediately. The abbess was allowed to remain in the convent with 'sufficient provision to meet her needs for the rest of her life and to keep her according to her social rank'....As for the monasteries: a document was drawn up and read to all the monks. Any of the Augustinians or Dominicans who would leave their order and take up a trade could have back any possessions they brought with them to the monastery. Those who had nothing were to be given help from the property of the monastery.

---

8   The Prohibition of the Mass in Zürich (12 April 1525)

Finally, the council moved to prohibit the celebration of the Mass in Zürich, 12 April 1525. This was the effective end of Catholicism in the city. One has some idea, from the following extract as well as the above, how very different the new services would have been from the old. The whole religious environment of worship would have changes: no more bells, statues, incense. On almost every sensual level the new service would have been different. Even the 'taste' of communion would have differed with the introduction of the cup for the lay-people and, in some cases, the change from unleavened wafers to regular bread. Church-goers would have been made dramatically aware of the sweeping extent of the changes and the degree to which the old ways had been repudiated.

[E1: no. 684; B14: 1. 147]

On Easter Wednesday the last celebration of the Mass took place in Zürich. God's Table was set up and the Sacred Bread and the holy oil were removed from the sacristies. Every alter which was left in a church was stripped bare. There was no singing or reading that week, rather all the books were removed from the choir and destroyed. However, while this pleased some men, it did not always please their neighbour.

---

9 M. de Watteville to Berne's Council on the Progress of the Reformation in the Pays de Vaud (28 September 1531)

The Reformation began to spread in Switzerland beyond Zürich. M. de Watteville reported to the Bernese council on the (less than peaceful) progress of the new teachings in the French-speaking lands controlled by Berne, 28 September 1531. Zwingli's successes should not lead one to assume that the Swiss happily and quickly rushed to embrace the new ideas. In fact, violence against the reformers continued unabated in many places despite the best efforts of officials to promote the new faith. This was often especially true in rural areas which suddenly found themselves with Protestant, urban overlords.

[K3: 489]

The faces of the [Protestant] preachers are torn to shreds. They look like they've been beaten with cats. Alarm bells are rung whenever they're around. It sounds like someone is organising a wolf-hunt.

---

10 Thomas More to John Cochlaeus

Zwingli's fame – or infamy – spread as widely as that of Luther. Although Zwingli's death in battle (leading Zürich's troops against rural Swiss devoted to Catholicism) was a blow to the Swiss reform he was but one among many and, in any case, the city remained faithful to the Protestant ideas. Once an area had accepted the new ideas it took more than the death of the leading minister to restore Catholicism.

Chelsea, 14 June [1532].

[R2: 189]

Dear Cochlaeus

Our friend, George, has come back with your letters as well as a packet of books which contain, among other things, your polemical works. In them, as a great defender of the Gospel and religion, you take on Luther, that great enemy of the Church. Your knowledge and godliness are as great as your courage. I have received other letters from you since George's return to England bearing various dates. The most recent tell of Zwingli and Oecalampadius. I was happy to hear that they were dead. Sadly, they have left behind a lot of reasons to be unhappy. I cannot talk about it without a cold chill going up my spine. Everyone knows about it and all godly people should sigh when they hear about it. Nevertheless, it is certainly right that we should celebrate that these men, such enemies of the Christian faith, have been taken away. They were thoroughly armed for destroying the Church. They were always looking out for a chance to root out godliness.

---

11   Pierrefleur on the Reformation at Grandson and Orbe in the Pays de Vaud (30 January 1532)

After the defeat of Savoy north of Lake Geneva, Berne shared control of the French-speaking lands of Vaud with Catholic Fribourg. It was necessary to come to some arrangement to allow for mutual religious toleration. The result, which shows the weakness of Fribourg (the junior partner in the alliance), was that every village was to vote annually about retaining the Mass. As long as the vote favoured the Mass it was to be kept while Protestant services (usually in the same building) were to be tolerated. Once the vote went against the Mass, Catholic services were to end entirely. This account, from 30 January 1532, reports on the situation in the villages of Grandson and Orbe.

[H2: 2. no. 371]

We the Ambassadors and Councils of Berne and Fribourg notify all present that there are serious differences...between our dear and faithful subjects at Grandson....Some wish to follow the Gospel and hear the preaching of God's Grace while others prefer the ceremonies and Mass of the Church. Having consulted about how to maintain order in the face of these difference and to allow our subjects to live in peace and harmony we have decided and commanded the following:

First, our subjects in Grandson...ought...to live in peace.

Next, since, as said, the differences relate to the Gospel and the Mass...we command that in the village of Grandson, in the monks church, the Gospel be preached every day without disturbance, obstacle or any trouble at the hour previously established. Namely, in winter from the Feast of St Michael to Easter in the morning, from seven o'clock to eight o'clock, and then in the evening, from six to seven o'clock. Likewise, in the same church, before the sermon, the matins, lauds and other canonical services, the Mass, ceremonies and offices of the Church will be allowed as before. This, on the condition that the Catholic services not impede the preaching and the Protestant services not disrupt the Mass. On Sundays and feast days [the Catholics] can preach in the Franciscan monastery one hour after dinner before vespers.

We also want everyone to be free to go to the sermon or the Mass or other services of the Church. Also, to avoid these differences which exist at Grandson, that the Mass and the Church ceremonies are not to be abolished in the parish until the majority of the parish vote to abolish them. In those parishes no longer wanting the Mass and where the Mass and ceremonies are no longer said, that is, where the majority no longer want the Mass and the Church ceremonies, they should cease and God's Grace be announced. In those parishes where the majority want to keep the Mass and the other services of the Church and where some wish to hear the Gospel, they ought not to be denied....

To keep either side from bothering the other we have ordered that anyone found mocking the other side should be jailed and held for 24 hours on bread and water and fined a gold écu before being released....

We have also ordered, under the same penalty, that the preachers must not call the priests 'liars, heretics, murderers, thieves' nor any other slanderous names which destroy rather than edify....Likewise, the priests should not curse the preachers or their supporters. Each side should allow the other to live in peace and tranquillity....

Also, we expressly forbid anyone from taking the authority to break, deface, destroy or cast down any images or decorations in the churches.

---

12   Disturbances at Grandson (23–24 September 1531)

Despite the best attempts of Berne and Fribourg to promote their respective faiths while preserving order, the reality was often less than peaceful. There were very practical problems with the attempt at mutual toleration suggested for Vaud. As one might have surmised, the need to share the parish church building was the most obvious focal point for violence and competition between the two sides. What is unclear is whether the Catholics were to leave their statuary, etc., in the building (and the Protestants ignore its presence) or were they to carry these into the building before each service and then out afterwards. Guillaume Pierrefleur, a Catholic sympathiser (who remained in village government even after the Mass was abolished) reported on disturbances at Grandson, 23–4 September 1531.

[H2: 2. no. 355]

The Catholics, deprived of all religious services for eight days, finally took heart and said the Mass. They celebrated it armed with weapons and clubs...on the Saturday before the feast of St Michael [23 September]. On the following Sunday [24 September], the [Protestant] preachers...preached three sermons one after another. When one finished his sermon, the other started....The Christians who wanted to celebrate the Mass, and aware of the slanders of the preachers, encouraged the women to enter the church which they did with a lot of noise and tumult....The three preachers were named Guillaume Farel, Marc le Rongneux, and George Grivat; they were wondrously badly dressed.

___

13   Roset on the Beginnings of the Genevan Reformation (9 June 1532)

The reforming ideas spread to Geneva in the wake of the Bernese army which came to 'liberate' Geneva from Savoyard control and was only persuaded to depart after lengthy negotiations. As in many cases, the appearance of the new ideas in Geneva was spectacular. It also had the very strong political advantage that Protestantism was linked to the city's military protector, Berne. Thus, association with the old faith could easily be seen as a longing for the return of the former political ruler, Savoy; in effect catholicism became anti-Revolutionary, treason. Michel Roset, a future city secretary and the son of the city's secretary during these troubled events recalled some of the first clashes in Geneva in his later chronicle. Here he recounts the events of 9 June 1532.

[H2: 2. no. 382]

There was a dispute between the priests and the Lutherans about the removal of some printed posters discussing the great, general grace of Jesus Christ. One of the canons [Pierre Werly of Fribourg] was wounded on the arm.

___

14   Jeanne de Jussie on the Beginnings of the Genevan Reformation (9 June 1532)

The same events were recorded by Jeanne de Jussie, a nun at the Franciscan convent in Geneva. She, and her sisters (except for one), remained loyal to the old faith and moved their convent to nearby Annecy Placards where Jeanne later became abbess. Again, as elsewhere, the level of popular interest in and violence towards the new ideas is apparent. People were strongly stirred by the issues and questions raised by the reformers; they were a matter of life and death for the people in a very real sense.

9 June 1532.

[H2: 2. no. 382]

In June on Sunday [the 9th] morning some evil young men placed some large printed posters on the doors of all the churches in Geneva. They contained all the major beliefs of the perverse Lutheran sect but the good Christians tore them all down. After the canons' matins service one of them, a determined and good Catholic, tore down the poster attached to the door of the church of St Peter right in front of the eyes of the heretics. These sinners were incensed. One took his sword and struck the canon's arm so badly that he almost bled to death. He was in bed a long time and almost despaired of his own life: all the good people pleaded with him [to live]. Eventually, with God's help (for whose honour he risked his life), he was cured by the care of the doctors. The following Tuesday, which was the feast of St Barnabus, the trumpet was sounded and a decree was read out banning anyone from putting up similar posters under pain of torture and banishment from the city for a year.

Catholic

15 Jeanne de Jussie on Farel's Arrival in Geneva (4 October 1532)

The moves to introduce the new ideas at Geneva began in earnest when the Bernese arranged for the introduction of Guillaume Farel, a Protestant preacher, into the city. Although Geneva had broken free of overt Savoyard control, the city's direct ruler remained the Prince-Bishop who was himself a protégé of Savoy. The Catholic position was dangerously compromised as a result. Nevertheless, the Church's leaders in the city were not willing to allow Protestantism to spread unopposed.

4 October 1532.

[J1: 48]

The following October there came to Geneva a vile, cursed preacher named Guillaume Farel, a native of Gap in Dauphiné. The day after his arrival he began to preach secretly in his lodgings. He was assisted by a large number of men who had heard of his arrival and who were already infected by his heresy.

Amedée de Gingin, Geneva's Vicar-général and abbot of Bonmont, hearing of this, called together all the canons to plot against the heretics. They advised that he question the said preacher. The abbot's secretary issued the order that the man appear at a set hour with two companions. The secretary, a very learned and eloquent man, named Guillaume de Vergio asked him who had sent him, for what purpose and by whose authority. The poor villain answered that he was sent by God, and that he came to announce grace. The secretary said to him:

How so? You show none of the signs such as one sent by God, like Moses showed Pharaoh who was able to show by clear signs that he was sent by God. Also, when you preached to us you could produce no license from our reverend overlord, the Bishop of Geneva. No preacher can preach in his diocese without his authorisation and blessing. Moreover, you do not wear the sort of clothes one associates with those who come to preach the grace of God, and the Holy Gospel. Instead you wear the clothes of a soldier and a thief. How can you be so brazen in preaching? It is forbidden by the rules of the Holy Church for lay people to preach in public, under pain of excommunication. This is in the decrees of Holy Mother Church. Thus, you are a liar and a sinner.

During this all the priests of the cathedral church were gathered together before the house of the Vicar. There were about twenty-five of them and they were all heavily armed. They were ready to defend the holy Catholic faith and to die for it. They were also ready to slaughter that sinner [Farel] like a dog, as well as his accomplices if they came near. After he had been questioned, the Vicar told him that he should leave his house, his presence and, within six hours, the city, under pain of burning at the stake – along with his two friends....When it became apparent that he did not want to leave, two of the canons threatened him violently. They said that if he did not wish to leave in the good graces of God then he should go to the Devil whose servant and minister he was. One of them gave him a good kick and the other punched him on the head and in the face.

---

16   Jeanne de Jussie on Froment's Public Preaching in Geneva (1 January 1532)

Antoine Froment, another Protestant preacher, arrived in Geneva to replace Farel who had been forced to leave the city after his sermons caused extensive turmoil. Jeanne de Jussie took note of the preacher's activities and the attempts by the clerical and civic authorities to control him. The disruption to Catholic services and the attempt to compete with them directly was a very provocative and, often, successful method employed by the advocates of change. It was also likely to produce the maximum number of occasions for violence and disorder, a consideration not lost on the magistrates.

[J1: 52ff.]

The next day, New Year's Day (1532), after the regular sermon at St Peter, the Lutherans wheeled out their idol to preach in the main market-place, Molard. The Vicar was notified and immediately demanded that the city council stop it. The council sent the lieutenant [chief criminal prosecutor] to tell them, under pain of punishment, to depart and take their idol with them. [The Lutherans] did not dare to speak back because they did not think they were strong enough. Then, the governors held a council to solve this problem and decided that the next day there would be a meeting of the general council.

The next day, after the insolence of the heretics was explained to the councillors, it was decided that this sect would no longer be tolerated to rule in their city. They wanted it categorically abolished and exterminated and that there was no need to take the matter to the people. The governors and councillors then issued an edict about this. No one, henceforth, could preach in the city in public without a licence from Geneva's overlord or from his Vicar except the ordinary of the Franciscans and the Poor Clairs. If anyone harboured such in his house or favoured [this sect] he would pay a large fine. Also, there was a heavy penalty on anyone who ate meat on Friday or at other times forbidden by the Church. By these means the troubles in the community were lessened.

---

17   Froment on his Initial Work in Geneva (1532)

Froment also produced an account of his early activity in Geneva. The role of women (which will be treated below as well) in the spread of the new ideas or resistance to them was of great importance and frequently noted by leaders on both sides. Also, they were frequently involved in the street-rioting which accompanied clashes between the two sides. In part this may well have been because, as they were seen as less responsible for the actions being women, they were less likely to face prosecution for involvement in rioting. Both sides realised the value of swaying both women and the young to their position.

[F2: 4, 7, 13f., 22, 39, 46, 54, 71, 163f.]

There wasn't even a woman there who was interested in the truth. They were infected by breath of the doctrine, behaviour, and conversation of their pastors who had taught them. These women were staunch opponents of those who brought the Gospel [to Geneva]. They were encouraged by their priests....

[*Understanding of particular peculiarities of a given situation could be of great value.*]

[Someone in the assembly said: 'Farel] deserves to die'. And then said: '[Throw him] into the Rhône, into the Rhône'...Farel replied: 'Talk like Christ, not Caiaphas!' The whole meeting was thrown into confusion. Many were shouting: 'Kill, kill this Lutheran!' However, Dominic Bergier, supplier of the [cathedral] chapter, was sneakier than the rest. He shouted out in Savoyard [that is, the local dialect]: 'Hit him, hit him!'...Even the most thick-eared could understand that...

[*More subtle methods were also employed by the reformers.*]

Notices were prepared and put up at every street-corner of the city so that [Froment] could start preaching in Geneva. This was the gist of the notice:

A man has come here who wants to teach French reading and writing for a month. Everyone who wants to come is invited whether from a rich or poor background, male or female—even if they've never been to school before. If you cannot read and write after a month [the lessons] will be free. He can be found in the large room of Mr Boytet's house, near the Molard [market-place] at the sign of the Golden Cross.

When these had been plastered all over the city there were different reactions among the people, some good, some bad. Some said: 'I've heard him speak and he speaks well'. Others: 'He wants no money. We should go and learn to read and write'....But others: 'He's one of those evil Lutherans we want to beat up'. And some: 'He's a devil who'll bewitch everyone who listens to him'....Nevertheless, he taught some of the children. But he didn't teach them just reading and writing but religion as well. Every day they got one or two sermons on the Bible. This sounded very impressive to them because they had never been taught doctrine before. The young people talked about this with their mothers and fathers and many people in the city. They encouraged them to come and hear the man....Because of what the youths said many men and women came to hear him preach in his large room. Some came because they were curious or to laugh, others to learn....Thus, day by day, the number of believers grew rapidly....

[*Public activities, especially preaching, to promote Protestantism were always likely to lead to violence.*]

By the day after Christmas, the crowd had become too large and the large room couldn't hold everyone....Some began to yell: 'To the Molard [market-place], to Molard!' They set him up on a bench in Molard and cried out louder than before: 'Preach to us, preach the Word of God'....He raised his hand to get their attention...the people saw that he was about to preach. They knelt down, looked to Heaven and folded their hands in prayer....

[Froment said:]

The clerics, lawyers, suppliers, officers, and commissioners gobble up the people. That is they get their property. I'm not saying that they're like cannibals who actually eat human flesh. What I mean is, how we say in our language, that they gobble up widows, the living and the dead, in other words their belongings....

[Froment] crossed the Rhône bridge and met a procession of priests...they saw that he wouldn't show proper respect to them, their cross, their relics or their statues. They were so angry that they began to chant, 'St Peter, St Peter....Into the Rhône, into the Rhône!' They stirred up the rage of the women [behind the procession] so much that the women wanted to throw him into the river.

[*Inevitably, the possibility of full-scale collapse of public order and a descent into communal civil war was never far away.*]

The two sides prepared for battle. They were determined to kill one another. Cannons were set up in the street. The muskets were loaded. The pikes and lances were levelled. The blow was about to fall....None can describe the cries, the tears, the weeping, the sorrow which filled the city as it looked on and listened to all of this. The son saw his father armed against him, brother against brother, neighbour against neighbour, each ready to kill the other....But God didn't want bloodshed and He restored calm....

[*The Protestants, as well as their Catholic opponents, had few qualms about engaging in the most provocative of activities to discomfort the other side.*]

But consider the sermon [preached] in Geneva by Dr Furbity of the Sorbonne University of Paris: 'These wicked Lutherans, sinful heretics are worse than Moslems and Jews'....Then Froment made his debut in the middle of the church and raised his hand. 'For the honour of God', he begged them, 'Listen to me!' He said that he was willing to die if he should fail to prove to them from the Bible that [Furbity] was wrong, that he was preaching lies against God....Furbity was so shocked and confused that he didn't say a word. When [Froment] was done speaking some said, 'he speaks well': others, 'Let [Furbity] answer, let him respond now....

[*Geneva, as Zürich, was confronted by the problem of what to do with monks or nuns after the adoption of the Reformation. The city was on occasion willing to take a very moderate line.*]

When [the Poor Claires] had been thoroughly admonished to live according to [Geneva's] reformation it was obvious that there was no point in saying anything else. They didn't drive these vixens out of their dens – out of the city. However, it was clear that they were the best and trickiest spies of the enemy in Geneva....The Syndics and many senators saw the stubbornness of the [nuns]. They had no excuse for their ignorance or any reason to complain about Geneva....They were repeatedly asked to live according to the Gospel and to abandon their papal ceremonies and to help spread [the Gospel] just like everyone else. The government offered to treat them as they wished. Unanimously they decided to leave the city, all except one...she married a former priest...and was given a dowry of one thousand florins which came from the sale of the convent's property. The [other] nuns were escorted to the Arve bridge under armed guard almost as though they were brides for the Syndics and senators. They were met by many priests, monks and others to lead them to the priests' warrens in Annecy.

---

18 Dentière's Account of the Early Genevan Reformation

Froment was not alone in his efforts. He was ably assisted by his wife, Marie Dentière (whose work will be discussed in greater detail below). She had been an Augustinian abbess in Tournai. Her lively account of the early reformation in Geneva (the only contemporary Protestant account published before the nineteenth century) was extensively used by Froment in his later chronicle (which the city refused to publish). Dentière's emphasis upon violence against Protestants contrasts well with the accusations levelled below against the Protestants by Jeanne de Jussie.

[D2: 55]

By the wish and instigation of the [Prince] Bishop [of Geneva] an untold number of gentlemen and priests from the vicinity committed murder, blackmail, rape, theft, pillage, house-burning, and – what is worse – people-burning.

19   Genevan Council Minutes of Jean Balard's Continuing Catholicism

Jean Balard, a leading civic official, was repeatedly warned for refusing to abandon his allegiance to the old faith. He was called before the council to account for his stubbornness. Although he never appears to have recanted wholly he was able to remain in the city magistracy. Thus, as with the nuns, the city could take a tolerant stance when the situation was not too threatening. The views of one individual seem to have been a low priority for the magistrates.

[K3: 559]

21 July [1536], council minutes: After Farel's exhortation it was decided to consider what was wanted by Jean Balard, Jean Louis Ramel and others who refused to attend the sermons. It was advised, after they were summoned, that they were ordered to attend the sermons or give a reason why they would not.

24 July, council minutes: Again Jean Balard was asked why he would not go to the sermon. He answered that he believed in God who taught by His Holy Spirit but that he could not believe our preachers. Then he said that it was not lawful to compel a citizen to go to a sermon against his conscience.... He said: 'I wish to live according to God's Gospel but I do not wish to use the interpretation of some certain people but only the interpretation of the Holy Spirit through Holy Catholic Mother Church. This I believe.' When questioned further he said that he did not want to go to the sermon because his conscience would not allow him to go.

20   Calvin's Sermon on the Micah

It is perhaps useful to end the discussion of the early Reformation in Geneva with a retrospective assessment of its success there. Calvin was very critical indeed of the extent to which the new ideas and beliefs had actually penetrated into the general populace and succeeded in altering behaviour – he was especially concerned at the (as he saw it) indifference of the city's rulers. This extract is taken from a sermon he preached on Micah in the 1550s as Calvin was preparing to clash with his opponents in the Protestant city government whom he believed were less than enthusiastic in their support for the [Calvinistic] new ideas.

[B5: 63f., 151, 163 – 16, 39, 40, 41, 63]

If the reception of God's Word makes a city famous then the rest of the world will think that, as a result, the city should have a better government. Moreover, that it should be so well ordered that fairness and justice should apply to everyone, equally. But, if the city appears to be just like anywhere else, in fact, worse than other places as though God's Word was not there at all, what will people say? Won't we appear to be the worst kind of people? Just listen to what the papists are saying:

Oh those Genevans, they say they are better than anyone else just because they want to make the whole world better. You might think they were actually angels. But look at how they live. You will find their shops are as full of trickery and theft as before, should you happen to visit the place. You will be robbed and conned – in ever situation not just in business deals. You cannot trust anyone there even in unimportant matters. If you shop in the main market-place to buy your necessities you will discover lies and hatred worse than what you would expect to find in a city which had never even heard of God. Then, if you sue, watch closely and you will see what happens: the really well-respected people will be the worst con-men of the lot!...

When everywhere you find filth, when you can see proof of a disregard for God and His Word, when scandal is not stopped, when adultery, drunkenness, loose-living, and all kinds of evil are allowed then all we can do is admit that everything is lost, ruined. True, not everyone behaves this badly and many people do the best they can to avoid such temptations. But there are not enough of these people who have enthusiasm. Thus we cry out: 'Why is God playing around with us, keeping us from relying on His Word? Why do we have to suffer so many problems when we call ourselves God's people?' We should all think very long and hard about this and try not to think this way. It is sad to see how frigid and uncaring our faith is. This is seen not just in the well-to-do in our city but especially among those who have power. The very people who should work to keep order just look the other way when they see evil people commit crimes. Either they do not care about crime because their hearts have become ice or they are sleeping at their posts and winking at the crimes because they do not want to have to disturb themselves long enough to do something about it....

No matter where you look all you can see is blasphemy, scandal, ruin. The world is such a mess that when I look at the godlessness in Geneva it looks so enormous that I feel like I am looking into a deep pit – the very mouth of Hell. There are a lot of people who like to be called Christian. They act the part well enough. But look closely and you will see that they are two-faced, it is all a lie. Maybe by looking carefully you could find about five per cent who are really serious and convinced that God is speaking to us. Undoubtedly, they used to be fools, drunk with their stupid traditional practices and their Mass. But they are worse now. The Word of God should have cut them to their hearts like a razor-sharp, two-edged sword. It should have jabbed them awake from sleeping through their own sins. But the opposite has happened. They have frozen solid – you would think they had never even heard about God's Word. You can tell that they are just out to get what they can for themselves. Fair play, honest business cannot be found. It is sad to see the state of things. Sexual immorality is viewed with so little concern that you might think it was perfectly acceptable behaviour. Worse, the people who should be bringing order, attacking such activities, and punishing these crimes are happy to allow them right next door. The filth of it all rubs off on them too. For example, they enthusiastically outlawed filthy songs. Then, they said that the new laws did not include nasty and disgusting songs about sex. These can be sung quite legally. See, they just want to make adultery acceptable. If that is the sort of thing they like well, then, they can have it. But they can stay out of God's House with their diseases, leave their filthy garbage outside. They can get on with their business in their dens and sewers – they could care less where they were. They are all just outright whores. I mean all of them when I say whores – the men and the women who go around making God look foolish. Their behaviour proves that they have always been two-faced especially when they are so hateful and derisive to God's Word – and to the sermons and prophetic warnings!

---

21   Marcourt's Placard

To put Geneva in its proper context, as well as to show the similarity in methods employed, it is worth recalling that Geneva was just one of the French-speaking areas touched by the new ideas. They caught the attention of the French nation in a very spectacular manner indeed. On the night of 17/18 October 1534, placards (or posters) condemning the Mass were put up in various places including the door to the king's bedchamber. The result was that the king was finally roused to move against the 'Lutherans' with determination.

[H2: 3. nos 485, 488; G2: 4. App. 59ff. – 72, 73]

I call upon heaven and earth to bear witness to the truth against the pompous and vain Mass of the Pope. By it the whole world (unless God intervene) is and will be totally destroyed, ruined, lost and sunk. In it our Lord is outrageously blasphemed and the people misled and blinded. It should not be tolerated or endured another minute....

The whole of the Christian faith is and ought to be very certain that our Lord and only Saviour Jesus Christ, as the great Bishop and Pastor eternally appointed by God, gave his body, soul, life and blood for our sanctification – a perfect sacrifice. That sacrifice cannot and should not ever be repeated by any visible sacrifice. This would totally renounce the original as though it were of no value or power, insufficient and incomplete. Also, that Jesus Christ had not fully satisfied the justice of God, His Father for us, and that He is not the true Christ, Saviour, Pastor, Bishop and Mediator. To think that, let alone to say it, is an horrible and inexcusable blasphemy....

The Pope, and his horde of cardinals, bishops and priests, of monks and other heretical Mass-sayers (and all those who agree with them) are like this: that is, false-prophets, damned cheats, apostates, wolves, false-pastors, idolaters, seducers, liars and inexcusable blasphemers, killers of souls, traitors to Christ, of His death and passion, perjurers, traitors, thieves, rapers of God's honour – more detestable than devils. By the great and glorious sacrifice of Jesus Christ, all external or visible sacrifice was abolished and eliminated, no other ever to be needed....

The result and methods of the Mass are wholly contrary to the result and methods of the holy Supper of Jesus Christ. This should not surprise anyone: Christ and Belial have nothing in common...The result of the Mass is altogether different as experience has shown us. By it all knowledge of Christ is erased, the preaching of the Gospel is rejected and impeded, time is wasted in bells, wails, chants, meaningless rituals, lights, incense, disguises and all manner of witchcraft. In this way the poor world (like lambs and sheep) is miserably deceived, diverted, and misled and by these wolves the world is rabidly chewed, chomped and devoured. Who can speak or think against the crimes of these fornicators? By this Mass everyone is imprisoned, everyone destroyed, everyone swallowed up.

4 The Conflict Intensifies
'At least the Turks leave the conscience alone'

[*Suggested readings:* 90, 93, 102, 103, 104, 105, 106, 107, 116, 121, 122, 124, 128, 142, 144, 145, 146, 151, 152, 157, 158, 159, 160, 161, 162, 163, 164, 165, 176, 181, 186, 191, 200, 201, 202, 206, 210, 211, 218, 219, 222, 226, 227, 228, 229, 232, 233, 238, 239, 241, 245, 248, 255, 262, 265, 278, 279, 282, 291, 294, 295, 296, 300, 302, 303, 320, 334, 335, 338, 340, 343, 344, 345, 346, 349, 350, 357, 358, 364, 369, 384, 385, 386, 387, 388, 403, 407, 428, 437, 438, 444, 449, 455, 468, 475, 482]

1 Erasmus on his Loyalty to Catholicism

Erasmus, although a great proponent of reform, remained loyal to the Roman Church. Here he defends his loyalty and denies his support for Luther. However, he remained critical of the methods used by the Catholics to defeat Luther. All of which highlights the quandary in which Erasmus and other moderates found themselves. Any calls for a moderate approach to Luther were seen to be pro-Lutheran and, therefore, anti-Catholic. Increasingly, extreme views were the only acceptable views.

[A2: 3. 402–9, passim]

Some say I helped [Luther] by telling him that he had supporters in England. I told him that to get him to listen to [their] advice. Not one single person has given him any friendly advice so far. No one has responded to his views or pointed out his mistakes. They have just yelled out 'heresy' and 'Antichrist'....

I have only said that he should not be condemned before he has been able to defend himself. Excommunication used to be the only penalty for heresy but nowadays it is punished more cruelly than any other crime. How can it be right for these men (who call themselves bishops and claim to be defenders of the truth) whose morality is terrible to persecute a man of spotless character? Moreover, so many distinguished and respectable people have found his writings admirable? The sole goal has been to destroy him and to blot out of everyone's memory his books. But this can only be done when he has been proved wrong by argument and the Bible and that in front of a fair commission. Undoubtedly the Pope's authority is far-reaching but the farther it reaches the less it should be guided by personal feelings. Godly, educated men ought to be heard; the Pope's worst enemies are his foolish supporters. He can destroy anyone he wants but empires based on terror do not last: the more important the Pope's decision and the worse the charge, the greater the caution should be. Every sensible person, whether monk or priest – even some Dominicans – agree with me in this. Those who want to condemn Luther dislike the methods being used. My advice on this is more for the Pope's benefit (and theology) than out of concern for Luther. If the Pope's decrees and the judgement of the leading teachers of the Church are to carry any weight then they must come from men of unquestionably good character. We must be convinced that their decisions will not be swayed by worldly concerns....

Everyone should be able to say what he thinks without fear, if we really want truth. If those on one side are to get bishop's mitres and those on the other the rope or the stake then truth will not be heard. Two out of all Europe's universities have condemned some of Luther's views and they could not agree. Then came that horrible Bull with the Pope's name on it calling for Luther's books to be burned and declaring him a heretic before the whole world. No act could have been worse or less wise. The Bull was out of character for Leo X and those who took the Bull abroad made the situation worse. Secular princes oppose the papacy at their peril and I do not plan on being braver than the princes, especially as I can do nothing. There may well be a need for a thorough and immediate reform of abuses at the Pope's court but I and those like me are not called to undertake such a task on our own. Better to leave things as they are, I think, than to start a revolution that may end up who knows where. If someone wishes to be a martyr, let them. I have no such aspirations. I am hated by some for being a Lutheran, by others for not being one. Rest assured, Erasmus has been and always will be a faithful subject of the Pope. However, many think as I do, that this situation could be resolved if there was less animosity and if the whole thing could be settled by serious, educated men and if the Pope would follow his own instincts rather than being swayed by others.

---

2 Heresy Trial in Lyon (29 April 1534) of Badichon de la Maisonneuve

Baudichon de la Maisonneuve, a leading merchant in Geneva, was also the city's premier local Protestant adherent. In 1534, he attended a trade fair in Lyon and was arrested by the archiepiscopal authorities. A lengthy heresy trial followed. The trial, and especially the testimony, brought against Maisonneuve provides detailed information on early Protestant activity in France as well as local views on the emerging movement.

[B3: 5–9, 16f., 28–32, 34f., 40f., 48–51, 66, 67f., 78, 94–6, 193]

[*Baudichon's willingness to accept Catholic fomulations is a clear indication of how seriously he viewed his predicament.*]

Baudichon de la Maisonneuve, a Genevan merchant, who says he is forty-six years old, swore to tell the truth and this his name and age were as stated. When asked, he said that he was a silk merchant and that he frequently attended the trade-fairs in Lyon. He also said he had been in the city since last Sunday evening and was staying at the [Golden] Cup.... When questioned, he said that he believed in the Mass and the sacrament of the altar, that is, the Holy Host and that God's body is truly there.... At Geneva he had seen a book in French entitled the *New Testament* and some others... he had not seen any other books except [that one] and one called *The Merchants' Book*.... He said he didn't know that some of these books had been brought into [Lyon] or anywhere else... He was asked whether he was of the Genevan party called Papists or the one called Evangelicals. He answered that he believed the faith which his ancestors had believed. He believed the sacrament of the altar, of confession, etc. Last Easter he was at Frankfurt and he went to confession and received Mass there. He said he kept last Lent, etc. He was asked if he would respond to witnesses who said he was in the Evangelical party in Geneva. He said he didn't think anyone could prove that....

[*Letter from Baudichon's wife found on his person along with a letter from Farel.*]

Baudichon,

I commend myself to you. There is no news here since you left except that [Jean] Portier and the Barber have been executed. Also, [Farel] is very successful in preaching God's Gospel and no longer needs our protection. No one opposes him. Our position is greatly strengthened. I've nothing else to write except may God protect you. From Geneva, third week before Easter. Ever yours, your wife, Anrite Baudichon....

[*Maisonneuve's brother rushed to Geneva to demand his brother's immediate release.*]

Thomas de la Maisonneuve, the accused's brother... argued with us. His brother the prisoner came here as a public merchant for the Easter trade-fair. [In Lyon] he intended to do a lot of valuable business. He couldn't do this because he was under arrest. But, he was supposedly protected by the safe-conduct of the fairs. Also, as a person with civic rights in Berne and Fribourg he was protected by the treaty between the King [of France] and the [Swiss] Confederation. He could not be arrested in [France] except for a crime committed inside [France]....

Jean Guilliaud, a councillor and Jean de la Bessee, the city supplier... argued that there were many merchants, foreign and native, in the city for the fair who had complained and said that this arrest was violating the rights of the fair and that many merchants also said [Baudichon's] detention had kept them from doing business [with him].... Thomas wanted... [Baudichon] to be able to do business as usual. The request was to be considered....

[It was approved and free access was allowed to Baudichon for merchants – and apparently legal advisors as well. Thomas received valuable support from civic and royal officials.]

Claude Granier, the royal notary, secretary of Lyon, was sent by the city council, along with Thomas de la Maisonneuve....They came and said that Berne's council had written to the king's deputy in Lyon, the Lieutenant General....

[Granier and Thomas returned with a request from the Lieutenant General for Baudichon's release. The enthusiasm of the Church for arresting and prosecuting heretics could easily be hampered by the practical concerns of politics and economics.]

We considered the entire case...with deliberation [and decided] it was a question of God's honour, and of the Catholic faith, of interest to the king and the public good. Thus, to the request:...we've written all about this to the King and await his pleasure. Until then we won't release Baudichon....

21 May 1534.

[It is perhaps amazing that Baudichon was never accused of Anabaptism despite the close resemblance between his methods of avoiding answering questions and the beliefs of the radicals. The Catholics seem to have been fully able to distinguish between the legal ploy which Baudichon was using and more radical religious views.]

Baudichon was called in and was asked to take the oath on the Gospel. he refused to swear. He said the Gospel didn't allow him to swear but said a person's yea should be yea, his nay, nay....He said the Prince-Bishop of Geneva was his lord and asked to be sent to Geneva and there see who would judge him....We noted his refusal to respond and told him that in this case we were his judges and demanded that he respond....

[Maisonneuve was overheard advising Colonier, his co-defendant.]

Jean Mochon...servant in the Archbishop's prison, aged about 20...swore...[that he heard] Baudichon say to Colonier something like: 'Colonier, I'm well; I'm holding out; I'm not giving up and I'm not saying a thing. It'll cost me over 100 écus to keep us from being harmed. Also, Berne's rulers won't let anyone hurt us'....

[Maisonneuve was accused, among other things, of selling relics. Since it was essential for the clerical authorities to convict Baudichon of a crime within France this charge became crucial to their case.]

Louis Joffrillet, a moneychanger, resident in Lyon, aged about 22, testified that...about four years ago...while he was working for Pierre Manicier...a citizen of Lyon...Baudichon came into [Manicier's] shop and sold a reliquary of St Jaques....Manicier took the reliquary, removed his cap, and kissed [the reliquary] with reverence. Then he said something like, 'Baudichon, I'm amazed that you've brought in a reliquary.' Baudichon answered with derision that this held lovely relics and that these relics were probably the bones of some road-kill. The priests had collected them to fool the people and to get their money. He said this and left. The witness went after him and said it was wicked to sell images and reliquaries. Baudichon replied: 'Go away, go away. God's blood!...relics are sold in Geneva at the butchers' shops'....

Florimond Pecoud, merchant, citizen of Lyon, aged about 40, testified... Baudichon sold a silver crucifix with images of Our Lady and St John, to the Dean of Lyon....He also testified that during the [previous] Easter fair a month ago, one of Lyon's royal sergeants, named Desraisa, had approached him in Moneychangers' Street and said that Baudichon's brother Thomas asked that he not say anything harmful about Baudichon....Baudichon was brought in...he said that he knew the witness. He was asked if the witness was a good man and if he had anything against the witness. He said he would hold his answer until after he had heard the deposition and then comment on the witness....After hearing the deposition he fled the courtroom saying we weren't his judges and he had nothing else to say...the jailer was sent to get him but returned and said that Baudichon claimed that he wasn't well and would return after dinner....[Later] Baudichon admitted that he had sold the crucifix to the Dean of Lyon. He also said that the witness was an evil man and shouldn't be allowed to testify. [Pecoud] had ruined other merchants. Also [Baudichon said] he was a fornicator as his wife was a whore. On one occasion her clients were forced to jump into the river out of her window....He also said that he got the crucifix from a very rich merchant in Nuremburg....

[*Pecoud began a separate slander suit against Baudichon. The charges were not limited to activity within Lyon nor to Baudichon himself. His wife was accused of a blasphemy committed at Geneva.*]

Antoine, Lord Dezimieux, aged about 32, testified...that during the last Feast of Corpus Christi [in Geneva] the precious body was borne through the city as always and went before Baudichon's house. [Baudichon's] wife stood in a window with her chambermaid....His wife said...about the priests: 'Look at these darling goats'. Then she said to the women following the procession: 'Hey! Whores! Just like mummers you follow after the priests'....

[*The innkeeper's widow testifies about the problems she had had with Catholic merchants at the trade fair as a result of renting a room to Maisonneuve. From this it is apparent that the ground was being prepared for later outbreaks of communal violence.*

Already in 1534 individuals were beginning to separate themselves, physically and mentally, from those of differing religious views.]

28 June 1534.

Jeanne, widow of Martin Bachelier, innkeeper of the Golden Cup, aged about 46, testified...that for the past seven years she had known the Genevan merchant, Baudichon de la Maisonneuve. He came to the inn during every fair in Lyon and in the inn he bathed, ate and slept in the company of many other merchants and other guests from various places.

She also said that during the last two years while at the inn eating lunch or dinner Baudichon had been involved in discussions with those present about various topics. He had discussed the Gospel and our Holy Catholic Church. He had said many inappropriate things and those present were offended. Amongst other things, Baudichon had said that one should only pray to God and not to the saints. That was all she could remember.

She had seen Baudichon in the company of Aaron and Hugh Cathelan, merchants from Auvergne. Once, after they had listened a while to Baudichon they told him it was evil to talk like that and that if he were in their home town he would be burned. She also saw...many other people there but couldn't remember their names. She testified that round about last Epiphany the [Auvergne] merchants were upset with the witness. They said that she was wrong to let [Baudichon] stay there. Also, they said they wouldn't stay at the inn during the next fair unless she promised not to let [Baudichon] stay there. During the past Easter fair these merchants returned to the inn. They saw that Baudichon was there. They were upset and told the witness that she had not kept her promise. They went elsewhere.

---

3 Roset on Genevan Involvement in the French Reformation

Lyon's clerics were right to worry about the threat of Genevan Protestantism spreading to France. Roset records the role of Geneva in spreading reform in France and the political and diplomatic troubles this brought upon Geneva. As a centre for Protestant printing, Geneva was a grave threat to French attempts to halt the spread of the new ideas. Later, with the foundation of the Academy in Geneva, the city also began to train ministers to serve in the nascent French Protestant Church.

[R3: 393 – on books: 76, 81, 82, 91, 130, 132, 169, 194]

The French who had gone to Italy with the Duke of Guise returned and passed near Geneva. Many of them threatened the city as they passed. They said that it would be easy to take the city. The [French] King was then over-seeing great persecutions [against the Protestants] and he hated Geneva. He saw the city as the source and sustainer of the doctrine he was persecuting. Also, [he hated] the ministers there as much for their books as for their private letters which they produced [in Geneva] in large numbers. Many poor people risked their lives to carry books from Geneva. Their blood testified to the [truth of the] doctrine found in the books.

---

4   Jeannie de Jussie on Religious Violence in Geneva

Jeanne de Jussie details the increasing animosity and violence accompanying the spread of the reforming ideas in Geneva. It is worthwhile comparing her account of the violence against the Catholics with the accounts of Dentière and Froment in the previous chapter. For the most part, in the Genevan situation, the Catholics were able to portray themselves as the helpless victims, a role which was reversed across the border in France.

[J1: 6, 9, 13, 23f., 33f., 89, 173, 199]

At this time, the gentlemen of the Cathedral, the parish churches and the monasteries...were forbidden from ringing the bells between seven in the evening and seven in the morning. Also, the city clock was not to strike to announce [the time for saying] the Hail Mary after compline. This was a bizarre rule and reminded people of the Time of Darkness....

[*She was particularly upset and angered by the behaviour of the Bernese army as it rushed to the aid of Geneva.*]

When the Bernese troops came to Morge some of them were lodged in the Franciscan monastery. There they committed enormous and unspeakable evils and torments. They desecrated the holy ground by stabling the cart horses in the cloister and the church. There were about 200 of them. They slept in the monastery and the poor monks had to sleep on the cold ground.

That night, these Bernese, just like evil heretics, got into the church's choir and in the middle of the nave they built a bonfire. Then, like so many treacherous dogs – rabid and mindless – they took the container which held the blessed sacrament of the precious body of Jesus Christ, our Saviour. They threw the whole thing into the fire....They were like the accomplices of Caiaphas who hit His precious face and the devilish soldiers of Pilate who whipped and crucified Him so brutally. They also broke the painting on the high altar...burned all the wooden statues, shattered the glass behind the high altar which was ornate and beautiful. Throughout the chapels they destroyed all the carved images of the Saints. It was a pitiful sight to see....

[The nuns appealed to the magistrates for protection from the increasingly violent Protestants in the city.]

Supplication of the Poor Claires to Geneva's rulers:

Our magnificent and reverend Lords, our fathers, our benefactors and protectors,

We have noticed the arrival of God's enemies into your city. Also, the evil deeds and insults committed in God's church and against the faithful people. We are very frightened. We beg you, on bended knees, with our hands folded in prayer. In the name of our Redeemer, and His sorrowful Passion, of the Virgin Mary, of St Peter, St Francis, St Claire and all the Holy Hosts of Heaven. Please keep us under your protection. Don't let us suffer any violence or violation from God's enemies. We don't want any changes to the Faith or the Law or anything removed from the Divine Service. We are determined to live and to die in our holy calling right here in our convent. We pray to our Lord for the peace and protection of this noble city. We beg you to protect us as your ancestors did. If not, we ask for your permission to leave our convent and your city in safety and that you give us guides to take us somewhere else where we can celebrate the Divine Service. In this we look to you as our fathers. We ask for your pleasure and response....

[Jussie returned to the theme of the destructiveness of the Protestant forces.]

These Swiss Germans descended on the countryside and committed innumerable sins. They were like lying dogs and heretics. Everywhere they went they pillaged every church, monastery and religious house. They broke all the containers which held the body of our Lord Jesus Christ. They took the sacred Host and trampled it underfoot or threw it into the fire or ground it into the mud. They also took the holy oil used in Baptism and the holy oil which is used to anoint all good Christians who are about to die. They poured it on to the ground – it was horrific and evil – like so many Turks or unbelieving Jews: they would not have done worse ...

[She was especially vehement in her denunciation of Luther.]

The Prince and great leader of heretics of this damned group was an Augustinian, named Martin Luther. The start of this great evil and arrogance was in 1517. [Luther] gave his soul to evil and error. He revived and renewed every heresy which has ever existed since our Lord's death. The [errors] were printed in Basel and taken everywhere. His venom poisoned every kingdom and country in Christendom. If the kings and princes had not been vigorous in punishing those who wanted to follow this cursed group then there was the chance that the souls redeemed by the precious blood of Jesus Christ would have been in danger of eternal damnation. But God will never abandon his bride the Church. He inspired our holy Father, Pope Leo X, to declare [Luther] an heretic and an enemy of the Holy Catholic Faith. He excommunicated him and all his followers. He condemned this heresy and decreed this throughout every kingdom. This infamous heretic, who had disturbed the whole of Christendom, was burned in effigy in Rome. Because of [Luther] many kingdoms, which had been faithful, were perverted and fell into heresy. The Duke of Saxony followed [Luther] with his whole country and protected [Luther]. Basel was perverted, the bishop deposed; Strasbourg's bishop was expelled; the whole of Berne both city and countryside; Zürich and two other cantons; the County of Neuchâtel and many other German cities and regions – I don't even know all their names....

[Her account is full of miraculous signs and wonders none more vivid than the following. It seems clear that her miracles are not to be understood literally but as parables, cautionary tales meant to awe and inspire the simple folk in their struggle against the new ideas.]

A miracle happened on 15 March....There was a woman who had been hanging on the gibbet for a year. She had died in the faith of Holy Mother Church. Miraculously her corpse turned to face [the body] of a Lutheran youth [executed for murder] who had been hanged on the gibbet after her. [Her] corpse turned and bit him. This was a wondrous event and was talked about everywhere in the city. Many came to see the sight and confirm the truth of the story. The Lutherans came along with their spears to separate them because the Christians were laughing at them. But the woman kept turning back to bite the youth. This was seen by more than four thousand people, from every level of society....

[A confrontation occured between the Syndics, two Protestant preachers, Marie Dentière and the nuns.]

In their company there was a nun, an abbess. She was a liar, an idiot. She had a diabolical tongue. She was married and had had children. She was named Marie Dentière. She was from Picardy. She was there to preach to – to pervert – the faithful. She was looking for sister Collette [who had seemed willing to convert]. She said to everyone: 'Are you sister Collette, my daughter? We want to talk to you.' The very first one she asked was [Collette] herself. But [Collette] said: I'm not the one you want. Try somewhere else.' She kept getting the same answer from everyone: 'Go away, you oath-breaking nun and take your poisonous tongue with you.' She was upset that she couldn't corrupt anyone. Her attacks were ceaseless,

Alas, poor creatures! You don't realise how nice it is to be married. How it pleases God. You've been in hypocrisy and darkness so long. God Himself showed me the error of my sad life. He led me to the very light of Truth. Listen! I lived in sadness. Among nuns there is only bigotry, mental corruption, laziness....I took 500 ducats from the Abbey's money-box and fled from that evil to God alone. Now I have five lovely children and live a wholesome life....

[*The nuns were finally forced to accept the inevitable. They refuse to adhere to the new faith and are granted permission to leave Geneva with their possessions. The magistrates arrange an escort to protect the handful of nuns from the violence of the Protestant enthusiasts.*]

The abbess fell to her knees and begged that the nuns be allowed to take with them their cloaks, coats and blankets to provide for their poverty. The Syndic and the lieutenant answered: 'Dear ladies, each of you can take whatever you want, and leave it at the door. We will provide eight carts to carry your cases. We swear to take you safely to the Arve bridge, the city's boundary....

[*They were mocked as they left.*]

[When an insult was hurled at the departing nuns] the Syndic, seeing the band of ruffians, (by God's will) became extremely angry raised his voice and swore horribly by God's blood that if anyone moved he would immediately have him cut down without mercy on that very spot. He also said to the archers: 'Gentlemen, do not falter in your duty, if the need arises.' Then, by God's will, they raged violently and ground their teeth and watched the nuns from afar as they took to the road trembling with fear (let none doubt that). When they reached the Arve River which marked the city's border they all stopped. Those who mocked, as they did our Lord, cried out: 'Where are the great nobles to greet you and the tents and pavilions to protect you from the rain?' Then others derisively wailed: 'Alas, Geneva, who will protect you? Your light has gone out.' Others cried to God: 'the mice are leaving their nest and going into the fields like poor lost wanderers'. But the good people wept bitterly and likewise the Syndic who, when he came to the farewell, was moved to pity, so that he wept greatly and grieved bitterly. All his companions took the nuns in order across the bridge and bid them farewell saying, 'Farewell, good ladies, truly your departure saddens me', and saying among themselves (like a latter-day Caiaphas): 'Oh Geneva, now your light is truly gone out!' And when they were all across the bridge he clapped his hands and said, 'it is all finished'....

This is the true story of the pitiful departure of the poor nuns from their convent and from the city of Geneva on Monday, the Feast of St Felix, 29 August 1535, at five o'clock in the morning.

---

5 Bonivard on the Popes

Unlike Jussie, one leading Genevan cleric, François Bonivard, embraced the new beliefs. He had been the Abbot of the Cluniac monastery, was widely educated in the humanist style and had been held in irons at Chillon Castle for six years because of his patriotic support for Geneva's political revolt against Savoy. He provided a lengthy treatise on the papacy which included biographical sketches of each Pope. His sketches give some idea of the more learned approach to criticism which very strongly recalls the work of Erasmus – an individual Bonivard even manages to mention in the sketches.

[B7: 40, 52, 67, 78, 86f.]

[Pope] Alexander [VI] was followed by a gentleman cardinal from Siena named Francesco Picolomini, a nephew of Pope Pius II who had made him a cardinal. He was considered a good man. Had he lived he might well have been better than the rest. However, he only lived for seventeen days after his enthronement in 1503. He was called Paul III.

Leo X, formerly John de Medici, followed Julius [II]....He was learned in Greek and Latin...a good musician (an art which delighted him)....But he had a hard and deformed face....If a King and his court spent a lot then the Pope and his did nothing less and were wholly carefree. There is no question but that priests, monks, bishops and cardinals found whores (whom they called courtesans) for farces and comedies and to go with them to costume parties....I was in Rome during his pontificate in 1518. I was told that the Pope got 11,000 ducats each year from the whores. Every whore with more than three lovers paid one ducat a head.

Pope Adrian VI...formerly Adrian of Utrecht, was from a poor family but well educated. He was Flemish, a star at Louvain University and a friend of Erasmus who praised him highly. He was also tutor to [Emperor] Charles [V]....After Leo's death there was a disagreement in the cardinals' meeting. They couldn't decide whom to elect as Pope. On one side, the Cardinal de Medici tried to buy the papacy while on the other the Cardinal Farnese...neither side would vote for the other....This is how Pope Adrian was elected in his absence....He didn't even arrive [in Rome] for seven months after his election. After his election the whole world hoped that he would reform the Church because of his beliefs and godly life...but he didn't live long enough and died in 1523.

6 Balard on Religious Violence in Switzerland

Jean Balard, who remained loyal to Catholicism while still a Geneva magistrate kept a diary which chronicled the early, violent clashes between the two faiths in Switzerland. The personal religious disputes noted above were simply part of a wider, more general conflict.

[B2: 325]

The difference [among the Swiss] came from the hurtful words which those who didn't want to be Lutherans said to those who did want to be Lutherans. Berne and Zürich were always trying to get [those opposed to Lutheranism] to allow the Old and New Testament to be preached in their lands. The others didn't want to allow this. They wanted to live like their ancestors.... This was the root of the great hatred and threat of war among them.... A few days later news arrived in Geneva that the Bernese army had marched out to join the armies of Zürich and the other Lutherans against the five [rural and Catholic] cantons mentioned above. The five were led by Lucerne. The Lutherans lost many men and artillery.

7 Regensburg Colloquy (1541)

Although there were frequent and violent clashes there were also a number of attempts made – at the insistence of political leaders – to force a reconciliation between the Catholics and Protestants (whether Lutheran or Calvinist). The overwhelming concern of the political leaders was to avoid a collapse of order within their states and the advent of civil wars or religiously motivated wars between states.

[B12: 88–154, passim]

[*The Protestant position is clearly set out.*]

Thus, though moderation is praiseworthy in everything and at all time – given that knowledge and goodness should always try to gain a middle and moderate way – nevertheless, God's Word and not men's opinions must be the ruler for measuring moderation in the Church. We should not, as St Paul warns us, be misled into believing ideas based on human wisdom. Clearly, the people in our party have studied the points under debate moderately. But they have been guided by God's Word and the well-known and commonly accepted teaching of the apostolic Church. We state that those views which have been added to the points where there are still out-standing differences are moderate and correct. Thus, we will not give ground on them. We ask that Your Imperial Majesty accept and honour our replies to the points under discussion.

First, we must not allow any worship service which is based on ideas which make the Gospel hard to see because we are dealing with things touching on God's glory and the Holy Gospel's light. It would be approving an abuse if we accepted... the invocation of saints and other styles of worship which cannot be found in God's Word.

Second, we are not able to accept or approve anything which goes against our consciences. They (and the consciences of our church members) have been taught and convinced in these issues (put forth in the published articles) by true Biblical authority and the Spirit-led opinion of the Apostolic Church.

Third, these issues concern the whole Church everywhere. If we change our minds now and condone some of the abuses which we have already attacked and rejected –

on the basis of God's Word – then our words would be used, now and in the future, against anyone who, with a godly conscience, believes the right thing in these matters....

The Church would be forced into an indefensible position if we now agreed that under no circumstances can anyone attack the mistakes of a council. For example, there is a statement by Pope Clement which was accepted by the Council of Vienne in France that he was the true lord of the [Holy] Roman Empire. These words sound mistaken and they are as anyone can see. The Popes and bishops have become more interested in worldly politics than caring for souls and serving the Church even when the present problems are so obvious. Councils have made worse mistakes which can be shown but we will stop the list here.

What can be said? Many people, in our city and country churches, in our homes have accepted our ideas. They would be hurt if we accepted opinions opposed to our confession. How many people could rebuke us fairly....We would stand guilty of corrupting the Gospel's truth....

So that there will be no doubt about what we teach in our churches we state again that we keep to and obey the confession and accompanying defence given at Augsburg to His Imperial Majesty. We are convinced that this is the correct, commonly-held teaching of Christ's Universal Church. That it can be found in the prophets' and the apostles' writings. That it was clearly taught in the early Church and the basis of the learning of the Church Fathers....As we have often said, we are always ready to clarify and explain each and every belief held by our churches whenever necessary.

[*The Catholics, while refusing to accept Luther and his ideas, were aware of the vital need to implement changes.*]

Cardinal Gaspar Contarini to the Imperial bishops and prelates,

Most honoured and renowned Lords. Your renowned lordships requested, after visiting me yesterday in a large group and hearing my views on several matters relating to a Christian reform, that I write down an account of what was said. This would allow you to think about it at your convenience. In response to Your lordships' request, I have written down, as briefly as possible, what I can remember about the meeting yesterday.

First, I would remind and encourage Your lordships that we must pay attention to our lives and behaviour. We must be sure that God is pleased with us, that we are faithful protectors and godly shepherds of the Lord's flock. It is most important therefore that we avoid any hint of scandal – no matter how unimportant – which might make people think that we love physical pleasures, promotion or greed.

Thus, inappropriate or extravagant cooking, interior decoration, or clothing (or anything else like that which might upset lay people or people generally) must be avoided.

Secondly, there must be concern about the manners and morals of our servants. Those who are Christian and godly will make others better. But, people will be annoyed and quick to criticise (based on their servants' behaviour) the manners and morals of bishops, if they are wicked. As St Bernard clearly warned...all church leaders must be extremely careful in getting a respectable household and in keeping it from scandal. It should be their goal that the behaviour of their servants will serve to better the godliness and wisdom of the people.

Thirdly, there is the issue of the sheep put in our care. This matter makes it essential that bishops live in their own diocese and have their residence in its population centre. This will allow them to direct and guard against the plague which is spreading at this time from Germany. If their diocese is already infected they should strive to cure it as soon as possible.

Also, in the areas where the bishop does not live, it might be useful to have spies. They can tell him where the disease might break out so that he can eradicate it quickly. It could also be helpful if the bishop travelled about his diocese frequently. Political rulers do this in territories which have been recently conquered. Moreover, they should see to it that the worship service is properly conducted in the churches and that godly and qualified men are given church positions.

Fourthly, the matter of the allocation of property and money by the bishop. People become very angry when they see poor people round about and the bishop and his group going around in expensive clothes living in rich houses. All such excess should be avoided. The greatest amount of resources possible should be given to aid the poor. This will gain us God's favour...and that of the poor. We will reap a good profit from such an investment of money.

Fifthly, the control and teaching of the people. Godly, educated men must be appointed as preachers and teachers for the people. They should teach proper behaviour and morals by what they say and do. They should not start fights, nor be overly rude to opponents which might make them appear to be hateful. Instead, they should want people to think that they love and care for everyone, especially for their salvation. People just become more stubborn the harder you attack them and this does no one else any good either.

Sixthly, with regard to language classes and liberal arts for the young. We have seen that in this area the Protestants leave no stone unturned in getting educated and famous people to teach in their schools. Their dedication and fame brings German youths – especially noble ones – to their schools. Once there, in addition to a liberal arts' education they are corrupted and when they leave they spread the disease everywhere. Therefore, Catholics should make a real effort to set up schools and universities staffed with people who are Catholic as well as well-educated in languages and liberal arts. Also, famous teachers should be hired whose fame will attract [noble] youths to the schools where they can learn liberal arts and true beliefs. Finally, bishops must warn parents not to let their children attend schools of the wrong faith especially if there is a Catholic one available.

Your lordships will find that these are the main points which I wanted to make. Many things could be added if everyone's memory was used. This shows that I am obedient to that highest lord, the Supreme Pontiff, who gave me the task of advising your lordships on a Christian reformation. Also, I have spoken by my authority as a papal legate who has responsibility for the whole Church.

---

8   Florimond de Raemond on Calvin's Fame

The papal legate was correct in worrying about the threat posed by the fame of the leading reformers – who became the celebrity stars of their day. Florimond de Raemond, an anti-Calvinist writer discussed the important role of Geneva in spreading Protestant ideas in France and the appeal Calvin had as an 'international celebrity'. This 'star status' was of great importance for the reformers in initially attracting people to their ideas.

[R1: 7.19.4.1393 – 97; 8.13.6.1534]

[*The appeal of the new ideas to specific segments of society was a feature of the spread of Protestantism noted by contemporaries.*]

Lots of people from everywhere poured into Geneva just to see Calvin....Whole French families freely went into exile just so they could go live in the outback of Savoy where he lived – in a city they call 'the Holy City', 'Hieropolis'. That is the name it gets in Etienne le Roy's little *Book of Martyrs*.

Painters, clock-makers, draftsmen, jewellers, booksellers, printers, all the people whose jobs required a high level of intelligence were the first to be seduced. White cloth dyes the best, since dark colours can fix and show better on it likewise, these new-fangled ideas sank more easily into minds that were already active and thoughtful than into minds which were simple and slow....

[*The difference between the reality and the idea of the reformers was also apparent to many.*]

Some say that medical scholars were the first thinkers to become unwilling to believe something without proof. Once all the various parts of natural science had been cut up and examined by them, they were still unable to find the real cause or the mysterious secrets behind the Christian faith. The latter are beyond nature and so, by definition, beyond the ability of Naturalists to know. They then decided that most things were of little concern and the rest impossible simply because they were not able to get to the heart of anything....

A very trustworthy fellow from Guyenne told me the following story: Once, while he was a student, he and his friends had been walking around the campus of the Toulouse Schools. Suddenly, the Holy Ghost descended on them....Immediately, the same thought came to all of them: they quit the school, packed their belongings, and set off for Geneva walking round the clock. They wanted to see [Geneva's] holy man so badly that they virtually flew. They were overwhelmed with joy when they saw Geneva's holy walls (or so the story-teller said) that it must have been almost same as when Godfrey de Bouillon, that religious, godly crusader looked on the walls of Jerusalem which he had sought for so long.

When they got into the city they heard that an 'exhortation' (the Genevan term for 'preaching') was taking place. Breathlessly they rushed to see Calvin in his pulpit. To their surprise, though, he seemed very ugly and unpleasant....

[One of the more shocking aspects – at least to contemporaries – of the Reformation was the splits which it caused within individual families.]

A certain nobleman from Languedoc, named Lord Clairé, was coming home from his army post in Piedmont...when an idea popped into his head: on the way he would stop off and see Geneva. A aristocrat from Saintonge and a noble from Guyenne, Lord Laval (who is still alive) went with him, all full of the same curiosity.

Although they were all good Catholics, as soon as they got inside Geneva, they rushed off to hear Calvin. Lord Clairé, let his eye wander over the host of women who were crowded near the pulpit. Suddenly he saw his own wife. He was so shocked he thought he must be dreaming. Could he be hallucinating? He kept staring and became surer and surer that not only was it his wife but that his daughter was sitting beside her. They must have left his house and come here. He managed to control himself until the sermon was over but then, as the people were leaving, he headed for his wife. She screamed when she caught sight of him coming through the crowd. She ran after Calvin (who was on his way out), yelling: 'Save me, sir, save me!' By the time that Calvin stopped and saw the nobleman he had already got hold of his daughter. The wife said: 'There is my lord, my papist husband who has tracked me down. Help me, God!' Calvin saw that a crowd was forming as people crowded around waiting to see how the show would end. So he took the man, his wife and daughter back to his own home to get the whole story. The noble was not allowed to speak directly to his wife without permission. Calvin heard them all later that day and the next day the whole affair was handed over to the Consistory. The noble argued that he had a right to take his wife and daughter back with him. They tried to convince him to accept the Gospel as they had. They pleaded with him to give up everything for Christ's love. Some people took him aside and told him that he was not going to get anywhere and that he had better get out of town quickly and in secret. So he left his family to Calvin's tender mercy – that is where they still are – and made his escape.

9 Pithou on Bishop Carraciolo's Visit to Geneva (1556)

The often violent and disruptive effect the new ideas had on Geneva and individuals there were in evidence elsewhere. Nicolas Pithou, of Troyes, was a leading Protestant preacher in the city. He made an extensive account of the spread of the movement in Troyes.

In 1556, Caracciolo, a member of a prominent Italian ecclesiastical family and a relative of the Pope attempted his own form of inter-faith ecumenism and reconciliation. He tried to get approval to become leader of the Protestant community in addition to being the Catholic bishop in the city.

[P1: fols. 90–92 – 216, 368, 370]

The bishop of Troyes, Caracciolo, who...had promised Michel Poncelet that he would make up for the weakness and disloyalty that he had shown towards God and His Church, acted at this time quite contrary to his promise....[Caracciolo]...assured that [the new] pope [Paul VI] had...been fond of the late Prince of Melfi, [Caracciolo's] father, resolved...to go and kiss his feet, making believe that...he would come away with a cardinal's hat at least....The Pope gave him a cool reception...and let him know...that his presence was not very agreeable to him. The bishop, disappointed in his expectations, decided to withdraw....Thus he passed through the city of Geneva...and did not wish to leave without hearing some of Calvin's lessons in theology...the day after his arrival, or the same day, Calvin was due to give a lesson after dinner. The bishop resolved to be there in the best array he could muster,...a long silk robe and four-cornered bonnet...in this gear he went to the auditorium where Calvin was giving the lesson. But this sort of outfit so strongly displeased the audience that they took little account of him, which he found very strange...he was enlightened by some people who told him frankly that it was none other than his outfit that had been so improper...[after changing clothes] he went to find Calvin in his house and spoke for a long time with him. Calvin did not forget to teach him a lesson as he deserved...he reprimanded him sharply for...recanting, and for...still...chanting the mass....The bishop...dithered and looked for vain excuses, thinking he could dazzle Calvin...by clever words and a big show....Calvin, finally annoyed by the bishop's futile and long discourse, seeing that he was getting nowhere, cut him short and took his leave....[The] bishop returned to Troyes...laden with huge debts...[from] his trip to Rome...[and by] a good number of very exquisite paintings, the subject of which for the most part was...unworthy....Having returned to Troyes...he plunged once again into the deepest quagmire of all idolatry, and began to chant the mass....He strove from then on to persuade...by his clever chatter and frivolous reasons...that to assist at the mass was an indifferent thing....In short, this poor creature behaved very badly following his return....Still no bad came of it. Although it caused some to be delayed from coming to a knowledge of the true religion as soon as they might have done.

10   Pithou on the Reformation Dividing Families (1558)

Pithou also presented details on the personal life of individual Protestants and the turmoil and difficulty brought to their lives by their adherence to the new ideas. Acceptance of the new beliefs did much more than effect the life of an individual. An entire family could flourish or fail as a result of the religious views of one member, especially if that member were the head of the household.

[P1: fols. 109v–113v – on death, wills and religious sentiment: 7, 197, 203]

There was at this time in the city of Troyes a tanner called Pierre Boissonnot, whom our God had called to an awareness of the truth through his brother, a doctor. Boissonnot, burning with a great zeal to advance the glory of God, had long since revealed himself to a scabbard maker from Troyes, Blaise Chantefoin....Boissonnot made Chantefoin promise that should he fall ill...he would prevent him...from being polluted by the customary papal superstitions. Boissonnot reciprocated this promise to Chantefoin....Eight days later Boissonnot fell sick; feeling pressurised he sent for Chantefoin...reminding him of his promise....Chantefoin replied that he remembered it well and that he wouldn't forget, but also that [Boissonnot] should for his part show himself to be Jesus Christ's true champion...which the sick man promised to do with God's help. Two or three days later, Chantefoin, warned by the doctor...that in his judgement [Boissonnot] wouldn't last long, sent for the invalid's brother, Claude Boissonnot, who had some knowledge of the true religion, and a leather worker, Girard Valleton, a God-fearing man....Having consulted together they promised neither to leave nor abandon the sick man until he died.

[Boissonnot's] wife, who was more concerned about the loss of her possessions than anything else, asked him (though she knew God) if he died...without speaking to a priest, what would become of her and his poor children....The sick man, having sent for Chantefoin, told him everything his wife had said to him and asked for his advice. He replied that he wouldn't wish to advise him to take the counsel of his wife...and that if he went along with [her] arguments and admonitions...it wouldn't turn out well. This situation prevailed until this poor man, feeling bothered and finally vanquished by the tears, entreaties and constant reproofs of his wife, let her do with him as she wished. She...sent immediately for the curate of St Jean, Le Rossignol....[The priest] questioned the invalid as to whether he wished to receive the sacrament of confession. The sick man, hearing the word sacrament, said nothing....Once the invalid agreed to [confession, the priest] made everyone leave the room, even Chantefoin, who nevertheless stayed by the door in order to hear what was said....The priest...asked [Boissonnot] again: 'Now Pierre my friend, do you wish to confess to God, to the blessed Virgin Mary and to all the saints in paradise, and to me?' Boissonnot responded that he would confess to God eternal, creator of heaven and earth, and to His only son our Lord Jesus Christ, who had suffered death and passion for all the sins that he had committed. 'It is not usual to confess in this fashion' (said the priest to the invalid). 'I have at other times confessed great lords and ladies, who did not confess this way. Do you believe an apothecary, a shoemaker and who knows what scabbard maker' (referring to Chantefoin), 'people of low status and ignorant, who don't know what they are saying and are abusing you.' 'I beg you', replied the sick man, 'to leave me in peace for the moment because my fever is tormenting me.'...The priest left the room. The invalid's wife...certain that her husband had confessed, taking the priest by the hand asked him how her husband seemed. 'Ha!' said the priest shaking his head....Chantefoin...broke in, 'What do you mean, "Ha!", don't you know what you said to him? You are a confessor of princes and of ladies, you wanted him to confess in the customary way.'...Valleton...interrupted them...saying to [the priest]: 'Abuser that you are, if you don't remove yourself fast, I will throw you down the stairs and break your neck.' This poor priest...preferred to leave quietly...extremely angry that he had no...witnesses.

The poor invalid...called Chantefoin and said...'My friend, I am damned'. 'What!' said Chantefoin...'Don't you believe that Jesus Christ died for your sins and was resurrected for your salvation?' 'Ha, my friend...there will be no forgiveness for me, for [Jesus] said that He will deny before God His father he who denies Him before men.' Chantefoin seeing him so terrified...cited some passages from the Scriptures to reassure him...in came [Boissonnot's] relatives and those of his wife, who admonished him to confess in the ear of a priest and to receive the host....He gave them no response....His relations...resolved between them to have the host brought to him. Chantefoin...warned the invalid...to remain firm...keeping himself unpolluted. The poor man...asked Chantefoin how he should behave...'if you are pressed...spit it straight out.' Hardly had he finished these words when the priest arrived with the host, finding the room decked out just the same as if he was not expected, which made him very angry, but he had to calm down quietly. Having harangued the sick man in the accustomed fashion, he exhorted him to prepare himself graciously to receive his blessed creator. The invalid remained silent throughout....[The priest] urged him to respond....He shouted at him that if he could not receive it with his mouth, that at least he could show by a sign that he received it with his heart. As he said this, he lifted the host to his mouth so he could take it, seeing which the sick man turned round and spat out the host. At which point the priest...departed....Chantefoin...told [Boissonnot]...that he had...shown himself to be a true champion of Jesus Christ....'I have done well', said the invalid, 'there is no pardon for me before God'. Chantefoin, seeing that he had not been of any benefit to this man...sent for some good people of the religion....But this was in vain, for whatever they said, they were unable to bring him round. Seeing which Chantefoin told him...'When Satan comes to assail you...reply to him, "In Domino confido [I trust in the Lord]"'. The invalid...had [these words] on his lips at all times. And as he heard the cock crowing at midnight, he cried out loud, 'In Domino confido', making the 'O' long in imitation of the cock's crow....

Soon after some signs of death appeared in him.... [The] brother of the sick man, began to wonder, and...told [Chantefoin] that his brother had not been confessed and that he had not received a single sacrament, and...he would be dragged into view and battered to death. Therefore...he had resolved to have extreme unction brought to him. Chantefoin replied that for his part, he would never consent to that, and would prevent it as far as he was able. The brother... sent for the priest and brought him with the unction. Now he found the invalid in a pitiful state...completely [without] sight, hearing and speech....The invalid allowed [the priest] to do all that he wished...but when it came to taking off his stockings in order to grease his feet, he jumped up...cast his gaze here and there seeing...the priest dressed in his surplice...regarding Chantefoin...said to him, 'Ha, comrade! Is this how you keep your promise to me? Isabeau' (he said addressing his wife) 'you haven't given [the priest] money? Don't you want', said he speaking to the priest, 'to be paid for your grease and your oil? Villain, if I was up and had my strength, I would throw you downstairs. Go, and clear out fast.' This amazed all those present, and they all gave differing accounts....The invalid, having finished speaking, lay back down quietly in his bed....Chantefoin... asked the sick man...whether he wished to place his total confidence in our Lord Jesus Christ. 'Yes indeed', he replied: 'I have spoken to Him, He has forgiven all my trespasses, and has told me that before midnight, I will be with Him in His eternal Kingdom.'...He turned towards his wife and said to her, 'It's a long time since God united us in marriage, and so blessed us that we have been led to his truth. I beg you to persist and live and die in this and instruct our children in it. If after my death you want to remarry, make sure it is with someone who knows God and fears Him'...he fell silent. And at ten or eleven in the evening, he rendered his spirit peacefully to God, on 29 January [1559, presumably].

Thus it only remained for the poor widow, so delicate and frail, to find out how to appease the curate of her parish...so that no one challenged...the dead man's inheritance. So, firstly, she...bribed [the curate of St Jean] to keep his mouth shut. And after, overlooked none of the customary papal ceremonies and superstitions in her husband's funeral procession; had many masses, vigils, obits and trentals sung. In this way she won the favour of the curate and all the parish clergy.... The [Franciscan] Morel, since his convent had gained nothing, began to play games.... As he was giving a sermon, he attacked the Lutherans...'They are', he said, 'without religion, denigrators of the holy sacraments of the Church, people worse than dogs. They die like beasts, without confessing.... Isn't it a great shame to suffer such people in this city?'...(pointing to where Boissonnot's body had been buried a few days before) 'there's one of them, who is buried there, who had as his confessor only a shoemaker and some scabbard maker, who are as worthless as he. His body must be disinterred and thrown in the fire with his two kind confessors.' That was the game Morel played.... God provided so well that he could not achieve what he aspired to, and the people contained themselves more modestly than one could have hoped.

---

11   Calvin to Jacob Sturm on the Death of Francis

The cause of reform in France was seen to be aided by the death of the French king. Calvin's comments are very similar to those (above) of More on Zwingli's death. In a letter to Jacob Sturm, Calvin discusses the death of Francis I of France.

Geneva, 16 December 1560

[B4: 18. 270–2, passim – 48]

Have you ever read or heard of anything happen at a better time than the news that the King has died? These terrible events had become so horrible that there seemed no cure. Then, suddenly, God shows Himself from heaven. The same God who lanced the father's eye has now boxed the ear of the son.

---

12   Colloquy of Poissy (1561)

Just as the meeting at Regensburg (discussed above) attempted to reconcile Lutherans and Catholics at the insistence of the Emperor, likewise at Poissy the Regent-Queen Mother of France tried to force an agreement between the Catholics and the Calvinists. Beza, Calvin's co-minister and successor in Geneva spoke for the Calvinists. The gulf which actually separated the two sides is readily apparent.

[B13: 15. 159–196, passim]

We all agree that a supernatural change must necessarily take place in the sacraments. We do not say that the baptismal water is just water. Rather, it is the sacrament which regenerates us and washes our souls in Christ's blood. Likewise, the Communion bread is not just bread. Rather, it is a sacrament of Christ's precious body which is given for us. The wine is not just wine; it is the sacrament of the precious blood spilled for us. Nevertheless, we do not say that this change is to the material of the sign itself but that the change relates to the use and goal which each has been given. Also, this change does not happen because a few words are said, nor that it relies on the wants of the person who says the words. It is the power and will of Him who established these activities (which are very divine and heavenly) whose words must be read aloud in a clear voice in words which can be understood and accepted by the people present. So much for the outward signs. Let us consider what the Lord intended for these signs.

We deny that we believe what some people have mistakenly said that we teach: namely, that Communion is just a remembrance service of Christ's death. We deny that we believe that this gives us a share just in the results of His death and suffering. We agree with St Paul who said in I Corinthians 10 that the bread we break by his command is actually communing with Christ's body given for us. That the wine we drink is actually communion with His blood shed for us—the very same material as He took in the Virgin's womb and which He took with Him into heaven. Gentlemen, be fair, in God's name, what do you want to find in this sacrament that we do not also want to find there?

I already know the answer to this. Some insist that we say that the bread and wine are transmuted not, I say, into sacraments of Christ's body and blood (we agree with this) but into Christ's actual body and blood. Maybe some will not ask for so much but will only insist that we admit that the body and blood are really, physically in, with, or under the bread. Gentlemen, for God's honour, give us a patient hearing, try not to be shocked, throw away the prejudged ideas you have about what we believe. Should anyone manage to prove either of these beliefs from the Bible we will accept it to our dying day. We think, with the little wisdom God has given us, that this change – transubstantiation – does not agree with the correct understanding and interpretation of our faith. It contradicts the very nature of a sacrament which must remain the same if they are to be true signs of Christ's body and blood. Also, it makes the humanity and ascension into heaven meaningless. The same is true of the other view – consubstantiation – which is not based on Christ's words and is wholly unnecessary for receiving the fruits of the sacraments....

Gentlemen, this is the sum total of our beliefs on this issue. This (and I am willing to be corrected) does not twist Christ's words, nor those of St Paul. It does not undo Christ's humanity, nor His ascension, nor the establishment of the sacraments. It does not invite idle and unanswerable questions or categories. It does not lessen our communion with Christ which is why the sacraments were set up....

We see no reason to discuss baptism as we are sure that none of you thinks we are Anabaptists – no one opposes them more violently than we do. As to particular questions on this we feel that these can be sorted out once we have agreed on the major points under review at this friendly, cheerful meeting.

As to the other five sacraments, as some call them. Undoubtedly, we cannot agree to use this term for them until we can be convinced from the Bible otherwise. Nevertheless, we believe that we have a real confirmation in that we catechise and teach those who were baptised as children and all others as well before we let them take Communion. True penitence is taught by us also. This is when someone honestly faces their sins and makes amends (in public or private) to those who have been hurt, and then absolution by Christ's blood and finally, changing one's behaviour. Marriage, as taught by St Paul, as the ideal for all who are not blessed with the gift of singleness is supported by us. We do not think that anyone should be forced to remain single by any vows. We condemn filthy, lewd speech, gestures, and actions. Church positions, as taught in God's Word, are taught by us. We agree that a large part of the Gospel ministry is the visitation of the sick. Like St Paul, we say that people should not be judged because of what they eat or what holy days they keep – God's Kingdom is not about these things which go away eventually. However, we do condemn all bad living, we always encourage people to be sober, to ignore the desires of their flesh and to pray regularly.

[Guise replied for the Catholics]

...our opponents have attacked those not here – that is, we are not in Germany – in that they have implied that we are defending consubstantiation. Since the French Church does not believe in this we are happy to leave it to the Empire's princes and preachers – the so-called Protestants – to defend it. They do agree with us, at least, in rejecting the sacramentarian view as we and the Germans call it. They keep to Christ's words and insist that His body and blood is present in the sacrament....Apparently, I am boring you by talking more than I had planned rather than persuading you as I wished. We allow you to stay without order or reason and to reject all of the past from the earliest days of the Church until you left it. If you want for no reason to hate us because of upholding our side and that if you make it publicly clear that you want to be so separate from us, that you cannot bear to look at us, live with us, share accommodations with us or (and this chills me to say it) even to pray and sacrifice to God, to administer the sacraments in the same buildings at least do not refuse to listen to the judgement of the Greek Church – if you are so repulsed by the Latin (Roman) Church and are so unhappy with the Universal Church that you need an individual one. But why the Greek church? Look to the Augsburg Confession on that and you will stand condemned by all the Churches which accept it.

You cannot even agree with those others who have separated from us on this one point about the sacrament although you can agree with them on almost everything else. What hope is there that we will be able to come up with some form of words which we can both accept when we disagree on this and so many other points? If you are so in love with your own ideas then why not become hermits? If you have no desire to come to some compromise with us in belief or behaviour then go farther away from us and stop bothering the sheep over whom you have no legal control – our authority is from God.

---

13 Pierre de l'Estoile on Catholic Extremists

Despite Guise's assertions, the French Church and nation were not as united as he might have liked. Pierre de l'Estoile (1546–1611), a Parisian magistrate, chronicled the pro-Catholic behaviour of the French monarchy. However, even the king was not spared the attacks of the more inflammatory Catholic preachers. Catholic extremists were as great a threat to French stability as the Protestants. Their calls for the violent eradication of the Protestants would have plunged the nation into even more religious civil wars.

[L1: 324, 326f. – 18]

February 1583.

The King and his closest friends walked around Paris on Mardi Gras wearing masks. They went from door to door insulting many until six o'clock on the morning of Ash Wednesday. Most of the Parisians' preachers attacked him for his conduct during the day's sermons. The comments of Rose, a doctor of theology, were especially annoying to the king. Rose was sent for. He tried to get out of going because he was afraid he would be mistreated....In the end he went and only got a warning from the King...telling him not to repeat the attacks....Thus the king forgave him. Also, he sent him 400 crowns a few days later [with the message that Rose should use the money] 'to buy sugar and honey to get him through the Lenten fast and to be used to sweeten his bitter mouth'....

[*On the king's new confraternity and Poncet's preaching.*]

In 1583 the king set up a new confraternity called the 'Penitents'. He was a member as well as two of his favourites [probably, in fact, his male lovers]....On 25 March, the Feast of the Annunciation, they held their first meeting. They made a solemn procession at four o'clock in the afternoon from the Augustinian monastery to Notre Dame. Two by two they went...in white robes made of Dutch cloth...the king, without any guards, was in the parade dressed just like everyone else. The cross was carried by the Cardinal Guise, the Master of Ceremonies was Duke Mayenne (Guise's brother)....

They all joined in singing the 'Hail, Holy Queen' when they got to Notre Dame....None of this was slowed down by the fact that the rain poured down all day. A nobleman was prompted to write a short poem about the king's wet clothes. People found it so appropriate that they are repeating it everywhere:

> When he had bagged France,
> And put it to the sack
> How fit the penitence
> He comes in a dripping sack.

On Sunday, 27 March, the king arrested Poncet, a monk. His Lenten sermon at Notre Dame the day before was the cause. In it he had attacked the king's new confraternity saying it was made up of hypocrites and atheists.

Also, over a hundred younger servants were ordered beaten at the Louvre by the king because they had made fun of the Penitents' procession. They had put handkerchiefs over their heads with eye-holes cut in them and then copied the ceremonies but in a way that was obscene and rude.

[*On processions in Paris which were seen to be slightly more proper.*]

On 10 September [1583], nearly a thousand people marched through Paris. They wore white with veils over their heads, barefooted. They carried either a large candle or a wooden cross. They went two by two just like pilgrims. They came from villages in Brie, St Jean des Deux Gemeaux and D'Ussy. Two village gentlemen rode on horses as escorts and their wives followed in a carriage. Parisians, in large numbers, watched them as they prayed and made their gifts at Notre Dame. Pity and admiration touched them as they thought about the long and godly trip they had made in their bare feet....

---

14 Pieter Titelmans, Inquisitor to Regent Margaret of Parma Kortrijk (17 July 1562)

France was not alone in experiencing serious violence as a result of clashes between the supporters of Calvinism and Catholicism. Similar excesses were noted in the Low Countries (in effect, Belgium and the Netherlands. Once again, the spread of Protestantism was a grave challenge to social order.

[C3: 2.61f. – 21]

My Lady,

I went to Ieper on Monday on business of the bishop, our reverend father in God. While there I heard gossip about some scandalous behaviour in the village of Boescepe, near Steenvoorde. So I went there on Tuesday to find out the truth of the matter. I looked into the situation and found out that on the previous Sunday, during High Mass a man (an uneducated layman from the village) named Gheleyn Damman, had climbed up on a spot from where one can preach in the churchyard. He then gave a sermon attacking our Holy Mother, the Church, the Pope's (our Holy Father's) authority, the Mass' holy sacrifice, the altar's sacrament, and other parts and rites of our Holy Catholic faith. He caused a lot of concern and shock among the good people and insulted our Lord Jesus Christ and the Church. Some of the people there estimated that there was a crowd of about 150 to 200 people from the local area. To protect the preacher some of the crowd carried rusty swords and stout staffs, some pistols. Also, it is said that there were other supporters in the nearby hills ready to help if needed but I could not be sure of that because I had to get back to Ieper that same day.

This same preacher, Damman, was arrested and publicly humiliated wearing only his shirt in the village a few years ago for his heresy. His brother, Willem, was recently freed by supporters from the bishop's prison in Ieper.

I thought I should pass along this news to advise that Your Highness act, although I have also reported the matter to the Council of Flanders. It is about time that everyone did as much as possible, or so I think, though I am not able to do as much as I would like.

The normal methods for maintaining law and order are inadequate as Your Highness will find out. This is especially true in the countryside and villages where the poor simple people have been misled by these people who can go back and forth to England and other places. The same is true of the Anabaptists – those from Amantières are especially prominent.

---

15 Maximilien Vilain de Gand, Baron de Rassenghien, Governor of Lille, Douai and Orchies, to Regent Margaret of Parma on Calvinism in French Flanders (June 1566)

The early growth of Dutch Calvinism was noted for the use of outdoor preaching especially to very large crowds, the so-called 'Hedge-preaching'. The involvment of these (often ill-educated) preachers was both a cause of scandal and concern to the Catholic leaders. It made the movement all the more difficult to contain and eradicate.

[D4: 215f.]

Lille, 30 June 1566.

... In addition, I am forced to tell Your Highness that last night there were two

more preaching. The largest had 4,000 people...on the road to Tournai and was led
by a preacher named (or so I believe), Cornille de La Zenne, a blacksmith's son
from Roubai. His beliefs have made him a fugitive from justice for quite a while
now....We fear that as soon as the harvest is in and the barns full (in two or three
weeks' time) they will take over the countryside and starve the cities. Thus they will
use poverty to force people to follow them. I think, therefore, that orders should be
given soon to find some way to stop these meetings. I have been told by some that
certain French gentlemen are ready to aid the treasonous rebellion when it
comes....I am hopeful that we can rely on the nobles of the Low Countries ...

16   'Hedge-Preaching' in the Netherlands

The popular interest in this activity is obvious. Crowds could be attracted merely by the novelty.

[V1: 1. 2–14, *passim*]

Sunday, 30 June 1566.

Another person also preached. He was dressed just like the first person, in a gown
trimmed with ermine and a good felt hat. He was short and about thirty years old
and, from his accent, may have been from Kortrijk. He gave his sermon on a small
hill surrounded by trees and orchards near the chapel outside of St Lievenspoort.
He preached with his hat off and spoke with modesty. He sat on a pile of cloaks
and hoods which had been given to him by his audience and had a book in front of
him. Now and then he would read from the book and then go on with the sermon.
Before he started he had knelt and folded his hands in a very devout manner. He
came into the meeting area in a group of about six others. No one could be sure
who would preach and this was designed to avoid any attempts to surprise and
arrest him. He explained the Gospel reading for that day, attacked sins, and prayed
for the civic leaders, the king and the Pope asking that God would open their
minds so that His Word (as they call their beliefs) could be spread in peace. He had
said that he would preach at three o'clock but he actually started at two o'clock.

The audience was divided into three groups huddled close together: men,
women and young women. There were about thirty in each – as many as the age of
the preacher. Each group had a teacher and everyone had a small book and every
now and then they would sing a Psalm. There were books with the Psalm in metre
on sale for a stiver. There were lots of bystanders. They were all there to see the
strange goings-on which was especially unknown in Flanders. All this was told to
me by my laundry woman. I gave her a stern talking-to. I told her that all of us
would be in danger from a great evil if it were not stopped very soon. However, like
many simple people she thought it was all very innocent and even good for
people....

On Sunday 7 July 1566 – despite the rules – there were more sermons, this time at noon in Stallendriesche. Thousands of people from the city and the country came along including many of the common people who had little training in the Bible and the Church Fathers. The [preachers] said that the truth was being presented and the Gospel preached correctly for the first time. To prove this the preachers quoted the Bible loudly and forcefully. They encouraged the audience to check what they said against what was in their Bibles to see that they were preaching truthfully.

---

17 Iconoclasm in the Netherlands

Large gatherings and the unstable political system which saw the Hapsburg regent pitted against the local nobility and magistracies inevitably led to conflict. Iconoclasm, or the destruction of religious statues and adornments was relatively common. Moreover, there was little either side could do to contain these outbursts of popular violence once they began.

[B9: 1. 192–6; B10: 1. 342–50 – 12]

Antwerp, Aug 1566

The city rulers of Antwerp were afraid that, since the Prince of Orange was away – he had been called to a meeting in Brussels by the Regent on the morning of 19 August – the wave of image-breaking might head this way. They were especially concerned as this was fair-time and there were a lot of foreigners in town. Because of this they took the statue of the Virgin Mary (which was normally on display for a week during the fair) from the main part of the church and put it in the choir. There it was less likely to offend anyone. These good precautions ended badly…the mob saw that the rulers were afraid and became ruder. Some of them sarcastically asked the statue whether she had left her post out of fear.…A group of youths were playing near the pulpit and one of them climbed up into it and began to imitate the sermons. Some wanted to watch the show but others wanted it stopped. The boy held his place by kicking at those climbing up until a young ship captain climbed up the other side and threw him out headfirst. People took the boy's side and daggers were drawn to attack the ship captain who managed to escape the church although he was wounded.…

Another dispute about the statue of the Virgin started the next day when the mob again gathered in and around the church. An old woman who sits in front of the choir and sells candles and begs scolded the people. She threw ashes and garbage at the boys probably because she was angry that they said that her products were out-of-date and that she would go out of business. The church officials saw that the crowd was growing and becoming more unruly the bigger it got so they decided to clear the church and lock it. No one paid any attention to them. When the city leaders...at the town hall heard about this riot they went to the church and warned the people to leave and some did. Others pretended that they were there to sing the 'Salve Regina' after the evening service. They were told that it was cancelled that evening. They said they would sing it alone then and immediately in the corner someone started to sing a Psalm or a hymn. Others joined in. Some of the youths played with balls in the church and others kicked stones around. Some threw them in the church while others threw them at the altars.

---

18   Maximilien Vilain de Gand, Baron de Rassenghien, Governor of Lille, Douai and Orchies, to Regent Margaret of Parma on Iconoclasm

Short of violent and harsh retaliation there was little the (Spanish) authorities could do in the face of iconoclasm. The use of (mostly Spanish) troops, which could easily get out of hand, played into the hands of the Protestants who were keen to paint their Catholic opponents as the supporters of (a foreign) tyranny.

[D4: 217f.]

Lille, Friday 16 August 1566

My Lady,

I must warn Your Highness immediately about events last night. Some of the followers of the new sect came over from the Pays de l'Alleu along the Leie River claiming they were on the way to one of their sermons. Instead they burst into Mesen, Quesnoy, Warneton and Comines and, with the support of some locals, they raided and rioted in the churches, hospitals and monasteries smashing the statues and grave monuments. They did not hurt or kill anyone, as far as I know, but then they met no resistance.... The solution, I think, is that Your Highness send several companies of regular soldiers and raise some more troops as soon as possible....I cannot be sure of holding the town nor even the castle here unless I get help because I increasingly fear that I do not actually control the cannons. If I had some help in this I could take the initiative. No matter what I will not surrender the town or the castle as long as there is some chance of help from Your Highness. I urgently beg Your Highness to do something to meet this problem to stop worse from happening. At least provide enough so that I can hold Douai if I have to leave here.

---

19   Marnix on Mob Violence in the Netherlands (1567)

Some Protestants, aware of the general revulsion in Europe to mob violence, were concerned to present iconoclasm in as positive a light as possible – indeed, to disassociate Protestants from it altogether.

[T1: 1. 98–109, passim – 20]

Philip Marnix, *A true narrative* ...

I admit that among the image-breakers there were people who claimed to be of the [Protestant] religion. However, I also assert that there were just as many who made, and never would make, such a claim. In some places only women and children were involved in the destruction. In other places the bishops and priests began to hide all their valuables – many citizens did the same – because they thought that an order had been issued to hide what could be saved until the children and street urchins had finished destroying everything else. Elsewhere, the magistrates sent along their officers, accompanied by commoners, to do the work. Even now no one knows who started it. However, there are good reasons for thinking that this was started by the priests themselves in an attempt to get the civil officials to turn on the followers of the [Protestant] religion. They had obviously done this a number of times before to provoke new persecutions. It was also intended to wreck the churches' plan to send a letter to Her Highness [the Regent]. The priests and their supporters realised that this letter would ruin their petty schemes and that time was of the essence. In fact, no sooner had the violence in Antwerp died down than some men forced their way into the Church of Our Lady and started another riot. Six of them were arrested and hanged the next day. Of these, four were known papists of whom one was a well-known nobleman who had been urging on the rest. Thus, we must conclude that they tried to ruin the churches' plan by this plan. Later events prove this correct. The plan was abandoned and from then on those of the [Protestant] religion faced nothing but disapproval and hatred.

---

20   'The Request of Those of the New Religion to the Confederate Nobles (8 February 1567)'

In addition to trying to distance themselves from the behaviour of the mob, the Calvinists were very concerned to enlist leading nobles to their cause. Although the mob was able to disrupt order, the nobles were the best means to victory for the Protestants.

[K4: no. 151]

Now, contrary to what we have expected (based on your promises), the edicts have been strenuously carried out. Some who would not promise to remain faithful to the Roman Church have been jailed or banished. The ministers of God's Word have been persecuted, some even hanged, others have had their beards torn off, they have been shot at, and some who were close by have been fatally wounded. The crowds which had gathered were attacked, some cruelly killed for attending the services, some for singing the psalms on their way home, some for baptising their children in the Reformed Church. Children of others who had been baptised were taken away and rebaptised in public. This looked more like an Anabaptist spectacle than the behaviour of those adhering to the old rules. Letters were circulated ordering death for those practising the [Protestant] religion. As a result preaching stopped in many places and many of the king's faithful servants fled the country and their families to escape persecution. Because of hatred towards our faith the people of Valenciennes and the vicinity have been attacked more cruelly than they were by their enemies in the last war [against France]. Clearly, if defeated, the same fate will befall all churches immediately. In Gelderland, Friesland and elsewhere there have been similar attacks every day. Not only are secret schemes used by the magistrates and the provincial States to destroy our religion in many other places but also the attacks are often open and force is used. Armed men swarm over the land. Supporters of the [Protestant] religion in several towns and villages are mistreated worse by [these armed men] than they would be by a foreign enemy. They are attacked, pillaged, assaulted, their wives and daughters are raped – many other horrible things take place which need not be mentioned.

21 Viret on Consistory Cases

In addition to turning to nobles for assistance, the Dutch Calvinists also sought practical advice on church organisation and government for other leading Calvinists. Here, Pierre Viret, one of Calvin's closest confidants, gives advice on Consistory cases. To restore order once they had triumphed it was essential that the Protestants be able to set up a strong system of church government quickly. To delay risked falling victim to the very violence and disorder which had undermined the Spanish position.

[S4: 72–78, passim]

The most common cases which the consistory deals with are the following: superstition, disrespect to God, heresy, disobeying parents, or the city rulers, treason, rebellion, assault, adultery, pre-marital sex, theft, greed, kidnapping, rape, fraud, perjury, lying, visiting drinking-houses, gambling, wild partying, dancing and other shocking behaviour…the punishments will normally be reprimands, that is brotherly rebukes – which will be as harsh and strong as the situation demands – not being allowed to take Communion, temporarily or for a longer period of time, and the people who keep repeating their crimes will be named in public so that everyone will know who they are.

22 Wesenbeke on Calvinist Gains in the Netherlands

The Calvinists were able to continue their advances. The positive role of the printed word and the

failure of persecution in this are both discussed by Jacob van Wesenbeke,
　Description of the events....

[K4: no. 147]

The Netherlands, 1569.

The printed works flooding into the country could not be stopped by legal prohibition. The more edicts issued by the courts, the more the booklets and papers increased. One person said that the common people were being denied their freedom to discuss and discover the truth openly. This included [discussions] in the provincial councils and the towns or by lists of complaints or publications. The country's prosperity depended on this [freedom]. People wrote that these abuses would produce worse evil results and they said that the men who wanted to use these means to rule over the king and the country were afraid that their treason would be revealed if the Estates General were properly constituted and allowed to discuss freely. The refusal, then delay, in calling the Estates eventually renewed the turmoil, bitterness and grumbling among the people which had already been seen before the nobles presented their [previous] petition.... Those who disagreed on religion despaired and forced them to resist the government publicly and to state their beliefs bluntly rather than to accept oppression and submission. This is the reason they started to hold their meetings each day more openly which only attracted more people to them. Others became bitter and opposed the [government's] tactics for dealing with the situation. In their opinion, these methods were the cause of all the trouble, turmoil and abuses.

23   Calvinists Appeal for a Truce

Although advancing on a number of fronts, the Dutch Calvinists were also willing to appeal to the king in an effort to arrange a truce. They hoped to be able to consolidate their position in the areas they controlled outright before beginning the final assault to 'free' the rest of the Low Countries.

[K4: no. 363]

22 June 1578.

The Protestants promise to accept all reasonable conditions and to maintain and conform to all conditions which Your Majesty might be pleased to suggest. They beg you to recall that they have suffered much for their country – indeed they are ready to give themselves, their lives and possessions for their homeland – and their loyalty and obedience has been great since the [Pacification of Ghent]. Appropriate action has been taken whenever one of them has behaved in a manner which did not command common consent. These errors are not like those done by the people who say they are for the common good and then openly side with the enemy. The Protestants, should any wrong befall them (one hopes it will not), are determined to continue to fulfil their duty to their homeland.

---

24   Beutterich on the Possible Consequences of a Truce

While appealing to the king there were also Calvinists (for example, Peter Beutterich), who were realistic in their pessimistic response to Catholic suggestions for a truce and mutual toleration. For the Spanish who advocated a truce there was always the possibility that the rebels would fall to fighting amongst themselves.

[K4: no. 392 – on toleration: 95, 173]

c. 1 October 1578.

One needs to understand exactly what has been hidden by the Roman Catholic Church under the guise of the guarantee of the Pacification of Ghent. This agreement is so well thought of that some of the most patriotic and many of the plain, honest people are blind to the tricks and plots associated with it. Their enthusiasm for common liberty lessens and actually ceases. They are afraid of resisting this tyranny lest they harm, in the least little bit, the Roman Catholic Church in any way, thereby troubling their peace of mind. This concern has been elevated to the greatest height possible by the defenders of the Roman Catholic Church.

Thus, preserving the Roman Catholic Church and preserving tyranny amount to the same thing here. I will say it again, preserving the Roman Catholic Church here is the same thing as preserving a tyranny which is worse than the one inflicted by the barbarians and Turks. At least the Turks, who are dictators over the body leave the conscience alone. The supporters of the Roman Catholic Church want to be tyrants over the body and the mind.

Keeping the Roman Catholic Church means bringing back banishments and confiscations, burning people at the stake again, re-building the gallows throughout the provinces, bringing back the Inquisition, and, finally, dredging up from Hell those vile, accursed laws. Remembering those laws fills every true patriot with dread and disgust. They recall the pouring of so much South Netherlandish [Belgian] blood from so many martyrs and that for one sole reason: the one and only Roman Catholic religion...

Maintaining real freedom and the Roman Catholic Church are mutually exclusive. Keeping the Roman Catholic religion means nothing less than restoring the Spanish tyranny. The goals of the Spanish and the Roman Catholics are identical. The Spanish want the Roman religion established, so do the Catholics.

The Catholics want the king to be accepted and given his due, so do the Spanish. We accept, rather than deny, that the king should receive his due as sovereign lord. However, there is a vast difference between what is lawfully due to the king and what the supporters of the Roman Catholic religion have in mind. They do not mean that one should obey the King in law, justice and fairness by keeping to the old customs and traditions. Rather, they mean that one should do everything the tyrant commands without a word of complaint, without a challenge, without resistance. In sum, it means being a serf and a slave.

This then is the goal these tin-pot dictators, the supporters of the Roman Catholic religion, have in mind; this has also always been the goal of the Spanish.

5   Conflict Among the Protestants
'We play dice at the foot of [Christ's] cross to see who gets His clothes'

[*Suggested readings:* 125, 217, 236, 254, 274, 275, 305, 306, 307, 436, 488]

1   Erasmus to Martin Bucer

Erasmus gives a concise evaluation of the competing reform movements. He is especially scathing of the tendency of the reforming to splinter. This constant fragmentation was one of the most damaging features of the Reformation from the Catholic point of view; it made the claim of the (various) Protestant group(s) to be the true Church seem rather questionable.

11 November 1527.

[**A2:** 7. 231–33 – 10, 36, 42, 60, 61]

You have given a number of guesses as to why I have not joined your Church. First and foremost, I want you to know that my conscience has held me back. If I could have been convinced that this movement came from God I would have enlisted long ago. Also, I can see that there are a number of people in your camp who are completely unknown to Evangelical truth. I will not repeat rumours and suspicions. I will speak from experience, indeed ones which have hurt me. Experiences taught me not just by the mob but by people of worth, indeed leaders. It is not my place to judge things I do not know; the world is a big place. I knew some people who were excellent before they joined your side; what has become of them since, I do not know. As far as human judgement will allow, it seems to me that many of them have become worse and none have improved.

The third thing which has held me back is the constant in-fighting between the leaders. Leaving aside the Prophets and the Anabaptists, just look at the spiteful pamphlets written by Zwingli, Luther and Osiander against each other. I have always condemned the venom of the leaders but they are egged on by the actions of certain people. In actual fact, if you were what you brag of being, they would have set an example of godly and patient conduct which would have made the Gospel widely acceptable. Laying aside everything else, what possible point was there in Luther starting up all that tomfoolery with the English king? [The king] was trying do something very difficult and was doing it with general support. Did [Luther] not think about how he looked? Did he not realise that everyone was watching him? This is the movement's leader! I am not overly upset with him for treating me so badly. However, his betrayal of the Gospel, inciting the princes, bishops, false monks and theologians against good people have made everyone's burden (which is already bad enough) twice as heavy – these actions drive me mad. I foresee a violent and bloody century should those who are angry get their strength back, as they surely will. You can say that every crowd has its unruly elements. But surely it was the responsibility of the leaders to pay special attention to conduct and not even to speak to liars, false-witnesses, drunks, and fornicators. The Gospel would have looked good to everyone if the husband had found it made his wife nicer, if the teacher saw his student more obedient, if the magistrate had seen better-behaved citizens, if the employer found his employees more honest, if the buyer saw the merchant less deceitful. But, as things are now, the conduct of some people has thrown cold water on the enthusiasm of those who initially supported the movement: the sort of people who loved godliness and hated Pharasaism. The princes, some of whom were hopeful at the start, are now cursing as they contemplate the host which has appeared full of vagrants, fugitives, bankrupts, the naked, the destitute, and, primarily, evil people.

2   Conrad Grebel to Münzer (5 September 1524)

Anabaptism, by calling for a voluntary, gathered church, was threatening the unified fabric of sixteenth-century society. There was a widely accepted assumption that everyone was, in some sense, part of Christendom, the Church. Everyone had been baptised but the Anabaptists undermined this universality of Christianity by questioning the validity of that baptism. To them, society was not Christian, only individuals. If there was to be a collective religious identity then it was that of the gathered and separated local church.

5 September 1524.

[C2: 2. 245 – on Anabaptism: 118, 123, 171, 177, 179, 230, 242, 251, 277, 284, 293, 304, 321, 326, 327, 330, 332, 339, 347, 351, 380, 383, 410, 422, 423, 424, 458, 459, 460, 461, 476]

We believe...that every child which does not yet know the difference between good and evil...is saved by Christ's sufferings....Also, infant baptism is silly, blasphemous outrage, contrary to the Bible....As...you have written against infant baptism we hope that you do not baptise children thereby betraying God's Word, wisdom and commands which says only believers should be baptised.

3   Balthasar Hübmaier to Oecalampadius

The Anabaptist attack on the traditional practice of infant baptism was a grave threat to other reform leaders. Without a clear Biblical passage to cite in defence of the practice they were forced to rely both on tradition and interpretations of the act which linked the New Testament initiatory rite with that of the Old Testament, circumcision.

16 January 1525.

[C2: 2. 245]

We have said in public that children should not be baptised. Why do we still baptise children? [Zwingli and Jud] say it is only a sign. We argue about a sign? However, the meaning of this symbol, the promise of faith unto death and the hope of the resurrection and the life to come is more important than the sign. This promise has nothing to do with babies and therefore their baptism is meaningless. In Baptism people give themselves to God. In Communion people give themselves to their neighbours, offering body and blood for another as did Christ. I believe, in fact, I am sure, that things will not improve in Christendom until the proper, pure meaning of Baptism and Communion are restored. Brother, this is my opinion. If I am wrong, correct me. If you and others can convince me from God's Word I would love to leave this belief, indeed, deny it altogether. Until then I will stick with my view because the Word of Christ forces me to – the Word, faith, truth, judgement and my conscience. Tell the truth; it will not offend me. I am human, I can make a mistake, that is being human, but I heartily want to be corrected. Write and tell me whether the verse in Matthew (19: 14), 'suffer the little children to come unto me', etc., applies only to infants. This question arises because Christ adds 'for such is the kingdom of heaven', not 'of them'. I have sent letters to Zwingli through the captain of our volunteers. I think the verse means that instead of baptism the church should be gathered and the children brought in and the Gospel be explained to them in German. 'They brought little children, etc.', and they were given names, the entire church prays for them on its knees and gives the children to Christ asking Him to be gracious and intercede for them. If the parents are weak and still convinced of the need for baptism then I baptise it. I am weak for the sake of the weak for now until things improve. As for what the Bible teaches I do not give in an inch.

---

4 Confessions from Fourteen Anabaptists (Zollikon, 7 February 1525)

Anabaptism represented the most radical wing of the increasingly fragmented movement for reform. In addition to calling for a separation of the church from society (by gathering only a voluntary membership) it also had numerous radical ideas on the relationship between the individual and society. For example, many (though not all) Anabaptist groups supported some concept of communal ownership of property and most (though again not all) were pacifist.

[E1: nos 622, 624]

They have confessed that they have been baptised and now call themselves 'servants, serfs and subjects of God'. They say that they do whatever God's Spirit encourages them to do and will not allow civil authorities to stop them from obeying the Spirit. They were willing to obey the civil authorities as long as this did not mean disobeying God's Word....Rudolph Thomunn of Zollikon admitted that he, the old assistant curate [Brötli] and the [pastor] of Wytikon [William Röubli] had had Communion and then gone to his house...they were joined by many people who filled the room, there was a lot of talking and lengthy readings. Hans Bruggback of Zumikon finally stood up weeping and shouting that he was a great sinner and he asked all of them to pray to God for him. Then Blaurock asked if he wanted God's grace. 'Yes', he replied. Then Manz stood up and said: 'Who will stop me from baptising him?' Blaurock said, 'No one.' So, taking a bowl of water, [Manz] baptised him in the name of God, Father, Son and Holy Spirit. After this, James Hottinger stood up and asked to be baptised, too. Felix Manz baptised him as well...Blaurock then looked at a loaf of bread on the table and said: 'Those who believe that God has redeemed them by His death and His crimson blood...let them come with me and eat this bread and drink this wine.' Several ate and drank with him.

---

5 Kessler on Total Immersion

More Anabaptist expressions which highlight that Anabaptist practice did not originally or necessarily involve total immersion. For them, the presence of faith, rather than the quantity of water was the greater concern.

7 February 1525.

[K2: 1. 262]

Wolfgang Uolimann met Conrad Grebel while going to Schaffhausen. He was so thoroughly convinced of Anabaptism that he was not content to have a little water poured on him from a bowl. Instead, stark naked, he was dunked in the waters of the Rhine.

---

6 Trial of Dr Hübmaier, Waldshut (7 February 1525)

More Anabaptist expressions. From the Catholic perspective it would have been very difficult to differentiate between the changes and behaviour in this extract and the actions of Carlstadt, Zwingli, and others (above). All involved radical alterations to traditional practices and methods of worship.

7 February 1525.

[K3: 455, modified]

[Hübmaier] said that baptism was introduced by William Röubli of Wytikon. He told how Röubli came to him while he was in Waldshut and told him what God had in mind for him. Several citizens came along with Röubli and then went with him to a nearby village where they were baptised by him. Later, they approached Hübmaier and asked why he was not willing to deal with the matter. He declined and put off a decision until Easter. Then, when it was customary to bless the baptismal font, he did not. Then Röubli baptised him as well as another sixty people. Later, during Easter itself [Hübmaier] himself baptised another 300 people.

7 Zürich Edict Against Anabaptism (7 March 1526)

The Zürich city council finally took action against the Anabaptists who were considered to be a grave threat to social cohesion and good order. They ordered Anabaptists drowned. This was perceived to be an appropriate punishment for those determined to be baptised 'again' – Anabaptists would say that they were being baptised for the first time. Anabaptists, because of their rejection of normally accepted economic and political structures and traditional practices meant to provide social cohesion and universally believed models for the Church, attacked the sixteenth-century world on every front.

[E1: no. 936]

For a long time now our Lords the Burgomaster, Council and Great Council have tried to convince the confused and mistaken Anabaptists of their errors. However, several...have refused to change and this has harmed the public good, the civic rulers as well as the common wealth generally and godly Christian living. Also, several of them (men, women, and young girls) have been punished by our rulers and jailed. Now, in this edict, command and warning our Lords, mentioned above, order that henceforth no one (man, women, or young girl) in this town, the countryside or the town's possessions is to baptise anyone else. If someone does baptise someone else in the future that person will be arrested by the state and, according to this decree, drowned without mercy. Everyone is clear about how to obey and what they need to do to avoid this punishment.

8 Marburg Colloquy (1529)

The fragmentation of the Swiss Reformation resulting from the break between the Zwinglians and the Anabaptists was not the sole breach in the reforming movement. There were also major theological differences between them which separated Zwingli and Luther from the start. The magistrates, both princely and civic, who supported the two men were concerned to repair the split. They were convinced that the new movement needed to present a united front when dealing with Catholicism and, especially, the Emperor. Thus, Luther and Zwingli were persuaded to attend a 'face-to-face' meeting to resolve their differences.

[K5: 48. 7–38]

Zwingli:

Let's turn to the Lord's Supper now. When our presentation is over we will be glad to talk about any and all points of dispute.

Luther:

Fine. But I want to say here and now that I do not agree with such things. I don't want anyone at home saying I sat here and said nothing. Your basic points are these: When all is said and done you want to say that a body cannot be in two places at one time. You bring forth proofs about the 'unlimited body' based on common sense. I do not ask how Christ can be God and man or how the two natures can be joined. God is greater than our ideas and we must simply accept his Word.

You have to prove that when the Bible says, 'This is my body', that Christ's body is not actually there. Rational arguments I will listen to but I completely reject those proofs based on physical or geometrical properties. For example, that a door cannot become a gate....God is beyond science and God's words must be revered and obeyed in awe. God says, 'Take, eat, this is my body'. What I want then is valid Biblical proof that this is not so.

[Luther wrote, 'This is my body' on the table with chalk and covered the words with a velvet cloth. This inability or unwillingness to depart from these words proved to be, in the final analysis, the major stumbling-block between the Lutherans and the Zwinglians.]

[Oecolampadius and Luther]

Oecolampadius:

John Chapter 6 makes all the other passages clear. Christ does not mean a local presence. He says, 'The flesh is of no avail' (John 6:63). I don't intend to use rational or geometrical arguments, nor do I deny God's power, but, while I have the whole faith in me, I will argue from it. Christ rose; He sits at God's right hand; thus, He cannot be in the bread. This interpretation is not new or sacrilege. It is based on the faith and the Bible.

One has to go from a physical meal to a spiritual one. The Bible uses figurative language, metaphors...where the words don't always mean what they say. Thus, words like 'This is my body' can be figurative just like 'John [the Baptist] is Elijah' (Matt. 11:14), 'The rock was Christ' (1 Cor. 10:4), 'I am the true vine' (John 15:1),

'The seed is the word of God' (Luke 8:11)....You believe that it is an obvious religious truism that Christ is in the bread. But this is actually only an opinion not a belief. Attributing too much to something physical is evil.

Luther:

I return to the words of the Lord's Supper. When I say, 'body which is given for us' this is not 'a limited understanding of the Bible'. Even if we only meant the bread alone this would not be 'a limited understanding of the Bible'. The least thing commanded by the Master is spiritual....For example, when a ruler orders that a shoe be put on a horse, the horseshoe is a little thing among little things....[But] when a prince tells a servant to shoe a horse then the iron becomes valuable when it is put on the horse's hoof....We would very much like to agree with you but we can't because your interpretation is a wanton mistake. I ask forgiveness, gracious prince and lord! But these words, 'This is my body' hold me captive....

Oecalampadius:

I can accept this illustration. Luther wants to say that God's word gives us Christ in the bread.

Luther:

Exactly. For example: a prince orders that a piece of iron be made into a horseshoe and then attached to something of value. Thus something unimportant becomes important. This is how to understand Christ's meaning.

Oecalampadius:

If we have this spiritual meal then why do we need a physical one?

Luther:

Your argument boils down to this: because there is a spiritual meal there is no need for a physical one. My answer is that we aren't denying the spiritual meal, in fact we insist that it is necessary. But this doesn't mean that as a direct result the physical meal is useless or unnecessary. I don't ask whether it is necessary or not, that isn't why we are here. It is written, 'Take, eat, this is my body'. Because of this one has to obey and believe no matter what the cost. One has to do this! One has to do this! Without this I could not be baptised, I could not believe in Christ! He gives Himself to us in many ways: in preaching, in baptism, in consoling our brethren, in the sacrament. Over and over again Christ's body is eaten just as He ordered us to do. If He were to order us to eat shit I would do it and be convinced that it was good for me. Servants don't sit around questioning their lord's commands. You just have to close your eyes.

Oecalampadius:

Where does the Bible say that we should wander through the Bible with our eyes shut, Master Professor?

Luther:

We could keep on arguing for a hundred years and it wouldn't get us anywhere! Until you can get rid of my verse I will not admit defeat. The same person who spoke in John chapter 6 said, 'This is my body'.

Oecalampadius:

John chapter 6 says, 'There flesh is of no avail'. Eating the flesh accomplishes nothing, but taking in the spirit does. We have to open our eyes to what is useful and then respect God's will. We insist on this open-eyed interpretation of the Bible and demand that verses interpret other verses. That is what Augustine did. I stand by what I've said.

Luther:

Well, I stand by my verse.

[Zwingli and Luther]

Zwingli:

Doctor Luther refuses to give ground on this point because he is prejudiced and has already made up his mind. He won't yield until someone quotes a passage which says that the Lord's Supper is figurative. This is the prejudice of an heretic like Helvidius who said that Jesus could not be Mary's only son because the Bible says, 'So his brothers said to him' (John 7:3). You can't use the Bible this way!...You yourself admit that it is the spiritual meal which is worthwhile. Since we agree on this, the most important point, I beg you for Christ's love not to label someone an heretic for these [other] differences. The [Church] fathers disagreed without condemning one another....You take a view opposed to that of the Gospel writers. Your comments on cutting up and chewing are bizarre and inappropriate....You mentioned taking the Bible literally. Some of that I can agree with but other bits I reject because they were completely silly, for example: 'If God told us to eat shit'. What God tells us to do is for our good. God is truth and light He doesn't lead us into darkness. Thus, he doesn't mean 'This is my body', literally, actually, physically because that contradicts the Bible. Satan's words are hard to understand, not Christ's. That isn't how God works. The soul is spiritual, the soul doesn't eat flesh. The spirit eats spirit.

Don't be offended by what I've said. I want your friendship, not enmity. I disagree with you willingly Doctor Luther, and with you Master Philip.

Luther:

Out of respect to God and our gracious lord and prince I will keep control of myself. The past is the past. Let's look forward! We may not be able to agree on everything but we can still have fellowship. I will return to that at the end.

As to Helvidius, you can prove from the Bible that 'brothers' can sometimes mean 'cousins'. That does not make 'This is my body' a figure of speech. When you say 'eating' you seem to mean anything and everything but 'eating'. 'Eating' to you means flesh, flesh. Even if you were right the whole thing would still be pointless. If God put rotten dried-up apples in front of me and said that I should eat them in a spiritual sense based on His word I would. When God talks to us faith is necessary. If He connects a physical meaning then we must accept it....

Zwingli:

Luther is just using the debating technique of exaggeration. His argument is powerful: When God speaks then you know He has spoken. If God says to eat His body as a memorial then we can be sure that it pleases Him when we do. Luther is not talking about what the Bible means – just what it says. The meaning shows us God's will. We claim that it is impossible for God to order us to eat His flesh in a physical sense....

Luther:

You're getting off the point in attacking my 'techniques' and 'exaggerations'...there are a lot of verses with a clear meaning rather than a figurative one....I am not deliberately saying that the meaning of the words is not obvious....I'll say again what I already said: your basic assumption is shaky. Admit defeat and give God the glory!

Zwingli:

We demand that you give God the glory and stop begging the question. This is the issue: Where is your proof? I am more than willing to consider your views with care – I mean no harm. You're trying to out argue me. I stand on my verse in John 6 and will not be moved. You'll have to change your tune.

Luther:

You're being rude.

Zwingli:

Can't you see that in John 6 Christ was trying to clear things up for those who are confused.

Luther:

You're trying to take over the debate. You want to judge. Let someone else do that. John says: 'This is a hard saying.' The Jews were talking about things which were impossible and ridiculous. Your view has to be proven, not mine. Let's stop this sort of carrying on, it's a waste of time.

Zwingli:

Exactly. You have to show that John 6 means a physical meal.

Luther:

You're making no sense and getting as far as a stick in a corner. You're getting nowhere.

Zwingli:

No, no, no! This verse will break your neck!

Luther:

Don't be so sure! Necks don't break that easily. You're in Hesse not Switzerland. Christ's body is deadly, poisonous, and satanic when eaten by an unworthy person....

Zwingli:

Please forgive me for what I just said. It is just a Swiss expression.

Landgrave Philip:

Apology accepted. Doctor Luther, please don't be offended by the expression....

Luther:

You have better arguments, let's hear them. It is only too clear that you have had enough time to make your points and yet nothing has come of it. I can't agree with you.

Oecolampadius:

If you aren't convinced by what has been said then a thousand quotations from the Church Fathers would do no good. Our text and our interpretation have failed to convince you. We want to stop.

Luther:

Fine. But you have proved nothing. Your conscience will testify against you on that.

Chancellor Feige:

Your assignment was 'to seek ways and means of achieving harmony'.

Luther:

The only way I know that this can be done is for you to keep God's word and agree with us.

Oecolampadius:

We can't believe or accept that Christ's body is there.

Luther:

I leave you to God and His judgement. I thank you, Mister Oecolampadius, for giving me your views not with bitterness but friendship. Mister, Zwingli, despite your anger I thank you as well. I apologise if I have been harsh to you. I am only human. I really wish that the issue could have been resolved to our mutual satisfaction.

Oecolampadius:

I pray that God's will will protect His poor Church.

Zwingli (tearfully):

Doctor Luther, I ask you to forgive my anger. I have always wanted your friendship and I still do. There is no one else, in Italy or France, whom I would rather see.

Luther:

Pray that God will open your eyes!

Oecolampadius:

Pray to him yourself. You need Him as badly as we do!

---

9 Münster Colloquy (August 1553)

There were also attempts to reconcile Anabaptism with the rest of the reform movement. At the Münster Colloquy (August 1533), Anabaptists were able to convince a significant portion of the populace. The result was that the city fell under the control of the Anabaptists who then introduced a very radical 'reformation'. This included prophetic contact directly with God, intense expectation that Christ's return was at hand and, even, polygamy. All those who refused to accept believer's baptism were forced out of the city. In the end, the city was besieged and taken in a violent and bloody assault by a combined Catholic and Protestant army. Thus, ended the sole successful Anabaptist takeover of a government. It is also worth noting that this also destroyed the only major Anabaptist group willing to support violent methods of advance or (even) of self-defence.

[H3: 20. 151–194]

Bernard [Rothmann, Anabaptist]:

It is more than clear from God's Word that infant baptism is an abomination. First, Busche admits that infant baptism is not set out in the Bible and fails to present any clear passage for it. Thus it is contrary to His Word and commandments. Various passages show that one should not add to or delete things from the Bible (Deut. 4:12; Prov. 30; Eccles. 3; Isa. 8). Since infant baptism is not commanded in the Bible it is illegal and an abomination to God....

Christ is the perfect source of salvation (John 1; Matt. 17): 'This is my beloved Son, listen to Him.' Christ frequently ordered his disciples to baptise believers – but belief comes from hearing and accepting Biblical teaching, which is God's seed. By this one must be born again before baptism (John 1, etc.). This makes it perfectly clear that infant baptism is an addition to the Bible and offends the faith. This is what makes it illegal – an abomination and a sin.

[Hermann] Busche [Lutheran]:

I return to my original assertion. If Bernard and his friends are correct and infant baptism without faith is an abomination then we're all abominations. If infant baptism is an abomination to God even if not a sin the fact remains that we're still unbaptised. If not being baptised is a sin doesn't that make us abominations in God's eyes?

Secondly, Bernard accuses me for supposedly admitting that infant baptism is an abomination because I agreed that there is no clear Biblical passage about it. I say again, a clear, obvious verse is not needed. It is much more necessary that those who oppose infant baptism produce a clear, obvious verse forbidding it. There are lots of things not mentioned in the Bible which are still perfectly acceptable. For example, the perpetual virginity of Mary or that the Bible nowhere mentions the baptism of the apostles but because it often mentions that they are baptising we can surmise that they were. How could they baptise someone if they weren't already baptised? Also, the Bible never mentions women taking the body and blood of Christ so why are women allowed to receive the sacrament? ...

Bernard:

Busche argues that it isn't necessary to support infant baptism from the Bible but that those who forbid it must have Biblical passages.

We will not accept Busche's sad argument...any more than we will agree that anything else not found in God's Word can only be rejected with clear Biblical passages. Doing this would mean accepting Masses, indulgences, requiems, holy days, Purgatory. None of these is clearly and expressly forbidden in the Bible and have been done for a long time. My opinion, however, is that what men should do or require must be based through God's name and command, on a positive word from God (as Peter says, I Pet. 4:11)....

Since this practise of great importance – some argue that it can turn heathen children into Christians by dripping salvation on them – it is essential that this have a clear basis in God's Word and command.

Turning to Busche's previous arguments. Infant baptism can be proven to be forbidden by the Bible. First, Christ's words in the last chapter of Matthew: 'Go forth', Christ said to His disciples, 'teaching all people, baptising them (who understand the teaching) in the name of the Father', etc., 'teaching them to observe all that I have commanded'.

Christ is commanding that everyone who has been taught is to be baptised and that the baptised are in turn commanded to obey everything which He commanded.

Now, infants can't be taught, therefore Christ has excluded them from baptism. He is clear about whom to baptise.

Also, look at the last chapter of Mark: 'Go into all the world, preaching to the whole creation. He who believes and is baptised will be saved; but he who does not believe the teaching will be condemned.'

This makes it clear that preaching is for everyone but that baptism is only for those who believe the apostles' teachings and God's Word.

---

10   Roset on Disputes between Geneva and Berne (1539)

Even when the disputes amongst the Protestants did not lead to an open breach they could be very dangerous. The Genevan and Bernese reformations were very much in the Zwinglian mould. Nevertheless, they differed in a number of areas which even Calvin considered intrinsically unimportant. However, attempts to reconcile the practices in the two cities were fraught with peril. For Calvin (and Farel), the issue at stake was whether or not the magistracy had the inherent power or right to make decisions about such matters without consulting the ministers. One can understand how the ministers would want to maintain their role in this process. One can also understand how the government which had deposed the Prince-Bishop, severed all links with Savoy and abolished the Mass and Catholicism by majority vote would think that it was more than competent in other religious areas as well.

[R3: 250f., 314–319]

At Geneva, plain bread was used for the Lord's Supper. And, as today, baptisms were conducted without baptisteries. Also, all holy days were abolished except Sundays. The customs adopted in Berne were not the same. They used unleavened bread...they baptised at the fonts which stood outside the churches. They had four high holy days: Christmas, Easter, Ascension and Pentecost [Whitsunday]. Many Genevans took the occasion of this difference of ceremonies to complain about their ministers....The Bernese magistrates called a meeting at Lausanne where they met with Farel and Calvin in a friendly fashion. When they were all there they demanded that [Farel and Calvin] adopt the [Bernese] practices....Farel and Calvin said the issue needed to be debated but [the Bernese] refused....It was suggested...that [the decision] should wait for a conference at Zürich....But, a Genevan citizen arrived with letters ordering the ministers to say whether they would conform [to the Bernese practices]. The ministers felt the letters violated the resolution to wait for the Zürich meeting. The Senate complained about the ministers' refusal to answer the letter and decided to adopt the Bernese practices.

At this point great blasphemies and excesses began....The ministers were threatened by the crowd. They were told they would be thrown into the Rhône River if they wouldn't conform to the [Bernese] ceremonies. This scandalous behaviour went unpunished. One of the ministers, who was blind, named Corauld, spoke from the pulpit like a prophet. He called Geneva a 'kingdom of frogs – rats in the hay'....He was arrested the day before Easter and expelled [from Geneva] six days later.

[*Even within the Genevan Reformation there were many possible areas of disagreement and conflict. In some cases these related to theological issues, for example, predestination, and in others to more practical concerns, for example, the correct relationship between Church and state in the area of social control. Also, for many Genevan leaders, there was a question as to how powerful the ministers should be. The ministers were foreign and, in effect, paid civil servants.*]

In February, a hateful and lying council member said that Calvin had been teaching false doctrine and other blasphemies for the previous seven years...the council member was condemned and ordered to carry a torch through the city to make up [for his offence]....Also, the taverns were closed down for a while....In the place the Senate set up fellowship halls....In three months the whole [tavern] situation was a mess and everything went back to the way it had been....In June, a comedy called *The Acts of the Apostles* was to be put on in Geneva. Some of the ministers were unhappy because it was very expensive and the times were hard....One of the ministers attacked the [play] from the pulpit. The actors and actresses claimed that he had insulted them greatly and they complained [to the Senate]. After an investigation it was decided that the minister had done his job well.

The Captain-General [the militia commander] and his relatives in the Senate claimed that the magistracy had control over [excommunication]....But Calvin resisted this view on behalf of the ministers. He complained to the Senate....Nevertheless, there were many excesses and bad behaviour. Many lies and threats were made against the ministers. At the end of June, the Captain-General's wife, who had been admonished for dancing (which was against the rules), called the minister, Abel Poupin, a 'pig's groin'.

---

11 Dentière on Disputes between Geneva's Ministers and Magistrates (1539)

Maire Dentière, as early as 1539, gives an example of just how bitter the breaks within the reforming movement could become. When Calvin and Farel were unwilling to implement changes bringing Genevan practices into line with those in Berne, they were fired by the city's magistrates. Dentière reacted strongly to this and sent a letter to Marguerite, Queen of Navarre (a famous supporter of, though not convert to reform) defending the ministers' stance. In the process she expressed her views on other Protestants as well. This letter was so provocative that it forced the city to introduce magisterial censorship of all publications in Geneva. So successful were they that only one copy of this letter has survived. It is most interesting, however, for highlighting the quandary which faced many reformers: how to maintain the right of individuals to study and interpret the Bible while upholding traditional societal views on the role of women.

[**D3** – on women: 31, 43, 71, 79, 92, 94, 112, 113, 114, 141, 183, 184, 196, 244, 292, 329, 355, 417, 445, 467, 471, 473]

A very useful letter composed and written by a Christian woman from Tournai addressed to the Queen of Navarre, sister to the king of France, attacking the Turks, Jews, unbelievers, false Christians, Anabaptists and Lutherans.

[sig., d2v°]

We see the whole world full of curses and the people are troubled. We see lots of fighting, debates, dissension, divisions. One against another…lots of envy, noise, malice, ill-will, greed, fornication, theft, blackmail, blood-letting, murder, tumult, rape, arson, poisoning, war, kingdom against kingdom, nation against nation….In short, every abomination abounds. Father against son, son against father. Mother versus daughter, daughter versus mother. Each selling the other – a mother handing her daughter over to every evil.

[sig., d4 – d4v°]

Not only do liars and enemies of the truth attack us with great boldness and arrogance but also even some of the faithful. They say that women are being too hasty in writing to one another about the Bible. One can quite correctly respond that all those [women] who wrote and are mentioned in the Bible weren't considered to be too hasty. Many [women] are mentioned and praised in the Bible for their morals, deeds, support, and example as well as for their faith and doctrine….I wonder who would dare to condemn Ruth because she was female.

[sig., facing c]

Obviously, many are called but few are chosen. Many believe truly but few are saved. Likewise, only a few are rightly called Christians, glorifying in God alone. But most call themselves Franciscans, Dominicans, Clairisses, Marians, Augustinians, sectarians, papists, Anabaptists and Lutherans. As such they have no part in Christ. Their fount is false and they are not baptised in Christ's name.

[sig., c2v°]

Nowadays some Anabaptists clearly and plainly reject and renounce God's election. They say that the will has the power and freedom to damn. This gives them lots of saviours rather than one Saviour, Jesus. They claim justification by works and merit. They set up a new form of papacy which is worse – and more dangerous – than the old variety.

[sig., facing d–d]

[They say] the Bible has lots of meanings and can be interpreted in many ways. Women and the uneducated can't understand it, only educated teachers. [The rest] should just believe without question.…But I ask you. Didn't Jesus die for the poor and ignorant?…Did he say go and only preach my Gospel to the wise, educated preachers?…Are there two Gospels, one for men and another for women? One for the educated and another for the uneducated?

---

12 Iwie Synod (1568)

Disputes within the reforming movement were not confined to Western Europe but were also a feature of the efforts to reform religious life in Eastern and Central Europe. Anabaptism was fairly successful in this area. Perhaps more importantly and interestingly, the area also saw dramatic success for Socinians, Unitarians and other groups which rejected many traditional Christian theological beliefs (for example, the Trinity). In the West, the groups were hounded out of existence (the execution of Servetus in Calvin's Geneva being the most spectacular example) but they managed to maintain a toe-hold in the East.

[K7: 181–216, modified]

23 January 1568.

Paul [of Wizna]:

We admit that there is no reason to expect anyone's religious teachings to be perfect. Everything, no matter how great or small, has been made false, altered, destroyed or totally contaminated. Since we have been born and raised in this mess we should pray constantly to God to lead us in such a way that mistakes will not be hidden among us. God's grace and the Spirit's enlightenment have allowed us to see that some things are nothing but pure papacy. For example, some brethren have servants and some bonded servants who are treated like slaves which is against God's Word. If someone disagrees let him say so and prove from God's Word that I'm wrong. I am convinced and believe that it is improper for a Christian to have serfs or, worse yet, to have bonded servants. It is pagan to own a brother and steal his sweat and blood. The Bible is clear: God made everyone of the same blood. Thus we're equal and brethren. If we're brethren how can one brother rule over another? I am more than willing to be corrected.

Szymon [Budny]:

You're exactly right in saying that Antichrist has confused...contaminated God's House. As a result, nothing can be trusted to be lastingly true. That much is correct, but when you go on to say that Christians should not have slaves or serfs you're totally wrong. You quote the Bible to prove that God made all men of one blood. I accept that Paul wrote that to the Athenians and Luke likewise but the apostle did not mean what you claim. He didn't say that God made all men of one blood and from one man so that, as a result, all would be equal and none could command another. This the apostle did not mean. He wanted the Athenians to realise that God had created them, that they came from Him and that, as a result, they should only pray to Him not idols. This [Paul] says a bit later.

Paul:

But brother, you can't deny that ruling over people came from an evil man, known as the tyrant, that is Nimrod....The Holy Spirit shows [Gen. 10:8 – 10] that Nimrod, the tyrant, was the first person to put people into slavery, ruling them and, without a doubt, forcing them to work for him.

Simon:

I don't discount what is known of Nimrod. I know he was a tyrant but that is hardly peculiar as the Devil often corrupts the good that God intends. For example, God gave to men a nature, an innate being, that they love their own bodies, that is their wives. But the Devil twisted that into adultery and worse. This is exactly the same as God ordaining the kindly superiority and authority of a father over a child...he also ordained that the king or master rule the land, administer justice, defend the subjects, keep the peace. In return, the subjects should obey and love the ruler, provide his needs, etc. Satan perverted God's order, he stirs up tyrants to beat people into submission, to demand unbearable service and taxes from the subjects and to treat them cruelly. This is not God's order but Satan's perversion.

Paul:

Doesn't the same thing happen today? Don't subjects – and there are a lot of them here in Lithuania and Poland – work hard for their masters without any rest? These poor people end up eating husks like pigs and save all their grain for taxes, tolls, levies and other exactions....

Earthly things, which change and wear away, which make people happy or (as we used to say) blessed. No in fact, only spiritual things do this, for example, knowing God and trusting Him alone. David, in the Psalms, makes this clear when he says that for most people a happy nation is one with many sons and well-dressed daughters, with an overabundance of food in storage, with lots of cattle covering the fields in their thousands (the cows all pregnant), and with city walls without cracks or any sign of wear. This is what most mean by a fortunate, blessed nation. But in reality a happy nation has Yahweh as its God. This clearly proves that the godly people of the past knew the meaning of true happiness and blessedness.

Joshua says the same...and Solomon, in the Proverbs: 'It is better to be an honest poor man than a wicked rich man.' He says that God made the rich as well as the poor and that anyone who makes fun of the poor is making fun of his own Creator as well. This shows that Solomon is praising the poor who have the Holy Spirit and attacking the evil rich, the stupid, the wicked. He even says that it is better to have a piece of bread and a clear conscience than a house full of meat and a bad conscience. He does add, however, that God's blessing makes a person rich.

For these reasons, Jesus did not attack those who got their wealth fairly or who were godly, rather those who had ill-gotten gains and used them wickedly. Solomon and the whole of the Bible condemns this: 'Wealth is worthless on Judgement Day but godliness saves from death', [Prov. 11:4] and also 'The person who leans on his riches will fall' [Prov 11:28] and elsewhere, 'Wealth gained by deceit is like a passing cloud and a death-trap' [Prov 21:6]. He then adds, 'the violence of the wicked will destroy them' [Prov 21:7]. He attacks the heartless here as well [Prov 21:13]: 'If you close your ears to the cries of the poor then no one will listen when you cry out.'

You are quite correct in saying that Christ was poor and had no place to sleep. But this doesn't mean that his followers should leave their houses and wander around like animals in the jungle or drift from city to city, village to village, bothering people by begging and being vagrants. This is clear because elsewhere He says that His followers should welcome guests and travellers into their homes....[Christ] was an apostle or rather God's messenger. Apostolic duty means not staying in one place....His messengers did the same...they moved from, place to place.

However, Christians who weren't apostles stayed where they were before they became Christians. They kept their houses, gardens, lands, servants, slaves, and everything else. They did this when Christ and the apostles were alive and long afterwards as is clear in the writings of the historians and others. For example: Lazarus of Bethany, Jesus' friend, lived in his home with his sisters, Mary and Martha, before and after he was raised from the dead; Lydia and the gaoler of Philippi kept their homes as well; Mary, Mark's mother, kept her home in Jerusalem. She did not sell her house though some sold their own homes.

Likewise, believers of today have houses, lands, property, male and female slaves. They must use them properly and with respect, getting a godly return from these. In this way the truism of Jerome will not apply here: 'A rich man is either a crook or the son of a crook.'

Jacob [Kalinowski]:

Brother, you have certainly talked for a long time but if you had talked ten times as long you would still never convince me that it is acceptable for a Christian to have servants let alone slaves. Christ doesn't want his followers to get wealth by treating people like domestic animals. Instead He wants them to sell what they have, leave it all behind, take up the Cross and follow Him. This is what the Lord commands; it is not what you want – to run things here and still follow the Lord. The Lord had nothing in this world and forbids His followers from having anything. 'Take no gold, nor silver nor copper in your [money]belts' [Matt. 10:9]. Elsewhere he says, 'Sell what you have and give it to charity; give yourselves money belts which don't rot, treasure in heaven which never runs out, which thieves can't get to, which moths won't eat' [Luke 12:33], etc. In another place he says, 'In short, if you don't give up everything you have you can't be my follower' [Luke 14:33]. Paul also said to the Hebrews [13:14], 'We don't have a permanent homeplace, but we are looking for one which will come'.

And that, brother, is the end of that. Plainly written without fancy phrases. Why draw this out with time-consuming stories or long-winded speeches which just make things more complicated.

Simon:

I'm all for short statements, Jacob, but you should stick to one point at a time if you want a short answer from me. When you take up lots of issues at once it is sure to confuse. For example, you have made four points. I will answer them as briefly as I can.

First, when Jesus sent the apostles out on their first mission he told them not to take any money. This has nothing to do with us nor do we have anything to do with it. Christ said this only to His apostles; it was not meant for all time. This was for the time when they were working in Judaea. What can this have to do with us? We aren't apostles, it was said only to apostles and only for a specific time. There, that is a short answer to your first point.

Jacob:

What are you talking about? Don't you remember what Christ said, 'What I have said to you I say to everyone' [Mk 13:37].

Simon:

I have not forgotten but what Christ says here is not about the same thing and the circumstances are different. He was telling them to be alert when He said to stand guard and He ended the command with these words: 'What I have said to you I say to everyone: Watch.' Being watchful is required not only of all apostles but of all Christians so they won't be found asleep on that day. As for having money, etc., this doesn't apply to everyone, only to the apostles and only at that one time. If you reject this interpretation, brother, you will have to say not only that Christians can have no money but also that they can't have two cloaks, shoes, etc. But, let the brethren decide about this.

Paul:

I think brother Simon has more than made his point. This command was for the apostles only and for that one time. For example, they later had two cloaks and carried swords while this example didn't even allow them to have a staff or walking-stick.

John Baptist:

I agree. It's late. Let's adjourn until tomorrow. Let us pray.

---

13   Comment on the Diet of Prague (1575)

The attempt to maintain a united front against Catholicism and the Emperor was especially complicated in Bohemia (the area of the present-day Czech Republic). Here there already existed the Hussite Church which had gained partial freedom from Rome a century before. There were repeated efforts to cement a union between the 'Protestants', whether Calvinist or Lutheran, and the various factions within the Hussite Church. The basic dispute in the Hussite Church was whether only bread should be given to the laity in Communion or the wine as well – hence, In-one-kind or In-both-kinds. These extracts as well as that above also highlight the tremendously complicated fragmentation which developed amongst Protestant groups in Central and Eastern Europe. Along with relatively weak political systems, this framentation made it easier for Catholicism to recapture much of the area later in the century.

[**B6: 4.343–48**, modified]

To His Majesty, Emperor of Rome, King of Bohemia.

A humble supplication and statement of adherence to the old, Catholic faith of those receiving communion in both kinds.

Most serene, most invincible Emperor of Rome, King and Master of Hungary and Bohemia, Our most gracious Lord.

Some nobles and friends of ours who used to adhere to the Augsburg Confession, have (along with others of another religion) presented a religious confession which they want to follow. Your Imperial Majesty has kindly permitted us (of the In-both-kinds) who keep the Holy Christian faith of our Czech ancestors, who are ruled by real clergy ordained by bishops, who obey God's law and the rules of Holy Church (set by councils), who live in peace with our nobles and neighbours of the In-one-kind. We ask that you examine this new confession to see what it means.... We see some things in it of our beliefs. Things which the In-both have always believed and still do...confirmed by many councils....

As far as those things are concerned which are really about keeping good morals among Christians. These are and always have been kept by the In-both-kinds long before anyone had thought about, knew about or heard about the Augsburg Confession. We would not bother Your Imperial Majesty about these. We hold to this old Christian faith of the In-both-kinds. We don't allow change or modification at all and stand by it to the death. We beg Your Imperial Majesty to maintain (without fail) your protection of the true and holy Christian faith of In-both-kinds and protect us, your faithful servants, as is the proper duty of the King of Bohemia and our Gracious Master.

But this confession also has some new – foreign – things in it which disagree with the order and practice of the praiseworthy godliness of our churches. We can no more accept these than any other new things. These nobles place themselves under the jurisdiction of the Prague consistory and ask that it be reformed. That is good and proper. For a long time now (and yet again) we have asked for the reform of the Prague consistory. We've asked that you allow for reform according to the old, proper and godly order and when it is ruled according to the old, proper, godly order and these nobles are under its jurisdiction then order will be established with regard to these new, foreign religious ideas....

The nobles...who presented this new confession to Your Imperial Majesty say in public that they don't want anything new, only what has been around since ancient times, in fact, they want...to return to the original godliness of the old Czech Christian faith In-both-kinds.

[B6: 4.343–48]

To His Imperial Majesty...

On Pentecost [Whitsunday], Your Imperial Majesty sent us the confession of faith which had been given to Your Imperial Majesty. It had been signed by nobles, gentry, representatives of Prague and other cities (that is, people for all three estates of the Kingdom of Bohemia). We have examined this confession carefully...we can now give our judgement of it.

First, this confession is wholly based on the Augsburg Confession. This latter disagrees almost totally not only with Catholic doctrine but also our ancient, true religion. [The Augsburg Confession] was quite rightly condemned for error and heresy from the start during the reign of Charles V....We state, as a result, that Your Imperial Majesty cannot justly allow those who sent this confession to introduce this confession into the kingdom. It contains a new and foreign religion.

Second, accepting this confession would mean accepting the confession and religion of the Brethren of the group called Picards [Calvinist]. They claim they are brothers and good Christians because they claim that they can agree to the basic points of the confession under discussion. The people who signed this very confession have no intention of suppressing the [Picards]. Most gracious Emperor, everyone in the kingdom knows the real truth of this: the Unity of the Brethren (that is, Picards) and its divisive religion have been disgraced, condemned and forbidden for years. This faith is a danger to the Church and to this kingdom. Councils and various edicts of this kingdom followed by strict decrees from their Majesties, the Kings of Bohemia, and also, in fact, from Your Imperial Majesty, have said so and even ended by prohibiting this group under penalty of death....

Third, this confession has a new practice and sectarian method of selecting clergy in the manner of the Augsburg and Picard Confessions. Young men who want to be priests will be ordained by having men – clerical and, it would seem, lay – who had been elected to the consistory laying hands on them. The In-both-kinds party in this kingdom have never followed this practice for ordaining men to the priesthood. It accepts as priests only men properly ordained by bishops of the holy, Catholic Church....

Fourth, this confession allows and approves of married clergy. This is against Church law, the laws of this kingdom, and against the ancient prohibitions of councils. This has never been allowed in this kingdom except by the old Taborite sect which was condemned in any case. Later the Picards supported this practice....

Finally, Your Imperial Majesty must decide if it is proper for a very few lay people to discuss religious and spiritual matters which relate to men's souls and consciences. Especially as this has been done without trained theologians to guard the clergy and the faith. It is proper for them to make decision for others when priests and monks weren't consulted or involved at all – as they clearly were not? Or, as far as we know, godly, educated and decent clerics were not part of this process.

Letter, Daniel Jindrich Svarc to Jan Kálef [6 June].

[B6: 4. 435–437]

They are all in a rage and ganging up against us....They have sent a petition to His Imperial Majesty and I enclose the beginning of it. I didn't have time to copy the rest.

The In-one-kind group have everything in their control and they are laughing and saying that there is a split among us. They say that they have always known that the various In-both-kinds groups were not united. It is clear what will happen: something horrible.

The Lutherans [the new In-both-kinds] have already sworn that they will leave the council and go home if the Emperor doesn't accept the confession presented. Some Czechs think everybody should become a 'Brethren' and then get rid of the chamberlain and the whole consistory. A few cities especially suggest this.

For the moment everyone is sitting around waiting for the Emperor's answer. He is in no rush to answer. He wants his concerns to be acted upon first. The Czechs don't want to do that.

Letter, Svarc to Kálef [13 June].

[B6: 4. 435–7]

Everything is getting very confused and it is impossible to figure out what is going on or predict what will happen. You may already know about what happened in the office of Dr Weber, the Imperial chancellor. Lord Kryspek [a new In-both-kinds, Lutheran] and Dr Mehl [Catholic] were arguing about religion but used their fists instead of words. Eventually they had to be separated and arrested. They are still under lock and key....

There are also strange whisperings heard among the Catholics, especially the Jesuits. They are promising a massacre like the [St Bartholomew's Day] one in Paris. This causes people to wonder. For example, today people in the council were talking about how the alarm bell was rung three times last night in St Jacob's Monastery (which is full of Italian monks). And, that a gun was fired in the Little Town. The elder of the Old Town was sent off to the monks to see for himself what was going on. His reply: the bell ringer was so completely drunk that he didn't know what he was doing. The answer seemed believable but some were suspicious.

On Thursday, the In-one-kind group submitted their opinion to His Imperial Majesty. This was the gist: none of this concerns them and as their religion is not touched they don't want to get involved in a matter which only involves the other groups. If the representatives of the In-both-kinds can come to an agreement then they will accept it....

When the Lord Chamberlain heard this from the In-one-kind group he fired off a letter to them. He said that he, and others, could not begin to express their surprise that the In-one-kind group were willing to abandon all the ancient agreements and council rulings and allow people who did to get their way.... So there it stands. Most people think that the result of these discussions will be pointless.

[B6: 4. 351f.]

Diary, Sixt von Ottersdorf.

[On 17 June] the representatives of the In-both-kinds group met in the green room. The chief justice told them that Lord Zdenoek of Vartmberk, mayor of Prague's New Town, had said that he had heard one gentleman from their group saying that they wanted to drive the Jesuits out of Bohemia, massacre the In-one-kind group and wash their hands in their blood. It was agreed that Lord Vartmberk should name the man to the chief justice and other witnesses so that action could be taken against such improper outbursts. Further, it was agreed that we should send an apology to the other group assuring them that such talk was idle and they should ignore it.

There was a second complaint. Supposedly, a certain priest called Franta, of the Royal Castle's St Vitus Cathedral slandered the In-both-kinds group in a sermon. He was said to have said that [that group] had drawn up a Picardish and thieving confession, that the agitators for the new confession would also want a new king and would then chase His Imperial Majesty out of his kingdom, and that the Emperor should ignore these sectarians and reject everything they present.

---

14   Emden Disputation (1578)

The need for all reforming forces to unite was equally important in the Dutch context. Any breaches in religion made it very difficult to maintain unity in the political forces rebelling against the King of Spain. This was even more important as the major alternative to 'Dutch Calvinism' (or magisterial reform) was Anabaptism. With the latter's commitment to pacificism, Anabaptism was seen as a dangerous – and very practical – threat to the Revolt. Although the need for unity was important in the Dutch context the desire to avoid internal conflict was greater and led to de facto toleration in the emerging Republic.

[A1]

Menso [Calvinist]:

To clear things up we would like to ask a few questions

First, do the gentlemen believe that the job of the government is related to the world or the Spirit? We say the Spirit.

Second, can a Christian hold a public office with a clear conscience? Can he judge and sentence? Can he protect the good and execute evil-doers with the sword? Can he hold such a post and still be a Christian and still be saved? We say he can.

Third, does the government have jurisdiction over the first [part of Ten Commandments relating to religious practice and belief] table of God's law as well as the second [part of Ten Commandments relating to public and private morality]? We say it does.

Fourth, can ministers of God's church command people to do what God and the government have forbidden? Also, can the Church forbid the ministers from doing what God and the government command? We say they cannot.

Peter of Cologne [Anabaptist]:

In answer to your first question, we say that we accept that God ordained government to run the world. In that sense we say that we agree and it is the only possible answer we can give.

To answer your second question, we state that we cannot find any New Testament example of a Christian holding a public office with responsibility for capital punishment. We cannot answer yes to Menso. If he can show us a New Testament proof – and we rely on the New Testament – we would happily agree with him. Until then our answer must remain no. As to that person's salvation we think that is a matter best left to God. We cannot think of anything else to say to this.

Presiding Officer:

The judges cannot accept this as an answer to the question. Since the gentleman says that he has nothing else to say we will have to be satisfied with that. When the ministers make their points we have decided that the gentleman should answer 'yes' or 'no'.

Brixius [Anabaptist]:

In answer to the third question about the scope of governmental jurisdiction over both tables of God's law. We answer no. On the contrary, we say that governmental authority only controls the public and other ordinances; it does not include matters of conscience or belief.

Presiding Officer:

The ministers say that this answer makes a meaningless distinction; they did not mean regulations of conscience. Therefore they want a definite answer. The judges would like one as well. However, as they have not been able to get one from the gentlemen (who claim they aren't able to say anything else) the judges feel that the discussion should continue. However, there is the condition that ministers will have the right to note the insufficient nature of the answer in their turn.

Brixius:

In answer to the first part of the fourth question about whether the ministers can command something that God and government have forbidden. We say no. But, that is only if the government forbid something which God has also forbidden. On the second part about whether the church can forbid. We also say no. But again, only when the government are commanding something which God has also ordered.

Menso:

It is clear that these gentlemen have given every appearance, to the authorities and uneducated, that they have proper beliefs about the proper role of the government. However, one realises that the exact opposite is true when one listens to their answers carefully. Thus, when we ask whether the work of government relates to the world or the Spirit they won't give a straight answer. They want to plead ignorance although they had plenty to say about the world and the Spirit before. Moreover, we have asked them if, in condemning to death a murderer who deserves to die many times over, the government is performing a worldly act. Such a worldly act would deserve condemnation from the Lord God since all works of this world are excluded from Christ's Kingdom. They will give no answer to this either. If one takes their view would not those who supported the 'King of Münster'...have deserved damnation? One wonders how these people can obey Paul (in I Tim. 2) and pray for governmental authorities. If government work is a damnable worldly work then one should not pray for it. Rather, one should beg God to end it and open the eyes of those holding public office so that they would resign.

As to the second question. Among their many comments they say that they appeal to the New Testament. However, they give no reason why they prefer to reject the Old Testament as an authority in this discussion when they have been more than willing to use it elsewhere.

Brixius:

Menso has inferred from our comments that we will use only the New Testament, that we condemn people in authority and deny their salvation. We say clearly that we never said this. What we said, and still say, is that we leave it to God to judge people not of [our group]; we don't judge them. For example, Menso, for whatever reason, said that our words seemed to mean that the people who supported the 'King of Münster' deserved damnation. Let the impartial reader judge his words. We never said this, and, as far as I know, the thought never passed our minds.

As for what Menso has said about how to understand what we said on praying for authorities. We say that Paul's teaching (as well as Christ in Matt. 5) in I Timothy 2 commands us to pray for the authorities even though they persecute and attack us. We think that Menso's interpretation would imply that he does not pray for authorities unless they support him and agree with his beliefs. He also says that we accept or reject Old Testament authority as is convenient for our argument. That is wrong. In fact we don't reject them, rather we say that Christ often upheld the letter of the law. In keeping with this interpretation we say that the Old Testament Church and the New Testament Church are the same people of God and united in Christ's salvation. However, they differ in form of government, worship practices, sacrifices, rituals, etc....

We don't share his idea that the New Testament says that public office belongs to the Church and that members of the Church served the state and were responsible for capital punishment. We have said that if he can show this – which he hasn't so far – then we would agree with him....

Menso also says that he thinks the words 'faith' and 'conscience' have a visible meaning as well and that the power of the government extends to controlling that. He then says that we should stop our activities as they promote division in this city where (he claims) God's Word is correctly preached. Our activities, therefore, are against God, the state and even the Imperial code. What he hopes to prove he may know, we can only say this: If we thought God's Word was correctly and plainly taught here and in other places then we would not be separate. This would certainly make our lives easier and safer than they are now. But, according to Menso's interpretation—with which we don't agree since it doesn't seem to agree with God's Word—we should not be allowed to continue with our activities. We would like him to give some thought to those who agree with him who live in other cities, perform their practices in secret, and face persecution because the authorities there think that God's Word is preached correctly. Are those authorities as right in persecuting Menso's co-religionists and stopping their activities as he is in doing the same to us?

Zwingli, when his views were as hated as those of others are now, never taught that the state had power over conscience of God's Word. He wrote in his book *The Works of Zwingli* (p. 77): 'If Christ wanted Himself or His Word defended by the sword he would have chosen an army of soldiers rather than an army of fishermen'...Menso might agree with these sentiments if he and his believers were now being treated the way Zwingli was then. He might think about this and have a little sympathy for people who don't share his particular interpretation of the Bible. Despite these differences they only want to live in peace and quiet with Menso and his supporters and the government.

Menso also says...that we don't want to serve as soldiers but are willing to pay others to fight for us. We answer this by saying that if the city were under attack we would not defend ourselves nor want someone else to defend us. However, when there is no battle at hand we have no qualms about paying taxes to employ guards....

15   Du Plessis-Mornay on Religious Intolerance

Philip du Plessis-Mornay, in his 'Discourse on the granting of religious toleration in the Netherlands' (1579), discusses the very practical problems encountered in the Low Countries as a result of attempts to create religious uniformity through force and coercion. Although his discussion is actually limited to Calvinism and Catholicism there were much wider applications and consequences of the acceptance of these ideas.

[K4: no. 425]

I would like to ask those who oppose the existence of two religions in this country how they intend to get rid of one of them. Obviously by this, I mean the one which they think is the weakest. Clearly, you cannot eliminate religious practice without force and civil war. Thus, we can fight each other rather than joining together to rid the country of Lord John [the Spanish military leader] and his supporters and delivering us from the indefensible tyranny of foreigners. If we set about destroying the Protestants we will destroy ourselves just like the French did. Therefore, it should be obvious that it is better to live peacefully with them rather than to destroy ourselves by a civil strife and a dangerous, disastrous, long and difficult – or rather a never-ending, hopeless war. If you consider all the possibilities there are two choices available: either we can let them live among us in peace or we can destroy each other; we can leave them alone or destroy ourselves by trying to destroy them.

16 Marnix on the Limits of Religious Toleration

The granting of 'religious freedom', however, was not always as generous as it seemed; a point made by Marnix in his Opinion of a noble bystander on the country and the republic about peace and war in the Netherlands. Toleration of conscience and beliefs when it required outward conformity to certain religious practices was toleration in name only.

[K4: no. 705]

I am well aware that they are offering freedom of belief but limited in that no one should be offended and no public worship is allowed. This is just a trick to catch us. Everyone knows that what someone thinks inside their head is always free, no one can tell what someone is thinking much less put it under control. In fact, there has never been an execution purely because of what someone thought. They are killed because they acted on their beliefs by committing some public act or demonstration. This can be words which supposedly offend or activities which are seen as public worship. What is falsely called freedom of conscience without public worship is no different from the old regime of rules backed up by the Spanish Inquisition. In addition, it is foolhardy of the Catholics to free the conscience while absolutely forbidding public worship. Everyone knows that the real differences between them and the Huguenots is not in the area of ceremonies or public worship but in doctrine: that is, issues of faith and conscience....

If someone doesn't go to Mass on holy days, or take communion at Easter or go to confession or doesn't genuflect to the host or holy oil, or doesn't have children baptised in the Roman Church, or isn't married by a priest, then the authorities will 'be offended'. What this means is that this so-called freedom of conscience will force people to go against their beliefs to avoid offending anyone else.

17 Bonivard on the Motives of Protestant Leaders

François Bonivard (discussed above in Chapter 4), in his *Deformed Reformers* (1560s), presents a very harsh verdict on the motivation and morality of many of the staunchest adherents of reform.

He highlights not only the splits which were increasingly weakening the movement but also the continued existence of a demand for religious change which was very much ethical, first and foremost. Thus, his views are in line with those expounded by Erasmus and other Humanists, views which tended to be squeezed between those of the Catholics and Protestants. If one sees Erasmus as the most extreme sort of reformer able to remain loyal to the Roman Church then Bonivard could well be seen as an example of the sort of Protestant closest to Erasmus yet outside the Roman Church.

[B8: 136f., 139, 148, 157–59 – 28]

Why have people received [Luther's teachings]? First, there is the dislike they have for the Pope and his supporters because of their obvious evils....Some want to eat meat on days forbidden by the Pope. Others because marriage was forbidden....Third, because the avarice of the princes was greater than that of their subjects. The princes really wanted to get the wealth of the churches, the movable and fixed goods. The subjects...thought they would no longer need to pay the taxes and dues...which they had paid to the churches. But they had their wishes frustrated because they had to pay to the princes what they used to pay to the priests....

How did the English king, Henry VIII, come to the Gospel? At the start the Pope was no less of an enemy of the Gospel than this king. Not only did he support the Pope's tyranny with his sword but also with his pen. He wrote and published a book against Luther. What sort of devotion made him change his skin and embrace the Gospel? A good friend of mine put it well in a poem:

> Why does King Henry,
> Who so opposed the Gospel before,
> By words, books, and words,
> Now embrace it as lovely?
> He lusted after the reliquary
> of St Thomas and sought to wed
> his whore. This made the change,
> bringing humanity from inhumanity ...

This then is the state of religion: some want to be saved by the Jewish law; some by the Islamic law; some by the Evangelical law. Everyone fights and struggles....

I can see two types of people who follow the Gospel. Some leave their possessions and risk their lives to follow the Gospel. For example, the French and others who have come to live in Geneva. Others have followed the Gospel to get the goods of others. For example, magistrates, whether elected or hereditary. I have already discussed why the English king embraced the Gospel. But what sort of holiness is visible in the acceptance of the Gospel by the Landgrave of Hesse, or Count William of Fürstenberg, or the two Albrechts of Brandenburg (the Marquis and the Grand Master of the Teutonic Knights)? We discussed the Landgrave...above. Everyone knows what sort of person Count William is: as wicked as a knight, as crooked as a Gascon – and he's raging drunk most of the time. Albrecht of Brandenburg, the Grand Master of the Teutonic Knights was a monk and a secular prelate. He was elected to his post; it was not hereditary. As soon as he heard Luther's interpretation of the Gospel, he grabbed it with his two lovely hands. But why? He wanted to get married. He also wanted some property to leave to his children – should his marriage produce any....He married the daughter of the Danish King...and changed his elective post into an hereditary one. This greatly damaged Christendom. This ancient office was supposed to be held by a man who could protect the Christian religion from infidels by force of arms. But [as an hereditary post] it can fall into the hands of an infant who can't wipe his own nose. His cousin, Marquis Albrecht, took the church property which he said should go to the poor but instead he gave it to the nobles....It is certainly true that the priests gobbled up the dead but we are worse – we gobble up the living...we leave Christ crucified and naked hanging on the cross while we play dice at the foot of the cross to see who gets His clothes. What do you mean? The poor represent Christ....The priests and we, their opponents, surely leave Him crucified. That is, we allow the poor to die of hunger, thirst, cold, nakedness and meanwhile we fight over their property – playing dice to see who'll get His robe.

6 Catholicism Reforms & Responds

'I support those who support the Pope; I just wish they were a little smarter'

[*Suggested readings*: 80, 96, 110, 127, 129, 131, 133, 134, 135, 136, 149, 154, 205, 207, 261, 285, 299, 317, 352, 353, 356, 389, 415, 450, 483]

1 Erasmus to Eloysius Marlianus (25 March 1521)

Erasmus's determination to remain faithful to the Catholic Church demonstrates the deep well of loyalty from which the Pope and his supporters could draw. It was crucial for them to mobilise this sentiment. There were many moderates like Erasmus who drew back from joining groups which they perceived to be not only potentially destructive to their vision of a unified Christendom but which also seemed wholly incapable of maintaining their own internal unity.

[A2: 4.459–61]

You suggest that I avoid being involved with Luther. I took your advice and did my best to calm things down. Luther's supporters encourage me to join him while those opposed to him have almost managed to convince me to do it by the violent sermons against me. Neither have succeeded. I know Christ; Luther I know not. I know the Roman Church and even death will not turn me against it, unless it turns away Christ. I hate treason. If only Luther and the Germans hated it too. One suspects they are in it together when one sees the way the two sides goad each other on. Luther's last outpourings have done him more damage than his enemies. On the other hand, many (in spite of their better judgement) think the Pope may be wrong because of the ridiculous attacks against Luther. I support those who support the Pope; I just wish they were a little smarter. They could gobble Luther up. For all I care, they can have him boiled or roasted. They are making a mistake in linking us together, however. They will find him easier to beat without me than with me.

2 The Emperor to his Ambassador at Rome (18 July 1524)

Most loyal Catholics argued that the most important action required was the convocation of a general council. In addition, advice was offered from every quarter on the best course of action to be taken to counter the Protestant threat. Even the Emperor was aware of the need to act. He was loathe, however, to initiate a repression which would almost surely lead to civil war in Germany. His preferred choice was a council which would somehow manage to draft a compromise statement of beliefs.

[S6: 2. no. 662 – 27]

There are two possible options available to the Emperor. First, he can go to Germany and put the heretics down by the sword. Second, a general council can be called. At the moment the Emperor cannot go to Germany so he asks the Pope to make a decision. He swears that as a faithful son of the Church he will give his life and his lands to crush this sect which is clearly so dangerous to all religious authority. The Germans are about to ask the Pope to call a general council in Germany. This request is being brought by the legate, Cardinal Campeggio. The Pope should anticipate this request for a council at Speyer by opening one at Trent. This council should be started in Trent by next spring. It is always possible that it could then be suspended and then moved to some other city in Italy, for example Rome, or wherever the Pope would like it to meet. The Emperor promises to obey the instructions of the Pope.

3 Curia's Views on Reconciliation

Despite the Emperor's obvious misgivings, the Church leadership in Rome preferred strong action. In general, the Roman hierarchy was distrustful of councils. In the previous century the Pope (and his court) had been involved in a life-and-death struggle for power against those who supported the supremacy of councils (the Conciliarist movement) over that of the Pope. The victorious papal supporters had no desire to see that Pandora's box re-opened. The Curia (in effect, the Pope's court) was clear about what it thought was necessary to stop the spread of Luther's ideas.

[K3: 139f.]

First: The Edict of Worms must be obeyed. This seems possible if the Emperor is encouraged to pursue this eagerly. Also, the Pope should work to encourage the kings of England and Spain to put pressure on the princes and citizens of Germany....

Second: One must be careful to ensure that the articles of religion are not changed at the meeting in Speyer....Especially care must be taken to see if the Emperor can stop the whole [meeting]. Failing that, the meeting should be delayed.

Third: There must be some response to the demand for a [general] council....

Fourth: Thought should be given about the Pope doing more about the Duke of

Saxony. Aleander has sent a lengthy report on this as ordered by the Pope. It was prepared before Campeggio left. Things have become so messed up that the mild approach needs to be stopped and the harsher penalties of the Church applied. [The Saxon Duke] should be removed as an [Imperial] Elector. But this has not been done.

----

4 Erasmus to Pope Paul III

Erasmus remained convinced that the Pope was being badly advised. He was sure that a conciliatory approach could restore unity and, simultaneously, introduce needed reforms to the Catholic Church. He seems to have been unable or unwilling to see that the process of disintegration was too far advanced and extremism too strong in both camps to allow such a policy to be tried, let alone succeed.

Freiburg, 23 January 1535.

Wanted a compromise

[A2: no. 2988. 51–91]

Far be it from me that I ever be so blindly foolish as to try to advise you when the whole world is supplied be your wisdom. Nevertheless, even an experienced ship captain caught in the midst of a bad storm will ask the opinion of anyone. I am sure that your human nature will allow you to accept my advice. I think that there is one important factor which will help to settle this trouble. The Supreme Pontiff, the father of every ruler and nation should not tie himself to one side only but should be fair to all. Everyone who has a spirit truly devoted to religion will be the best supporter of unity. Secondly, rulers and princes should work together to make this the goal of their efforts. This ought to be especially important to all rulers and princes although everyone owes this duty to Christ, the King of Kings, as they have all taken an oath of allegiance to Him. Unless this lack of control is stopped the princes risk losing what is important to them. To stop the fighting between the people with power there might need to be a six- or seven-years' truce. Then, these leaders could join forces to defeat the people who keep stirring up rebellions and who spread the troubles far and wide and make them worse. It is not necessary, I feel, for the council to state its views on every fine point but only on those matters which are crucial for the Christian faith. St Paul wants everyone, as he is able, to agree to certain things but then says that there are other issues about which, 'if there are some matters on which you differ, God will clarify it for you'. Different rituals do not destroy the unity of the Church. Likewise, there are matters on which people can disagree and yet keep Christian peace among themselves. Also, it would be useful to encourage the leaders of the various sects to believe that they actually have a chance of getting what they want. Also, since this plague seems to be very deadly, it would be useful if those who were willing to conform to the council's decisions could be offered a complete amnesty. But most of all I think that everyone has to put aside their own wishes and remember that there is one very important goal here: Christ's glory and the advance of the Christian religion. If this is done, God will bless the actions of those who seek for His Kingdom and His justice then those things which each person wants will be added on top – and more besides. Moreover, we should not give up hope that all will come out well although this vile disease has, sadly, spread everywhere. The overwhelming majority of men, especially those in important posts and those who are well educated, have not yet been infected by the plague. Not only that, but many of those who have inhaled this foul air have begun to regret what they have obtained and wish they had back what they gave up.

---

5 Bull of Paul III Convoking the Council of Trent

After strenuous and contentious negotiations the Pope finally convened a full-scale council of leading clerics and theologians to address the issues raised by the reformers. For the Pope, the greatest concern was that he maintain control over the direction and final outcome of the council. Thus there was much debate over where the council would be held and when. The Emperor favoured a site in Germany from which he would be able to exert pressure for the adoption of a conciliatory line towards the Protestants. The Pope wanted to avoid Imperial control as far as possible.

[S3: 281–89, passim – 19, 74]

From the very beginning of our pontificate...we have seen how seriously things have been troubled everywhere and how much our pastoral care and vigilance are needed. We have also wanted to cure the ills that have disturbed and almost destroyed Christendom. But, like all men *compassed with infirmity*, we are aware that our power is not enough to do this alone. We saw the need for peace...but we found everyone full of hate...especially the princes...who were fighting each other. We saw the need for unity in the Christian religion...but we found it was almost torn asunder by schisms....We wanted to see Christendom protected from the infidel but because of our sins and guilt and the wrath of God hanging over us...Rhodes is lost, Hungary devastated, attacks by land and sea are being prepared against Italy, Austria and the Adriatic coast. The Turk...has seen our divisions and internal wars as an opportunity to carry out his evil plans. Thus, as we have said, called to face so many storms, heresies, divisions and wars, to pilot Peter's ship on seas so tempestuous – we looked to those who served before us who were wise and godly and saw that they often turned to universal councils and assemblies of bishops in times of trouble. We have decided to do the same. We then consulted the princes because we felt it important to get their support. They were agreeable at that time. We...then summoned a universal council...of bishops...to meet at Mantua on 23 May 1537...however, the city was not willing to host the meeting unless certain conditions were met which could not be reconciled with Papal rules, present circumstances, our position and freedom....Thus, we had to find another city. Since none was immediately available, we decided to postpone the start of the council until 1 November [1537]....We did continue to ask the princes about where they thought the council should meet. But, their views were unclear and contradictory and time seemed to be slipping away. Therefore, we decided with the best will in the world, and wisely as we believed, to choose Vicenza. It is a large city, which is protected by Venice who offered to make it available. It is thus easily accessible, and has free and safe lodging for everyone....Once this was decided...we felt it would be best if the princes were at peace. We thus asked for a meeting with both Charles, Holy Roman Emperor, and Francis, the Most Christian King [of France], the two main supports of Christianity. They were continually urged...to lay aside their envy and hate, to make an alliance and treaty, to aid the crumbling bastions of Christendom....At last, they gave in to our requests and met at Nice....However, a lasting peace couldn't be arranged...at the Nice conference, although a ten-year truce was signed....We urged the princes to come to the general council in person along with the church leaders in their retinues and to call others to join them there. However, they said they couldn't come as they had to get back to their kingdoms and the churchmen who were with them were very tired and their money nearly exhausted and needed to reorganise themselves in preparation. They requested another postponement but we weren't in favour of this. By then we had letters from Vicenza saying that although it was well past the council's starting date, only a couple of prelates had arrived from other countries. Since it was clear that no council was going to start, we agreed to the princes' request and postponed the start until Easter [1538]....The princes then said that any council should wait until the peace negotiations were finished....This view was supported by Ferdinand, King of the Romans...and especially the Emperor who said that he had promised those who dissented from the unity of Catholicism that he would put their views to us and attempt to come to compromise. This could not be done until he had returned to Germany....In the light of this and the lack of delegates at Vicenza we decided to avoid the word postponement, which was getting overworked, and suspended the project completely....We notified the princes of this by letter on 10 June 1539....The situation in Christendom became worse and worse. When their King died the Hungarians invited the Turks into their country. King Ferdinand declared war on them. Part of the Low Countries rebelled. To crush this revolt, the Emperor rushed through France, where he was treated in a very friendly and peaceful manner. Thence, he went to Germany and started holding meetings with the German princes and representatives of the cities to discuss the compromise he discussed with us. But any chance of peace began to fade, and as it became clear to us that these meetings would only produce a worse situation, we decided to return to the original plan: a general council...and proposed this to the Emperor....We were afraid that we might be asked to tolerate certain [Protestant] beliefs until they could be discussed and judged by a universal council. However, that was completely incompatible with our will and that of the papal position as well as Christian and Catholic truth. We felt it better to call a council immediately....Since the Vicenza was no longer available, we felt we should choose a new place which would be more convenient...for the Germans. Some had proposed Trent, which we accepted, although we were of the opinion that some place closer to Rome would be better....Let [the princes] arrange for the church leaders to attend without delay...especially those from Germany since they are the reason for the council and the city they wanted has been chosen....Here we can restore what is good and correct morality, to bring peace, unity...to Christians...so that the attacks of the barbarians and infidels who want to overthrow Christendom can be repulsed.

6 Severoli on the Council of Trent (1545)

Not only had there been grave difficulties in arranging a general council but the meeting itself was hampered and disrupted by intense rivalry and disagreements between supporters of the Pope and the Emperor. This split was more than a debate over the correct way to deal with the Protestants. There were also important power-political issues relating to the control of the Italian peninsula where the Pope and the Emperor were the major diplomatic and military players.

[M2: 1.95.100]

[A dispute arose about whether the delegates had actually agreed for a definite date to start the sixth session.]

Cardinal of Jaen [Imperial supporter]:
   The votes should be presented and counted in front of everyone so that we can know the true result.

[The secretary read the votes and said that many delegates did not give straightforward answers. The two sides tried to claim some of these for themselves. He was finally asked to count only the clear votes but said that they all needed interpretation and he could not do that. Some began to shout that a definite date was required but the chairman, Cardinal del Monte refuted that. The Cardinal of Jaen and other Spaniards began to get out of hand. Jaen continued.]

   What is the point of asking us what we want in the meetings if you, the chairman, will do what you want and not what the majority wants?

[Del Monte denied this and said that nothing he had done before would support such a

charge. However, he added that in important matters it was often better to listen to the group with the clear minds rather than the group with the most votes. Jaen replied:]

Obviously you mean to insult me and all those who agree with me, honourable lord, by implying that some people's opinions are worth more than ours. Surely we should not be treated or insulted in this way!

Cardinal del Monte [Papal supporter]:

I think the various views should be weighed since the chairman disagrees.

Cardinal of Trent [Imperial supporter]:

I shudder to hear you speak in anger and beg you to treat us with polite and Christian conduct.

Cardinal del Monte:

I always speak politely and in a Christian manner!

Cardinal of Trent:

I only spoke to caution you as a brother. [This he said repeatedly, then:] I am only human, I know that, and I don't want to be forced to say something I will later regret.

Cardinal del Monte:

I don't know what you're getting at. I don't think I've been rude or unchristian in what I've said. For all that, it is clear to me that I'm now being told what to do and that I'm no longer actually presiding over this meeting. I would suggest that if you want me to speak more courteously then you should make your requests more politely. I will always respond just as I am addressed.

[Jaen whispered to Trent who said:]

I did not mean, when I cautioned the chairman, that he was less polite or less Christian. Rather I only wanted him to treat us more gently as befits our status. I see that others are free to say what they want and think I should be as well. I can't see what the dispute is all about. If someone is worried then out with it. As for me I can assure the council that even if the Pope or the Emperor were to order it I would never do anything to undermine the freedom of this council. It's true that one Prince of the Church has said things which are not really appropriate. The delegates must know from their own experience that all I want to do is serve – not, I hasten to add, satisfy – everyone here.

I admit that I sent that clergyman's boat away. I wasn't trying to keep him or any other prelate here. I was just concerned that the city, which has been very concerned about all this, would have a chance to calm down. The cleric had no plan to leave but just wanted to keep his boat handy – as though ready for a hasty retreat. This offended and worried my people. That's why I ordered the boats to leave. I wasn't trying to restrict anyone's freedom of movement. This is obvious in that the boats were sent away but horses and carriages are readily available.

Del Monte:

I am more than willing to be corrected – in private – and advised by anyone no matter how lowly when my duties require it. However, I cannot allow anyone to speak to a doctor or a master the way Jaen and Trent have. I always respect them and treat them like masters but not here. So, when Trent said, 'I don't want to be forced to say something I will later regret' then I have to say that this is how a person speaks when he means to command or threaten. These are not the words of a prelate speaking his mind at a synod, which is the point they are so keen on. He should be certain that no threats, even those of an enraged Cardinal of Trent, will be able to move the Cardinal del Monte....What would be the point then of someone being the chairman if everyone was of the same power? Also, when there is a dispute amongst the clerics about something and the vote is close then the views of the delegates from the Pope must be considered and be counted as the determining votes. Further, the people who want a definite date are not in the majority if you examine their wishes carefully. Some want to resume in a week, some in a fortnight, some in three months, some in six. Since the desire for a definite date is all conditional on the date chosen they don't really mean anything and can't unless they can agree on one date. If you subtract these qualified votes then those who don't want a definite date far out-weigh the rest.

[Jaen rejected this whole line of argument. Also, he said the chairmen should preside only until the delegates came to a conclusion then the chairmen were duty bound to follow that course.]

Del Monte:

There is no point going on until my co-chairman returns, as there is nothing I can do without him. So let's wait till he comes back, which shouldn't be very long.

[The meeting was adjourned until 5 p.m. Jaen got up and asked Del Monte to forgive him if he had caused any offence. Del Monte nodded agreement. Trent said the same and Del Monte nodded again. Trent took offence because Del Monte would not speak and said:]

You can read whatever you like into my words. It doesn't matter to me because I am a nobleman.

Del Monte:

If you're what a nobleman is then I'm not one, but I will go to some place where noblemen can't lord over me.

[The meeting ended in uproar and Del Monte swore he would never again serve as a chairman.]

7 Venetian Ambassador to France Reporting the Situation in France (1561)

While the Roman Church tried to organise a unified response to the threat of the reforming movement the situation worsened. This deterioration focused the minds of the churchmen and led them to respond and present, as far as possible, a unified front. With the loss of England, the Netherlands, Scandinavia and large sections of Germany and Central-Eastern Europe, the Church was very concerned not to lose France or Northern Italy. Italy remained loyal to the Catholic Church but there was every reason to believe that Calvinism might carry the day in France.

[Cl: no. 272 – 57]

Unless God intervenes soon the religious situation in France will be very evil indeed. Every single province has been infected. Congregations and meetings, which [the Protestants] call assemblies are held in provinces which make up seventy-five per cent of the Kingdom: Normandy, most of Brittany, Touraine, Poitou, Gascony, a large part of Languedoc, of Dauphiné, and of Provence. In these assemblies they read [the Bible] and preach using the rites and practices found in Geneva. They have no respect for the king's officials or even for the king's orders. This plague has spread into every layer of society; strangely enough, even the clergy are tainted. I don't mean that the disease has spread only to priests, monks and nuns – only a few monasteries are unpolluted. Even bishops and princes of the church who have never shown such an interest before are affected. So far the rigorous application of the law and the fear that their property and their lives might be lost has kept most people from coming out [as Protestants] though this has not restrained the common people. For the most part, Your Serenity [the Doge], the general people are fervently devoted to the Catholic practices and attend church regularly. But, all the other levels of society are heavily infected – the nobility worse of all, it would seem. The situation is especially severe amongst people who are under forty. Some of these, for show and to avoid prosecution, continue to go to Mass and attend Catholic services and pretend to be Catholics outwardly. But, as soon as they think they aren't being watched they avoid church and the Mass especially. This is even worse since it has become clear that prison, threat and burning are not working. It has now been decided that people won't be prosecuted unless they're preaching, proselytising or attend a public assembly. Everyone else is tolerated and some have even been let out of prison in Paris even as well as other sections of the Kingdom. Many of those let out of prison now preach and speak in public. They brag that they have beaten the papists as they like to call their opponents. None of them fears questioning. A silent truce has taken hold. Before, anyone who was suspected had to flee to Geneva, or Germany or England. Now, not only do they stay in the country, but many of the former refugees have come back. When I was going to Italy I went by Geneva and was told that many of the gentlemen who had fled to Geneva after the failure of the conspiracy of Amboise had returned to France after the late King died. For example, M. de Mombrun who caused the troubles in Provence and Dauphiné and who was burnt in effigy. Also, about fifty men were called from all over France to go about preaching and teaching the 'Word', which is what they call the Gospel and their doctrines. The power and prestige of the chief minister in Geneva, a Frenchman named Calvin from Picardy will seem unbelievable to Your Serenity. His authority is amazing. His style of life, his beliefs, his writings made him stand out from all the rest. The amount of money which is sent to him secretly from France is incredible. I can only close by saying that if God does not intervene one of two things will happen:

1 A truce, which is openly called for, will give the heretics the freedom to have churches where they can preach, read [the Bible], and worship according to their beliefs. This will be exactly like what happened when the king last August at Fontainebleau agreed to the terms of a petition from the Admiral [Coligny].

2 It will be necessary to use violence and wash our hands in noble blood to restore obedience to the Pope and see that the rites of the Catholic Church are kept.

I am sure that there will be a sharp break in the kingdom and civil war will follow. The result will be the destruction of religion and the kingdom since any change in religion always requires a change in government.

8 Diary of Giambattisti Casale (Milan, 1564)

Once the Roman Church was able to arrive at a consensus (at Trent) about what 'Catholicism' was to be, it was able to initiate its own reforms in those areas still under its control and to contemplate beginning a counter-offensive to reclaim those areas lost to Protestantism. These efforts were theological, institutional and practical. Even in those areas (such as Milan) where Protestantism had been wholly unsuccessful, the Tridentine reforms meant substantial changes to the pre-existing religious structures and traditions.

[M1 – 29, 30, 101]

29 August 1564.

The Pope, Pius IV, has sent the vicar general, Signor Nicolò Ormaneto, to publish the decrees of the Council of Trent in Milan and throughout the diocese of Milan. He is also ordered to put the decrees into operation in the smallest degree. Therefore, he called together all those priests of the diocese who were in charge of souls: the provosts, the abbots, the curates. They all submitted to him. That same day the vicar ordered a general procession. Many children, especially those from the Schools of Christian Life, took part. The procession went to the cathedral. The monks went home but the other priests stayed in the cathedral to get the vicar's blessing. The priests were reviewed one at a time. When the supper bell was rung everyone went back to the cathedral in their liturgical clothes. A platform was set up in the middle of the cathedral so everyone could hear. Here the vicar and the leading clergymen sat down. Everyone was registered and ordered to obey the decrees of the holy council. They had all been locked in the cathedral. This meeting lasted for three days...father Don Benedetto preached every time an assembly session began. A committee of twelve prelates was set up to settle disputes which might arise. A panel of four theologians examined every person who heard confessions to ensure that they were qualified.

1564.

On 10 December the Jesuits came to Milan. Thirty Jesuits were sent here by Pope Pius IV. They were to live in the city by order of the Pope, the council and the archbishop of Milan, Cardinal Borromeo, so that they could set up a seminary. There they will gather together students to study holy, apostolic, divine doctrine so that, in time, they will make good and godly priests. When a parish priest or curate dies one of their students is to be put in that post because they are more in keeping with the spirit of these days and will be good examples of doctrine and morals....That same day there was a general procession...to go with the [Jesuits] to the place chosen for the seminary...in the procession were Milan's vicar general, Ormaneto, the illustrious prince, Signor Gabriello Cuovo...the whole Milanese Senate...to the joy of the men and women who followed along. There were also about a hundred priests. One of these Jesuits, Don Benedetto, preached in Milan's cathedral. He was an exceptional man and a great preacher. God showed His goodness on the day of the procession by stopping the rain which had been falling for a number of days. It was a beautiful, clear day. God thus showed His approval of the events.

---

9 Bull of Pope Paul III Founding the Jesuits

One of the greatest institutional reforms was the establishment of the Society of Jesus. This organisation became the front-line in the efforts of the Church to extend Tridentine reforms throughout Catholic areas and to reintroduce Catholicism to areas lost to the Protestants. The military discipline and structure of the order along with their commitment to preaching and teaching at every societal level proved the key to restoring Catholicism in many areas, especially in Central and Eastern Europe.

[K3: 337–39], passim – on the Jesuits: 3, 17, 23, 37, 66, 68, 69, 83, 89, 99, 108, 111, 147, 269,

270, 271, 272, 273, 287, 324, 325, 361, 362, 391, 487]

We want our Society to be called after Jesus [i.e., Jesuits]. These are the tasks we see for members. They will fight for God and God alone under the banner of the cross. They will serve the Roman Pontiff who is [God's] representative on earth. They will solemnly swear to avoid all sexual relations. To be part of this best of all societies is to care for the souls of Christians in life and doctrine, to spread the faith by public preaching and the ministry of God's Word. Spiritual exercises will form a part as well as charitable works. Charity will be especially apparent in providing education for the young and the unlearned in Christianity and the Christian faith. Spiritual consolation will be provided by hearing confessions. In brief, any member must first look to God and then the foundation of this society – in short, to keep their eyes and goals fixed on the path set by God for all men.

10   Diary of Giambattisti Casale (Milan, 1565)

Casale continued to chronicle the practical impact of the Tridentine reforms in Catholic Milan. Tridentine reforms even reached into individual households. Although there was a clear desire to avoid the sort of individual religious practices (for example, private Bible reading) which were associated with Protestantism, there was an awareness that lay Catholics had to be trained in their religion if they were to resist Protestant teachings.

[M1]

On 16 February, I introduced family prayer into my house. The prayer was written by the priest, Hieronomo Rabia who had been prior general of the Confraternity of the Christian Life in 1564. I got permission for this from Father Catellino da Castello who had been my confessor for eighteen years. He praised this prayer as inspired by the Holy Spirit....He said that such prayers keep peace, unity and harmony in a house....This is the prayer: I kneel down and so does my wife, Cathelina, and my children Zanevera and David, and also my servant, Ioan Antonio. Then, in Latin, I say 'In the name of the Father, Son and Holy Spirit', then 'Come Holy Spirit', then the grace of the Holy Spirit, then 'Send Your Spirit', etc. I say each word and then the rest repeat it. We then say the Lord's Prayer and the Hail Mary three times, word by word....I make everyone say all of this, one word at a time, on their knees.

On 16 September, a free school for small children was set up in San Michele al Gallo. The children were to go there for Christian beliefs and good morals. The school was set up by Mr Rinaldo di Lanzi, Mr Ioan Paolo d'Andiera and Mr Christophoro Robio. This did great honour to God and amazed everyone. The founder of the institution, Father Catellino da Castello was there as well along with some of his spiritual sons, namely, myself and Ioan Antonio di Raymondo. He had been confined to a bed for seven years but it pleased God that morning to give him the strength to attend.…The whole of Milan was amazed since many thought he was long dead. He was embraced by many priests and lay people because he was a great servant of God and was well-liked and respected by everyone.

11　Fourth Session of the Council of Trent (8 April 1546)

In addition to practical and institutional reforms such as insisting on clerical celibacy and establishing the Jesuits, the Roman Church also responded to the theological teachings of the reformers. It was essential to tread a fine line between educating the laity sufficiently to answer Protestant criticisms while not allowing them to conclude that religious issues were subject to personal interpretation.

[S3: 296–9, passim]

Decree on the Bible:

It is clear that [Gospel] truths and rules are in the written books [of the Bible] and in those unwritten traditions. These have come through the Apostles from Christ's mouth or direct from the Apostles.…If someone refuses to accept those books mentioned above totally with all their parts, which have been normally read in the Catholic Church in the old Latin Vulgate Bible, or willingly and wilfully rejects the traditions mentioned let that person be declared thrown out of the faith.

Decree on the Form and Use of the Bible:

The same holy council…declares and orders that the old Latin Vulgate edition, which has been approved after centuries of use in the Church should be used for lectures, debates, sermons, and preaching. It is the authentic edition and no one, no matter what the reason, should reject it.

Furthermore, no one, relying on their own ideas…should interpret the Bible in any way not acceptable to Holy Mother Church who has the sole right to interpret the correct sense.…

From now on, it will be illegal to print…books about religious matters without the author's name, to sell them or even to own them.…

Moreover, to stop the shocking way in which sections of the Bible are corrupted and twisted to all sorts of unacceptable uses…for superstitions, for ungodly, demonic incantations, for divinations, for lot-casting…to stop all this…it is ordered and encouraged that these people be punished for violating and profaning God's Word by the bishops with every legal means at their disposal.

12　Diary of Giambattista Casale (Milan, 1565)

Giambattista Casale's Diary shows the popular interest in, and enthusiasm for the introduction of the Catholic reforms. The popular response seen below is analagous to that seen (above) in cities as they adopted the Reform.

[M1]

On 23 September...archbishop [Borromeo] preached in person in the cathedral which was so full no one else could get in. After the Mass another famous man preach'ed another sermon. The archbishop ended the service with a benediction to everyone. All the people there that day got a plenary indulgence from Pope Pius IV, the archbishop's uncle. On the next Sunday, 7 October, the archbishop and prince [Cuovo] led a procession...there was also a three-day fast ordered...everyone was ordered to go to confession and take communion the next Sunday. Everyone who did this was to get a plenary indulgence. The archbishop wanted to follow the example of St Ambrose who said that anyone who wants a favour from God must do three things: charity, fasting, and prayer. The archbishop was the first to do these things to set a good example. Therefore, he gave gifts to the poor monasteries, to the prisoners and to the poor.

On 14 October, the archbishop, on the order of the Pope, was made a bishop cardinal in the cathedral. After the celebratory Mass a wonderful sermon was given by Father Basileo on the Gospel story about the woman taken in adultery....The archbishop, many bishops, the prince, the Senate, magistrates, and many people were all there. They all listened with attention and devotion. This was a great example and made the people very happy since it was so rare, even unheard of.

On 15 October the diocesan council began. The archbishop and all his bishops were there and he officiated at the Mass with a godliness and honour...which has never before been seen in the cathedral. All the decrees of the Council of Trent were then read...and sermons were said in the cathedral every day....

The first session of the council lasted from 15–23 October...the second session lasted from 24 October to 3 November. The people at the council were there each day from early in the morning until an hour after sunset. They had nothing to eat in that time. All the bishops swore aloud and in writing that they would obey the [Tridentine] decrees. There were spectacular ceremonies...the people were so edified that it was marvellous, more marvellous than anything ever heard of.

---

13 Final Decree of the Council of Trent (Pope Pius IV, 18 November 1564)

Final Decree of Trent, Pope Pius IV. For the first time there was a clearly defined response to the question, what must one believe to be a true Roman Catholic? This need for confessions was an element apparent in almost every group. As the religious unity of Europe disintegrated it was essential for each fragmentary group, no matter how large or small, to be able to define themselves.

[K3: 357]

I confess most firmly and embrace the apostolic and ecclesiastical traditions of those other rites and rules of the Church.

Equally, that holy interpretation of the Bible which Holy Mother Church holds and has held. It is the Church's place to judge the correct meaning and interpretation of the Bible. This I confess. And [I admit] no interpretation apart from the one held by the unanimous consent of the [Church] Fathers.

Also, I confess that there are seven correct and proper Sacraments. These were set up by Our Lord Jesus Christ to save humanity. Not all are necessary for everyone. They are: Baptism, Confirmation, Eucharist, Penance, Last Rites, Ordination, Marriage. These confer grace. Of these, Baptism, Ordination and Confirmation cannot be repeated. To do so is sacrilege.

I receive and confess also the rites accepted and approved by the Catholic Church which are set to administer the above sacraments.

I embrace and receive everything and any thing defined and stated by the Holy Council of Trent about original sin and justification.

Likewise, I affirm that God is actually sacrificed in the Mass. It is a proper and effective sacrifice for the living and the dead. The Body and Blood of Our Lord Jesus Christ – at one with His spirit and divinity – is really and substantially in the most holy Sacrament of the Eucharist. The entire substance of the bread is turned into [His] body and the entire substance of the wine becomes [His] blood. This change is called transubstantiation by the Catholic Church....

I hold firmly that Purgatory exits and I swear that the souls of believers are kept there for judgement.

14   Diary of Giambattista Casale (Milan, 1568–9)

Giambattista Casale's Diary also shows that the Tridentine reforms were not universally accepted or appreciated. Many clerical leaders were unwilling to adopt drastic changes to traditional practices.

[M1]

On 4 July 1568, Cardinal Borromeo laid the cornerstone for the rebuilt church of San Fidele...which the Jesuits used later....He gave a sermon...then went into the church and said Mass; he himself gave communion to a large number of people and this astonished everyone at the service....Later that day he gave a banquet for the virgins of Santa Ursula...this was meant to honour God and provide a bit of recreation for the virgins.

On 31 August 1569, the cardinal went to conduct a visitation of the church of La Scala in Milan. The clerics there didn't want to let him in. When his servant arrived on a horse with the cardinal's banner the clergy there...threw him out. The archbishop, amazed, sent another servant with a cross to go to the church but the clergy went towards him to keep him out as well. When the archbishop saw how disrespectful they were, even of the cross, he got off his horse, picked up the cross himself with great reverence and started walking towards the group of clergy (priests and monks) who were blocking his way, equipped with various weapons.

Like a true knight of God he defended himself with the cross in his hand. It was enough to make a person weep, to see children against their loving father, sheep against the shepherd, servants against their loyal lord. Miraculously he was not injured though he was not able to get in. He then returned to the cathedral and personally excommunicated...all the clergy who had resisted him.

---

15   Final Decree of the Council of Trent (Pope Pius IV)

Trent was also determined to reform the morals and conduct of the clergy which had led to so much anti-Roman feeling. Here one is faced, most dramatically, with the problem of whether one should see this movement as a reaction to Protestantism (that is, a Counter-Reformation) or a natural development of late medieval and Humanist call for change (that is, a Catholic Reformation). There are certainly elements of both in the work of Trent and one might be forgiven for thinking that the council ordered and enforced many of the changes originally demanded by the reformers. Nevertheless, these areas of dispute were very much the product of pre-existing debates. It is in Trent's response to specific Protestant doctrinal beliefs (for example, Predestination) that one sees most obviously a direct reaction to the new ideas.

[S3: 436–8, passim]

On reform:

As to clerical residence....So there will be no misunderstanding about the wishes of the holy council...the council orders that every cleric...even cardinals...are bound to reside personally in their church or diocese where they should do their job which has been given to them and they cannot be absent...without written permission from the Pope or metropolitan or, if he's absent, the oldest resident suffragen bishop....Moreover, suitable arrangements should be made in their absence so that their flocks don't suffer...in any case, for whatever reasons, the absence should not exceed a period of three months in any one year....Also, unless required by diocesan duties, bishops should be in their cathedral churches for Advent, Quadragesima, Christmas, Easter, Pentecost, and Corpus Christi.

For all other lesser clergy whose duties put them in charge of souls...should not be given leave to go for longer than two months except in exceptional circumstances.

On the authority of the Pope:

Finally, the council declares that nothing in any form has been established by this holy council in the areas of moral reform or Church discipline under the pontificates of the late Paul III and Julius III or under the present Pope, Pius IV, which can be understood to undermine or limit the authority of the Pope.

[S3: 313f., 316f., passim]

On free justification:

When the Apostle says that a person is justified by faith freely, people should understand this as the Church has always understood it with complete agreement....

On the heretics' false hope:

Clearly one has to believe that all sins are, and have always been, forgiven by free grace for Christ's sake. However, a person's sins should not be said to be forgiven just because the person relies solely on the belief that sins are freely forgiven. This belief is currently preached furiously by the heretics and schismatics against the Catholic Church....However, no one can know with certainty...that God's grace has been given to them.

On avoiding rash views about predestination:

No one...should ever say with certainty that he is one of the elect. This would mean either that the person doesn't think they will sin again or if they do that they are sure that they will repent. Without a special revelation it is impossible to know whom God has chosen.

On perseverance:

Let people who think their standing is safe beware lest they fall. They should work out their salvation with fear and trembling, with work, with carefulness, with almsgiving, with prayer, with fasts and charity.

On penitence:

People who have lost the grace of justification can get it back when God moves them and they work to get it back through the sacrament of penance.

---

16 Diary of Giambattista Casale (Milan, 1567–75)

Giambattista Casale's Diary once again highlights the immense popular enthusiasm for the introduction of Tridentine reforms in Milan where they were brought in by Cardinal Borromeo, a Catholic reformer every bit as charismatic and enthusiastic as Protestant leaders.

[M1]

On 16 February 1567, at the start of Ambrose's carnival [this variant of Lent, based on a Latin liturgy of St Ambrose, in Milan begins the Sunday after Ash Wednesday. Borromeo successfully resisted attempts of the post-Tridentine Church to bring the

Milanese Church into line], the archbishop thought that...Milan should have a wholly godly and spiritual carnival....He asked...that the cathedral's deans and the religious teachers should receive communion every day as an example to all the people and that they pray that God would stop the immoral behaviour which normally marked [carnival]...we all consented...he offered to give us communion himself...because we had agreed....He asked all the other penitential confraternities to join in...and they quickly agreed. A general announcement was made to the people...1,300 people came to get communion directly from the archbishop's hand. This number was recorded by the official who counted communicants. Those who received, in order, were: [the archbishop's] household, priests and monks, senators, preachers, ladies and gentlemen, merchants, artisans, and everyone else. There were 300 people from the confraternities. The archbishop said low Mass at St Agnes' altar in the cathedral; the altar was dressed with tapestries, silver plate and other lovely things....The Schools of Christian Belief had all the male students line up in the cemetery and then marched them into the church where the archbishop waited to bless them. They all had on [white] and wings. It looked like Milan was full of angels, just like in Heaven, when they streamed back to their own schools. Milan was so moved by this that everyone forgot about the normal lewdness of the carnival and went around talking instead about heavenly matters.

On 4 September 1571, Augustino, my nephew, became a monk in the monastery of St Jerome. But after a month he left because he said he couldn't stand praying all day.

On 18 October 1571 [Augustino] went to become a monk at the monastery of San Vitore. He was accepted and was re-named Brother Luca.

On 13 September 1571, Cardinal-archbishop Borromeo had a midnight procession with about 500 people from all levels of society: gentlemen, merchants, artisans. They met at San Francesco at Signo Tomasco da Marino's grand house....There they began to beat themselves. They marched back and forth to the cathedral beating themselves the whole time. It was a beautiful sight to see: the devotion and order was amazing. [Borromeo] waited for the group in the cathedral and blessed them one at a time while prayers were said that God might protect Christians from the Turks who were then preparing to attack Venice. They did this every Friday night for two months. They were barefoot and everyone carried a torch. This continued until God gave us victory over the Turks [at Lepanto]...when the news arrived there was a great celebration in Milan with fireworks and cannon-fire....

On 11 November there were more fireworks and lights were set in every window for three hours after sunset. It was a beautiful sight to see. The archbishop ordered three days of processions to thank God for the victory over the Turks.

On 6 April 1572, the archbishop organised a prayer which was taught to everyone by the preachers. People were supposed to say the prayer every night when the cathedral bell was rung. He said that Pope Pius V had asked that this be done...to protect us from evil, especially the Turk, the great enemy of Christendom. So, that day, the first day of Easter, the bell rang half an hour after sunset and all the people began to pray.

On 30 October 1575, the governing board of the Congregation of Christian Doctrine and an equal number of assistants (twenty-four in all) began to visit the old, as well as the new, schools to reform them. This was ordered by Rev. Franceso, the prior general and had been approved by the Congregation. The visitors were ordered not to take any food or drink from the schools they were inspecting. All the people were edified by this....I was assigned to inspect the area outside the New Gate...and I set up a school for boys and girls in the church of Santo Martino a Balsamo.

17   Erasmus to Julius von Pflug

Erasmus's comments on the polarisation of the opposing camps and the failure of attempts at compromise demonstrate how early despair of reconciliation had set in for many. Despite the success of the Catholic retrenchment and subsequent counter-offensive, the conclusions of Erasmus should be borne in mind. The unity of Christendom was shattered forever and bloody battles were to be waged across Europe in the name of religion for over a century.

Freiburg, 20 August 1531.

[A2: no. 2522. 20–64, passim]

No age has ever been as wild as ours. It seems as though a host of demons has spilled out of Hell. Everyone is totally insane, lay people and clergy alike. I am not as powerful as you seem to think; I can't perform miracles. I don't know what the Pope is planning. The priests want to turn to war since burning the heretics has so far failed. It's not my place to judge whether or not they are correct. They may not have time to test their theory if the Turks attack. It would just be better to return to the Gospel as the rule for living. Then, 150 men could be chosen from the Christian world to decide the finer doctrinal points being disputed. Different views on some areas do not have to be set down as Articles of Faith. Some of the Church's laws will need to be changed and the clergy should certainly be better qualified for their jobs. Right now, the wealth of the Church does nothing but support a few Oriental despots while the bulk of the people are left to the leadership of the new preachers who simply want to get rid of the whole structure. If Pope Adrian had lived for about ten years then there might have been the chance that Rome would have been cleansed. He asked my advice. I sent it but got no reply. I assume he did not like it. Melanchthon is a man with a gentle nature. Even his enemies say kind things about him. Your plan was tried by him at Augsburg and if I had not been ill

I would have been there supporting him. You know the result. Men of learning and character were accused of heresy just for speaking to him. Imagine: if the two of us were to come up with some compromise plan, neither side – leaders or followers – would accept it. Do you remember Brother John's visit to the theatre? Being from the country he had never seen such a thing. Two boxers were play-acting on the stage. John rushed up to stop their fight and was, of course, killed.

Unable to reach a compromise

7 Talking Pictures

[*Suggested readings*: 2, 4, 5, 25, 26, 62, 148, 396, 398, 399, 413, 464, 465, 480, 411]

The effect of the wide availability of the written word as a result of the invention of the printing press on the spread of the Reformation is well known. Moreover, the spoken word, whether from travelling merchants, missionaries or ministers, was of great importance as well. However, the majority of the people were illiterate and, during the early decades of the Reformation, not well served by ministers.

It is important, therefore, to recall the value and power of illustrated posters and pamphlets – in effect, the visual word. While the modern reader may not be well equipped to 'read' these illustrations – which were similar to present-day political cartoons – people in the Early Modern period would be more than able to understand such drawings. For example, ethnic clothing would identify a person's nationality; also, the appearance or absence of certain religious symbols – such as rosary beads – could effectively label someone as a Catholic. Such visual symbols provided a code fully legible to contemporaries. They could read the wealth of details included in these pictures while modern readers, because of their lack of familiarity with classical and Biblical myths and imagery, are often functionally illiterate when viewing the drawings.

1 'Iconoclastic Assault on the Virgin and Child' (Illustration 1 [G1])

On initial examination, one might conclude that this was an anti-Protestant illustration, displaying iconoclasm. But, a more careful 'reading' of the drawing would note the peculiar hats, the exaggerated facial features and the pseudo-Hebraic letters on the spearman's hem. In fact, then, this is an anti-Semitic illustration meant to anger Christians against the supposed iconoclasm of the Jews. Of course, by altering the most obvious 'coding' elements in the picture (the Hebrew letters, for example) one could turn this into an anti-Protestant work.

Figure 1 *Iconoclastic Assault on the Virgin and Child*
SOURCE: P. Gengenbach, *Das ist ein erschreckenliche Historie* (n.d., n.p.).

Figure 2 *The Wolf's Sermon*
SOURCE: Anon., *Ein Predigt vom Wolf zu Gäusen* (n.d., n.p.).

[on Jews in the Reformation: 109, 131, 190, 231, 268, 281, 314, 372, 432]

---

2 'The Wolf's Sermon' (Illustration 2 [A4]) and 'The Lutheran Cat-Fight' (Illustration 3 [A3])

The first is anti-Catholic (note the rosary beads of the geese), the second anti-Lutheran and anti-German (the clothing is distinctive). Both illustrations, however, play on visual images identifying the opposition with various animals or beasts (ravenous wolves, cackling geese, sly foxes, randy goats in the first; barking dogs, randy goats, slimy snails, filthy rats, smelly swine, stubborn asses in the second). The finer details must be 'read' correctly to understand the image. In both, the words above would have been within the grasp of the barely literate who, reading them aloud (all reading in this period was aloud), would assist others in understanding the full import of the message.

---

3 'The Sufferings of Christ and Antichrist' (Illustration 4 [L44]) and 'The Church Besieged' (Illustration 5 [D11])

Both of these are well-developed illustrations. In the first, the passion of Christ is presented in an image which would have been instantly recognisable (recalling various Passion/Mystery Plays as well as the Stations of the Cross). The second image is easily 'readable' as it shows the papal chair, triple crown and coat-of-arms – Peter's crossed-keys.

The second illustration, which is anti-Protestant, is equally clear. The words (originally in Latin) were for the benefit of the well-educated. Nevertheless, the 'message' would be widely accessible. The clothing and accessories of the bishops/teachers, priests, monks and angels are easily identifiable. Likewise, the Turks, Jews and Heretics (here as German) are clearly identified by their clothes. The demons are as obvious as the angels. In addition, the central figure of Christ is holding a wafer (the sacramental Host) which makes the message all the more powerful: the very Body of Christ is under assault.

Die Luterifch Strebkatz

Figure 3 *The Lutheran Cat-fight*

SOURCE: Anon., *Die Luterische Strebkatz* (n.d., n.p.). ['Strebkatz[e]' refers to a form of 'tug-of-war' in which the contestants tie the rope around their neck. My thanks to Dr Beat Kümin for the meaning.]

Figure 4 *The Sufferings of Christ and Antichrist*
SOURCE: M. Luther, *Passional Christi und Antichristi* (n.d., n.p.).

Figure 5 *The Church Besieged*
SOURCE: Dangersheim, *Etliche Büchlein wider den Luther, der[en] Titel balde hernach folgen* (Leipzig: V. Schumann, 1530).

Sources

A1   *Alle handelinge Protocol. Dat ist des Gesprechs tot Embden in Oostvrieslant met der Wederdooperen die hen Vlamingen noemen gehouden begonnen den 27. Februarij Anno 1578. ende den 17 Mey desseluen Jaers gheeyndicht* (Emden: Goosen Goebens, 1579).

A2   Allen, P.S. (ed.), *Opus Epistolarum Des. Erasmi Roterodami* (Oxford: Clarendon Press, 1906–58) 12 volumes.

A3   Anon., *Die Luterisch Strebkatz* (no place, publisher or date).

A4   Anon., *Ein Predigt vom Wolf zu den Gäusen* (no place, publisher or date).

A5   Anon., *Epistola Luciferi ad malos principes ecclesiasticos* (no place, publisher or date).

A6   Arnaud, E. (ed.), *Documents protestants inédits de XVIe siècle* (Paris: Grassart, 1872).

B1   Balan, P., *Monumenta Reformationes Lutheranae* (Ratisbon: Pustet, 1884).

B2   Balard, J., *Journal* (Geneva: Jullien, 1854).

B3   Baum, J.G. (ed.), *Proces de Baudichon de la Maisonneuve accusé d'hérésie à Lyon, 1534* (Geneva: Fick, 1873).

B4   Baum, J.W., Cunnitz, E., and Reuss, E. (eds), *Joannis Calvini Opera quae supersunt omnia* (Frankfurt: Minerva, 1964), 59 volumes.

B5   Benoît, J.D., *Jean Calvin. Sermons sur le livre de Michée*, in E. Mühlaupt, et al. (eds), *Supplementa Calviniana: Sermons Inédits*, 5 (Neukirchen: Neukirchener Verlag, 1964) 7 volumes.

B6   *Böhmischer Lantagsverhandlungen und Landtasbeschlüße* (Prague Valecka, 1886).

B7   Bonivard, F., 'De lestat ecclesiastique', in his *Advis et devis de la source de lidolatrie* (Geneva: Fick, 1856): 1–131.

B8   Bonivard, F., 'Des difformes Reformateurs', in his *Advis et devis de la source de lidolatrie* (Geneva: Fick 1856): 133–162.

B9   Brandt, G., *The History of the Reformation and the Other Ecclesiastical Transactions in and About the Low Countries* (London: T. Childe, 1720–23) 4 volumes.

B10   Brandt, G., *Historie der Reformatie en andere kerkelyke geschiedenissen in en omtrent de Nederlanden* (Amsterdam: Boom, 1671–1704) 4 volumes.

B11   Brieger, T., *Aleander und Luther in Quellen und Forschungen zur Geschichte der Reformation*, 1 (Gotha: Perhtes, 1884).

B12   Bucer, M., *Alle Handlungen und Schriften zu Vergleichung der Religion durch die Key. Mai.* (Strasbourg: W. Rihel, 1541).

B13   Buchon, J.E.C. (ed.), *Choix de chroniques et mémoires sur l'histoire de France avec notices biographiques* (Paris: Desrez, 1836).

B14   Bullinger, H., *Reformationsgeschichte* (Frauenfeld: Ch. Benel, 1838) 3 volumes.

C1   *Calendar of State Papers: Venetian, 1558–80* (London: Longmans, 1864–1947) 38 volumes.

C2   Cornelius, C.A. von, *Geschichte des Münsterischen Aufruhrs in drei Büchern*, 1 (Leipzig: Weigel, 1855).

C3   Coussemaker, C.E.H. (ed.), *Troubles religieux du XVIe siècle dans la Flandre maritime, 1560–1570* (Bruges: A. de Zuttere, 1876) 4 volumes.

D1   Dangersheim, *Etliche Büchlein wider den Luther, der[en] Titel balde hernach folgen* (Leipzig: V. Schumann, 1530/31).

D2   Dentière, M., *La Guerre* (Geneva: Ch. Schuchardt, 1881).

D3   Dentière, M., *L'epistre tres utile...* (Geneva: Girard, 1539; falsely labelled, Anvers: Martin).

D4   Doyen, S. and Lottin, A., (eds), *Les "casseurs" de l'été 1566. L'iconoclasme dans le Nord de la France* (Paris: Hachette, 1981).

E1   Egli, E. and Finsler, G. (eds), *Huldreich Zwinglis Sämtliche Werke* (Leipzig: Heinsius, 1908).

F1   Friedensburg, W., *Der Reichstag zu Speier 1526 im Zusammenhang der politischen und kirchlichen Entwicklung Deutschlands im Reformationszeitalter* (Berlin: Gaertner, 1887) Appendix 11.

F2   Froment, A., *Les Actes et Gestes* (Geneva: Fick, 1854).

F3   Froude, J.A., *Life and Letters of Erasmus. Lectures Delivered at Oxford, 1893–4* (London: Longmans, Green & Co., 1894).

G1   Gengenbach, P., *Das ist ein ershreckenliche Historie...* (no place, publisher or date).

G2   Gerdesius, D., *Historia Reformationis* (Gröningen: Spandau & Rump, 1744–52).

G3   Günther, F. (ed.), *Quellen zur Geschichte des Bauernkrieges* (Munich: R. Oldenbourg, 1963).

H1   *Handlingar rörande Skandinaviens Historia* (Stockholm: Elméns & Granbergs, 1816–60) 40 volumes.

H2   Herminjard, F. (ed.), *Correspondance des Réformateurs dans les pays de langue français* (Nieuwkoop: De Graaf, 1965–66) 9 volumes.

H3   Hölscher, B., 'Nachlese zur Geschichte die Widertäufer in Münster', in W.C. Giesers and B. Hölscher (eds), *Zeitschrift für vaterliche Geschichte und Alterthumsk* (Münster: F. Regensberg, 1858) vol. 20, pp. 151–94.

J1   Jussie, J. de, *Levain du Calvinisme* (Geneva: Jullien, 1865).

K1   Kern, F. (ed.), *Deutche Volkslieder des Mittelalters* (Berlin: Wegweiser, 1922).

K2   Kessler, J., *Sabbata mit kleineren Schriften und Briefen* (St Gall: Fehrische, 1902).

K3   Kidd, B.J. (ed.), *Documents Illustrative of the Continental Reformation* (Oxford: Clarendon, 1911).

K4   Knuttel, W.P.C., *Catalogus van de pamflettenverzameling berustende in de Koninklijke Bibliotheek* (Utrecht: HES, 1978) 9 volumes.

K5   Koehler, W., 'Das Marburger Religionsgespräch 1529. Versuch einer Rekonstruction', in *Schriften des Veriens für Reformationsgeschichte*, 48: 148 (Leipzig: Heinsius, 1929).

K6   Koller, H. (ed.), *Reformation Kaiser Siegmands*, in *Monumenta Germaniae Historica 500–1500. Staatschriften des späteren Mittelalters*, 6 (Stuttgart: Hiersemann, 1964) pp. 50–353.

K7   Kot, S. (ed.), *Szymon Budny. O Urzedzie Miecza Uzywaja (1583)*, in *Zabytaki Literatury z doby Reformacji*, 1 (Warsaw: Instytutu Popierania Nauki, 1932).

L1   Lefèvre, L.R. (ed.), *Journal de L'Estoile pour le règne de Henri III (1574–1589)* (Paris: Gallimard, 1943).

L2   Leitzmann, *Kleine Texte*, in H. Böhmer, *Urkunden zur Geschichte des Bauernkrieges* (Bonn: Marcus & Weber, 1910).

L3   Loescher, V.E., *Vollständige Reformationsacta, Document und Nachricht* (Leipzig: Grossens, 1720–29).

L4   Luther, M., *Passional Christi und Antichristi* (no place, publisher or date).

L5   Luther, M., *Works*, ed. S. Pelikan, and H.T. Lehmann (Philadelphia, Pa.: Concordia, 1955–86) 55 volumes.

M1   Manacorda, C. (ed.), 'Il diario di Giambattista Casale (1554–1594)', in *Memorie storiche della diocesi di Milano*, 12 (1965).

M2   Merkle, S., Ehses, S. Buschbell, G., Jedin, H., Postina, A., and Schweitzer, V. (eds), *Concilium Tridentinum, Diariorum, Actorum, Epistularum, Tractatuum. Nova Collectio* (Freiburg: Herder, 1901).

M3   More, T., *Ornamenti Eximii, Lucubrationes ab innumeris mendis repurgatae* (Basel: Episcopium F., 1563) pp. 365–428.

M4   Myconius, F., *Historia Reformationis* (Leipzig: Weidmann, 1718).

M5   Myconius, F., *Historia Reformationis*, in J.C.L. Gieseler (ed.), *Lehrbuch für Kirchengeschichte* (Bonn: Marcus, 1855).

N1   Nichols, F.M. (ed. and trans.), *The Epistles of Erasmus from his Earliest Letters to His Fifty-first Year* (London: Longman, 1901) 3 volumes.

O1   Olin, J.C. (ed. and trans.), *Desiderius Erasmus, Christian Humanism and the Reformation: Selected Writings* (New York: Harper & Row, 1965).

P1   Pithou, N., *Histoire Ecclésiastique* (Bibliothèque Nationale, Paris, Collection Dupuy, Ms 698).

R1   Raemond, F. de, *L'histoire de la naissance, progrez et decadence de l'heresie de ce siècle* (Paris: C. Chastellain, 1605) 2 volumes.

R2   Rogers, E.F. (ed. and trans.), *The Correspondence of Sir Thomas More* (Princeton, N.J.: Princeton University Press, 1947).

R3   Roset, M., *Les Chroniques de Genève* (Geneva: Jullien, 1854).

S1   Schmidt, A. (ed.), *Aeneas Silvius, 'Germania' und Jakob Wimpheline 'Respons...'* (Cologne–Graz: Böhlau, 1962).

S2   Schmidt, A. (ed.), *Enea Silvio Piccolomini, Deutschland, Der Brieftraktatan an Martin Mayer...* (Cologne–Graz: Böhlau, 1962).

S3   Schroeder, H.J., *Canon and Decrees of the Council of Trent* (London: B. Herder, 1941).

S4   Seidemann, J.K., *Die Leipziger Disputation im Jahre 1519* (Dresden: Urnoldischen, 1843), Appendix 11, pp. 119–121.

S5   Seitz, O. (ed.), *Der authentische Text der Leipziger Disputation (1519)* (Berlin: Schwetschke, 1903).

S6   Callender, F., *State Papers: Spanish* (London: Longmans, 1862–1954) 17 volumes.

S7   Strobel, G.T., *Miscellaneen literatischen Innhalts: Gröstellens aus ungedruckten Quellen* (Nuremberg: Bauer, 1778–82) 6 volumes.

T1   Toorenenbergen, J.J. van (ed.), *Ph. van Marnix van St Aldegonde: Godsdienstige en kerkelijke geschriften* (The Hague: M. Nijhoff, 1871) 3 volumes.

V1   Vaernewijck, M van., *Van die berderlicke tijden in Nederlanden en voornamelijk in Ghendt, 1566–1568*, ed. F. Vanderhaegen (Ghent: Vanderhaighen, 1872) 5 volumes.

W1   Willson, T.B., *Church and State in Norway* (London: Constable, 1903).

W2   Wrede, A. (ed.), *Deutsche Reichstagsakten, Jüngere Reihe*, II (Gotha: Perthes, 1896).

List of Abbreviations

AHSJ	Archivum Historicum Societatis Jesu
ARG	Archiv für Reformationsgeschichte
BHR	Bibliothèque d'humanisme et renaissance
BQ	Baptist Quarterly
CEH	Central European History
CH	Church History
CHR	Catholic Historical Review
EHR	English Historical Review
FH	French History
FHS	French Historical Studies
HEI	History of European Ideas
HR	Historical Reflections
HTR	Harvard Theological Review
JEH	Journal of Ecclesiastical History
JIH	Journal of Interdisciplinary History
JHI	Journal of the History of Ideas
JMH	Journal of Modern History
JMRS	Journal of Medieval and Renaissance Studies
JRH	Journal of Religious History
LQ	Lutheran Quarterly
MQR	Mennonite Quarterly Review
NAK	Nederlands Archief voor Kerkgeschiedenis
P&P	Past & Present
R&R	Renaissance and Reformation
RQ	Renaissance Quarterly
S&S	Science and Society
SCJ	Sixteenth-century Journal
SH	Social History

Suggested Reading

1. Adams, G., *The Huguenots and French Opinion* (Waterloo, Canada: Wilfrid Laurier University, 1991).
2. Aiken, R., 'Christian Soldiers in the Sala dei Capitani', *SCJ*, 16:2 (1985) pp. 206–27.
3. Alves, A.A., 'The Christian Social Organism and Social Welfare: The Case of Vives, Calvin and Loyola', *SCJ*, **20**:1 (1989) pp. 3–21.
4. Amaru, B.H., 'Martin Luther and Jewish Mirrors', *Jewish Social Studies*, **46**:2 (1984) pp. 95–102.
5. Anderson, C. and Talbot, C., *From a Mighty Fortress: Prints, Drawings, and Books in the Age of Luther, 1483–1546* (Detroit, Mich.: Detroit Institute of Arts, 1983).
6. Arnal, O.L., 'Luther and the Peasants: A Lutheran Reassessment', *S&S*, **44**:4 (1980/81) pp. 443–65.
7. Arthur, A. G., 'Rural Faith and Wills as Evidence of Popular Religion in France, 1500–1650', *Historical Papers* (1983) pp. 113–35.
8. Atkinson, J., *Martin Luther: Prophet to the Catholic Church* (Grand Rapids, Mich.: Eerdmans, 1983).
9. Augustijn, C., *Erasmus: His Life, Work and Influence* (Checktowaga, N.Y.: University of Toronto, Press, 1991).
10. Augustijn C., 'Erasmus and Menno Simons', *MQR*, **60**:4 (1986) pp. 497–508.
11. Aune, M. B., *Rhetoric and Ritual in the Theology of Philip Melanchthon: To Move the Heart* (Bethesda, Md: International Scholars, 1994).
12. Backhouse, M.F., 'Guerilla War and Banditry in the Sixteenth Century: The Wood Beggars in the Westkwertier of Flanders (1567–1568)', *ARG*, **74** (1983) pp. 232–56.
13. Bagchi, D.V.N., *Luther's Earliest Opponents: Catholic Controversialists, 1518–1525* (Minneapolis, Minn.: Fortress, 1991).
14. Bainton, R.H., 'Thomas Müntzer, Revolutionary Firebrand of the Reformation', *SCJ*, **13**:2 (1982) pp. 3–15.
15. Baker, J.W., *Heinrich Bullinger and the Covenant: The Other Reformed Tradition* (Athens: Ohio University. Press, 1980).
16. Balke, W., *Calvin and the Anabaptist Radicals* (Grand Rapids, Mich.: Eerdmans, 1982).
17. Barthell, M., *The Jesuits: History and Legend of the Society of Jesus* (New York: Morrow, 1984).
18. Baumgartner, F.J., 'Crisis in the French Episcopacy: The Bishops and the Succession of Henry IV', *ARG*, **70** (1979) pp. 278–3 01.
19. Baumgartner, F.J., 'Henry II and the Papal Conclave of 1549', *SCJ*, **16**:3 (1985) pp. 301–14.
20. Beemon, F.E., 'Calvinist Conscience and Rebellion: Marnix of St Aldegonde's Justification of the Dutch Revolt', *Fides et Historia*, **24**:3 (1993) pp. 91–9.

21. Beemon, F.E., 'The Myth of the Spanish Inquisition and the Preconditions of the Dutch Revolt', *ARG*, **85** (1994) pp. 246–64.

22. Benert, R.R., 'Lutheran Resistance Theory and the Imperial Constitution', *LQ*, **2**:2 (1988) pp. 187–207.

23. Benkert, G., 'The Spiritual Legacy of Garcia Jimenez de Cisneros, Abbot of Montserrat', *American Benedictine Review*, **38**:2 (1987) pp. 178–91.

24. Bergin, J.A., 'The Crown, the Papacy and the Reform of the Old Orders in Early Seventeenth-century France', *JEH*, **33**:2 (1982) pp. 234–55.

25. Bergmann, R., 'Hans Sachs Illustrated: Pamphlets and Broadsheets in the Service of the Reformation', *RACAR*, **17**:1 (1990) pp. 9–16, 89–91.

26. Bergmann, R., 'A "trölisch pictura": Luther's Attitude in the Question of Images', *R & R*, **5**:1 (1981) pp. 15–25.

27. Bireley, R., *The Counter-Reformation Prince: Anti-Machiavellianism or Catholic Statecraft in Early Modern Europe* (Chapel Hill, N.C.,: University of North Carolina Press, 1990).

28. Biskup, M., 'The Secularization of the State of the Teutonic Order in Prussia in 1525. Its Genesis and Significance', *Polish Western Affairs*, **22**:1–2 (1981) pp. 3–23.

29. Black, C., 'Perugia and Papal Absolutism in the Sixteenth-Century', *EHR*, **96**:380 (1981) pp. 509–39.

30. Black, C., 'Perugia and Post-Tridentine Church Reform', *JEH*, **35**:3 (1984) pp. 429–51.

31. Blaisdell, C.J., 'Calvin's Letters to Women: The Courting of Ladies in High Places', *SCJ*, **13**:3 (1982) pp. 67–84.

32. Blickle, P., *Religion, Politics, and Social Protest: Three Studies on Early Modern Germany* (Boston, Mass.: Allen & Unwin, 1984).

33. Blickle, P., *The Revolution of 1525: The German Peasants' War from a New Perspective* (Baltimore, Md: Johns Hopkins University Press, 1982).

34. Blickle, P., 'Communalism, Parliamentarianism, Republicanism', *Parliaments, Estates and Representation*, **6**:1 (1986) pp. 1–13.

35. Blickle, P., 'Communal Reformation and Peasant Piety: The Peasant Reformation and its Late Medieval Origins', *CEH*, **20**:3–4 (1987) pp. 216–28.

36. Blough, N., 'Pilgrim Marpeck, Martin Luther and the Humanity of Christ', *MQR*, **61**:2 (1987) pp. 203–12.

37. Blum, P.R., 'Apostolato dei Collegi: On the Integration of Humanism in the Educational Programme of the Jesuits', *History of Universities*, **5** (1985) pp. 101–15.

38. Bornkamm, H., *Luther in Mid-Career* (Philadelphia, Pa.: Fortress, 1983).

39. Bouwsma, W.J., *John Calvin: A Sixteenth-century Portrait* (Oxford: Oxford University Press, 1987).

40. Bouwsma, W.J., 'John Calvin's Anxiety', *Proceedings of the American Philosophical Society*, **128**:3 (1984) pp. 252–56.

41. Bouwsma, W.J., 'The Quest for the Historical Calvin', *ARG*, 77 (1986) pp. 47–57

42. Boyd, S.B., 'Anabaptism and Social Radicalism in Strasbourg, 1528–1532: Pilgrim Marpeck on Christian Social Responsibility', *MQR*, **63**:1 (1989) pp. 58–76.

43. Boyle, M., *Christening Pagan Mysteries: Erasmus in Pursuit of Women* (Toronto: University of Toronto Press, 1981).

44. Boyle, M., *Rhetoric and Reform: Erasmus' Civil Dispute with Luther* (Cambridge, Mass.: Harvard University Press, 1983).

45. Boyle, M.J., 'Stoic Luther: Paradoxical Sin and Necessity', *ARG*, **73** (1982) pp. 69–93.

46. Bracewell, C.W., 'Marc' Antonio de Dominis: The Making of a Reformer', *Slovene Studies*,

6:1–2 (1984) pp. 165–71.

47. Bradshaw, B., 'Interpreting Erasmus', *JEH*, **33**:4 (1982) pp. 596–610.

48. Brady, T.A., *Protestant Politics: Jacob Sturm (1489–1553) and the German Reformation* (Philadelphia Humanities Press, 1994).

49. Brady, T.A., 'From the Sacral Community to the Common Man: Reflections on German Reformation Studies', *CEH*, **20**:3–4 (1987) pp. 229–45.

50. Brady, T.A., 'Peoples' Religion in Reformation Europe', *Historical Journal*, **34**:1 (1991) pp. 173–82.

51. Brann, N.L., 'Pre-Reformation Humanism in Germany and the Papal Monarchy: A Study in Ambivalence', *JMRS*, **14**:2 (1984) pp. 159–86.

52. Brann, N.L., 'The Proto-Protestant Assault upon Church Magic: The "Errores Bohemanorum" According to the Abbot Trithemius (1462–1525)', *JRH*, 12:1(1982) pp. 9–22.

53. Brecht, M., *Martin Luther: His Road to Reformation, 1483–1521* (Philadelphia, Pa: Fortress, 1985).

54. Brecht, M., *Martin Luther: The Preservation of the Church* (Minneapolis, Minn.: Fortress, 1993).

55. Brecht, M., *Martin Luther: Shaping and Defining the Reformation, 1521–1532* (Minneapolis, Minn.: Fortress, 1990).

56. Brendler, G., *Martin Luther: Theology and Revolution* (Oxford: Oxford University Press, 1991).

57. Britnell, J., 'Jean Lemaire de Belges and his List of Schisms', *Durham University Journal*, **73**:1 (1980) pp. 53–8.

58. Brooks, P.N., *Seven-headed Luther: Essays in Commemoration of a Quincentenary* (Oxford: Oxford University Press, 1983).

59. P.N., 'A Lily Ungilded? Martin Luther, the Virgin Mary and the Saints', *JRH*, **13**:2 (1984) pp. 136–49.

60. Burnett, A.N., *The Yoke of Christ: Martin Bucer and Christian Discipline* (Kirksville, Mo.: Sixteenth-century Essays and Studies, 1994).

61. Burnett, A.N., 'Church Discipline and Moral Reformation in the Thought of Martin Bucer', *SCJ*, **22**:3 (1991) pp. 438–56.

62. Burnett, S.G., 'Calvin's Jewish Interlocutor: Christian Hebraism and Anti-Jewish Polemics During the Reformation', *BHR*, **55**:1 (1993) pp. 113–23.

63. Butin, P.W., *Revelation, Redemption, and Response: Calvin's Trinitarian Understanding of the Divine–Human Relationship* (Oxford: Oxford University Press, 1995).

64. Cameron, E., *The European Reformation* (Oxford: Clarendon Press, 1991).

65. Cameron, E., *The Reformation of the Heretics: The Waldensis of the Alps, 1480–1580* (Oxford: Oxford University Press, 1984).

66. Caraman, P., *Ignatius Loyola: A Biography of the Founder of the Jesuits* (New York: Harper & Row, 1990).

67. Carroll, M.D., 'Peasant Festivity and Political Identity in the Sixteenth Century', *Art History*, **10**:3 (1987) pp. 289–314.

68. Case, T.E., 'The Year 1588 and San Diego de Alcalá', *Journal of San Diego History*, **34**:1 (1988) pp. 16–28.

69. Châteller, L., *The Europe of the Devout: The Catholic Reformation and the Formation of the New Society* (Cambridge: Cambridge University Press, 1989).

70. Clark, H., 'The Publication of the Koran in Latin: A Reformation Dilemma', *SCJ*, **15**:1 (1984) pp. 3–12.

71. Classen, A. and Settle, T.A., 'Women in Martin Luther's Life and Theology', *German Studies Review*, **14**:2 (1991) pp. 231–60.

72. Coats, C.R., *Subverting the System: D'Aubigné and Calvinism* (Kirksville, Mo.: Sixteenth-century Essays and Studies, 1990).

73. Coats, C.R., 'Restructuring Protestant Scriptural Space in Sixteenth-century Catholic France', *SCJ*, **25**:2 (1994) pp. 341–52.

74. Cochrane, E., 'Caesar Baronius and the Counter-Reformation', *CHR*, **66**:1 (1980) pp. 53–8.

75. Cochrane, E., and Kirshner, J. (eds), *The Renaissance* (London, 1986).

76. Cole, R.G., 'Reformation Printers: Unsung Heroes', *SCJ*, **15**:3 (1984) pp. 327–39.

77. Coogan, R., 'Petrarch's *Liber sive Nomine* and a Vision of Rome in the Reformation', *R & R*, **7**:1 (1983) pp. 1–12.

78. Cooper, J. W., 'The Outlines of Political Theory in the Protestant Reformation', *Teaching Political Science*, **10**:1 (1982) pp. 43–51.

79. Correll, B., 'Malleable Material, Models of Power: Women in Erasmus's "Marriage Group" and Civility in Boys', *English Literary History*, **57**:2 (1990) pp. 241–62.

80. Crimando, T.I., 'Two French Views of the Council of Trent', *SCJ*, **19**:2 (1988) pp. 169–86.

81. Crofts, R., 'Books, Reform and the Reformation', *ARG*, **72** (1981) pp. 21–36.

82. Crofts, R., 'Printing, Reform and the Catholic Reformation in Germany (1521–1545)', *SCJ*, **16**:3 (1985) pp. 369–81.

83. Dalmases, C. de., *Ignatius of Loyola, Founder of the Jesuits: His Life and Work* (St Louis, Mo.: Institute of Jesuit Sources, 1985).

84. D'Amico, J.F., *Renaissance Humanism in Papal Rome: Humanists and Churchmen on the Eve of the Reformation* (Baltimore, Md: Johns Hopkins University Press, 1983).

85. D'Amico, J.F., *Roman and German Humanism, 1450–1550*, ed. P.F. Grendler (Aldershot: Variorum, 1995).

86. Daniel, D.P., 'The Acceptance of the Formula of Concord in Slovakia', *ARG*, **70** (1979) pp. 260–77.

87. Daniel, D.P., 'The Fifteen Years' War and the Protestant Response to Habsburg Absolutism in Hungary', *East Central Europe*, **8**:1–2 (1981) pp. 38–51.

88. Daniel, D.P., 'The Impact of the Protestant Reformation of Education in Slovakia', *Slovakia*, **34**:62–3 (1989–90) pp. 9–27.

89. Darowski, R., 'John Hay, SJ, and the Origins of Philosophy in Lithuania', *Innes Review*, **31**:1 (1980) pp. 7–15.

90. Davis, N.Z., *Fiction in the Archives: Pardon Tales and their Tellers in Sixteenth-century France* (Stanford, Calif.: Stanford University Press, 1988).

91. Davis, N.Z., 'Beyond the Market: Books as Gifts in Sixteenth-century France', *Transactions of the Royal Historical Society*, **33** (1983) pp. 69–88.

92. Davis, N.Z., 'Gender and Genre: Women as Historical Writers, 1400–1820', *University of Ottawa Quarterly*, **50**:1 (1980); 123–44.

93. Davis, N.Z., 'The Sacred and the Body Social in Sixteenth-century Lyon', *P&P*, **90** (1981) pp. 40–70.

94. Davis, N. Z. and Farge, A. (eds) *A History of Women in the West*, vol. 3: *Renaissance and Enlightenment Paradoxes* (Cambridge, Mass.: Harvard University Press, 1993).

95. DeKroon, M., 'Martin Bucer and the Problem of Tolerance', *SCJ*, **19**:2 (1988) pp. 157–68.

96. Delph, R.K., 'Polish the Papal Image in the Counter-Reformation: The Case of Agostino Stenco', *SCJ*, **23**:1 (1992) pp. 35–47.

97. DeMolen, R.L., *Leaders of the Reformation* (Cranbury, NJ.: Susquehanna University

Press, 1984).

98. DeMolen, R.L. (ed.), *Erasmus* (London: E. Arnold, 1973).

99. DeMolen, R.L. (ed.), *Religious Orders of the Catholic Reformation* (New York: Fordham University Press, 1994).

100. DeMolen, R.L., *The Spirituality of Erasmus of Rotterdam* (Nieuwkoop: DeGraaf, 1987).

101. Deutscher, T., 'Seminaries and the Education of Novarese Parish Priests, 1593–1627', *JEH*, **32**:3 (1981) pp. 303–19.

102. Diefendorf, B.B., *Beneath the Cross: Catholics and Huguenots in Sixteenth-century France* (Oxford: Oxford University Press, 1991).

103. Diefendorf, B.B., *Culture and Identity in Early Modern Europe, 1500–1800: Essays in Honor of Natalie Zemon Davis* (Ann Arbor, Mich.: University of Michigan Press, 1993).

104. Diefendorf, B.B., *Paris City Councillors in the Sixteenth-century: The Politics of Patrimony* (Princeton, N.J.: Princeton University Press, 1983).

105. Diefendorf, B.B., 'The Catholic League: Social Crisis or "Apocalypse Now"', *FHS*, **15**:2 (1987) pp. 332–44.

106. Diefendorf, B.B., 'Prologue to a Massacre: Popular Unrest in Paris, 1557–1572', *American Historical Review*, **90**:5 (1985) pp. 1067–91.

107. Diefendorf, B.B., 'Simon Vigor: A Radical Preacher in Sixteenth-century Paris', *SCJ*, **18**:3 (1987) pp. 399–410.

108. Dimler, G.R., 'The *Imago Primi Saeculi*: Jesuit Emblems and the Secular Tradition', *Thought*, **56**:223 (1981) pp. 433–48.

109. Donnelly, J.P., 'Antonio Possevino and Jesuits of Jewish Ancestry', *AHSJ*, **55**:109 (1986) pp. 3–31.

110. Donnelly, J.P., 'Antonio Possevino's Plan for World Evangelization', *CHR*, **74**:2 (1988) pp. 179–98.

111. Donnelly, J.P., 'The Jesuit College at Padua: Growth, Suppression, Attempts at Restoration, 1552–1606', *AHSJ*, **51**:101 (1982) pp. 45–79.

112. Douglass, J.D., *Women, Freedom and Calvin. The 1983 Annie Kinkead Warfield Lectures* (Philadelphia, Pa: Westminster, 1985).

113. Douglass, J.D.,'Calvin's Use of Metaphysical Language of God: God as Enemy and God as Mother', *ARG*, **77** (1986) pp. 126–40.

114. Douglass, J.D., 'Christian Freedom: What Calvin Learned at the School of Women', *CH*, **53**:2 (1984) pp. 155–73.

115. Dugan, E.T., 'The Funeral Sermon as a Key to Familial Values in Early Modern Nördlingen', *SCJ*, **20**:4 (1989) pp. 631–44.

116. Duke, A., Lewis, G., and Pettegree, A. (eds) *Calvinism in Europe, 1555–c. 1620: A Collection of Documents* (Manchester: Manchester University Press, 1992).

117. Dust, P.C., *Three Renaissance Pacifists: Essays in the Theories of Erasmus, More, and Vives* (Zürich: P. Lang, 1987).

118. Dyck, C.J., 'The Suffering Church in Anabaptism', *MQR*, **59**:1 (1985) pp. 5–23.

119. Edwards, M.U., *Luther's Last Battles: Politics and Polemics, 1531–46* (Ithaca, N.Y.: Cornell University Press, 1983).

120. Edwards, M.U., 'Lutherschmähung? Catholics on Luther's Responsibility for the Peasants' War', *CHR*, **76**:3 (1990) pp. 461–80.

121. Eire, C.M.N., *War against the Idols: The Reformation of Worship from Erasmus to Calvin* (Cambridge: Cambridge University Press, 1986).

122. Eire, C.M.N., 'Prelude to Sedition? Calvin's Attack on Nicodemism and Religious Compromise', *ARG*, **76** (1985) pp. 120–45.

123. Epp, A.R., 'Calvin Reveals an Early Anabaptist Position Statement', *Mennonite Life*, **41**:1 (1986) pp. 12–15.

124. Evans, G.R., 'Calvin on Signs: An Augustinian Dilemma', *Renaissance Studies*, **3**:1 (1989) pp. 35–45.

125. Evans, R.J.W., 'Rantzau and Welser: Aspects of Later German Humanism', *HEI*, **5**:3 (1984) pp. 357–72.

126. Faber, G. S., *The History and Theology of the Ancient Vallenses and Albigenses* (Gallatin, Tenn.: Church History Research and Archives, 1990).

127. Falconi, C., *Leone X: Giovanni de' Medici* (Milan: Rusconi Libri, 1987).

128. Farr, J.R., 'Popular Religious Solidarity in Sixteenth-Century Dijon', *FHS*, **14**:2 (1985) pp. 192–214.

129. Farr, J.R., 'The Pure and Disciplined Body: Hierarchy, Morality and Symbolism in France During the Catholic Reformation', *JIH*, **21**:3 (1991) pp. 391–414.

130. Feld, M.D., 'The First Roman Printers and the Idioms of Humanism', *Harvard Library Bulletin*, **36**:1 (1988) pp. 1–91.

131. Ferraro, B., 'Form, Reform and Counter-Reformation in G. M. Cecchi's "Commedie Osservate"', *BHR*, **47**:2 (1985) pp. 321–41.

132. Flood, J.L., 'Subversion in the Alps: Books and Readers in the Austrian Counter-Reformation', *Library*, **12**:3 (1990) pp. 185–211.

133. Forster, M., *The Counter-Reformation in the Villages: Religion and Reform in the Bishopric of Speyer, 1560–1720* (Ithaca, N.Y.: Cornell University Press, 1992).

134. Forster, M., 'The Counter-Reformation and the Traditional Church in the Villages of the Bishopric of Speyer', *Fides et Historia*, **21**:2 (1989) pp. 30–7.

135. Forster, M., 'The Elite and Popular Foundations of German Catholicism in the Age of Confessionalism: The *Reichskirche*', *CEH*, **26**:3 (1993) pp. 311–25.

136. Fragnito, G., 'Cardinals' Courts in Sixteenth-century Rome', *JMH*, **65**:1 (1993) pp. 26–56.

137. Friedman, J. (ed.), *Regnum, Religio et Ratio* (Kirksville, Mo.: Sixteenth-century Society Essays and Studies, 1987).

138. Friedman, J., 'Jewish Conversion, the Spanish Pure Blood Laws and Reformation: A Revisionist View of Racial and Religious Antisemitism', in *SCJ*, **18**:1 (1987) pp. 3–30.

139. Fuller, R., *The Brotherhood of the Common Life and Its Influence* (New York: State University Press, 1994).

140. Fumaroli, M., 'Jaques Amyot and the Clerical Polemic against the Chivalric Novel', *RQ*, **38**:1 (1985) pp. 22–40.

141. Furcha, E.J., 'Women in Zwingli's World', *Zwingliana*, **19**:1 (1992) pp. 131–42.

142. Furcha, E.J. (ed.), *In Honor of John Calvin, 1509–64: Papers from the 1986 International Calvin Symposium* (Montreal: McGill University Press, 1987).

143. Gäbler, U., *Huldrych Zwingli: His Life and Work* (Philadelphia, Pa.: Fortress, 1986).

144. Gamble, R.C. (ed.), *The Biography of Calvin* (Columbia, Ga.: Garland, 1992).

145. Gamble, R.C., *Calvin's Opponents* (Columbia, Ga.: Garland, 1992).

146. Gamble, R.C., *Calvin's Work in Geneva* (Columbia, Ga.: Garland, 1992).

147. Ganns, G. E. (ed.), *Ignatius of Loyola: The 'Spiritual Exercise' and Selected Works* (Mahwah, N.J.: Paulist, 1991).

148. Gawthrop, R. and Strauss, G., 'Protestantism and Literacy in Early Modern Germany', *P&P*, **104** (1984) pp. 31–55.

149. Gentilcore, D., 'Methods and Approaches in the Social History of the Counter-Reformation in Italy', *SH*, **17**:1 (1992) pp. 73–98.

150. George, T., *Theology of the Reformers* (Nashville, Tenn.: Broadman, 1988).

151. Gerrish, B.A., *Grace and Gratitude: The Eucharistic Theology of John Calvin* (Edinburgh: T&T, 1993).

152. Gerrish, B.A., *The Old Protestantism and the New: Essays on the Reformation Heritage* (Chicago, Ill.: University of Chicago Press, 1982).

153. Gingerich, B.N., 'Property and the Gospel: Two Reformation Perspectives', *MQR*, **59**:3 (1985) pp. 248–67.

154. Goldblatt, H., 'On the Language of Beliefs in Ivan Vysen'kyj and the Counter-Reformation', *Harvard Ukrainian Studies*, **15**:1–2 (1991) pp. 7–34.

155. Golden, R.M. and Kuehn, T. (eds), *From the Ancient Near East to the Seventeenth Century*, in *Western Societies Primary Sources in Social History*, **1** (New York: St Martin's, 1993).

156. Gordon, F.B., *Clerical Discipline and the Rural Reformation: The Synod of Zürich, 1532–1580* (Zürich: P. Lang, 1992).

157. Gordon, F.B. (ed.), *Protestant Identity and History in Reformation Europe* (London: Scholar, 1996).

158. Gray, J.G., *French Huguenots: Anatomy of Courage* (Grand Rapids, Mich.: Baker, 1993).

159. Graham, W.F. (ed.), *Later Calvinism: International Perspectives* (Kirksville, Mo.: Sixteenth-century Essays and Studies, 1993).

160. Greengrass, M., *France in the Age of Henri IV: The Struggle for Stability* (London: Longman, 1984).

161. Greengrass, M., *The French Reformation* (Oxford: Blackwell, 1987).

162. Greengrass, M., 'The Anatomy of a Religious Riot in Toulouse in May 1562', *JEH*, **34**:3 (1983) pp. 367–91.

163. Greengrass, M., 'The Sainte Union in the Provinces: The Case of Toulouse', *SCJ*, **14**:4 (1983) pp. 469–96.

164. Greengrass, M., 'The Sixteen: Radical Politics in Paris During the League', *History*, **69**:227 (1984) pp. 432–9.

165. Grell, O.P., *Dutch Calvinists in Early Stuart London. The Dutch Church in Austin Friars, 1603–1642* (Leiden: Brill, 1989).

166. Grell, O.P., *Medicine and the Reformation* (London: Wellcome, 1993).

167. Grell, O.P., *The Scandinavian Reformation: From Evangelical Movement to Institutionalisation of Reform* (Cambridge: Cambridge University Press, 1994).

168. Grell, O.P., 'The City of Malmo and the Danish Reformation', *ARG*, **79** (1988) pp. 311–39.

169. Grendler, P.F., *Books and Schools in the Italian Renaissance* (Aldershot: Variorum, 1995).

170. Gritsch, E.W., *Martin – God's Court Jester: Luther in Retrospect* (Philadelphia, Pa.: Fortress, 1983).

171. Gross, L., *The Golden Years of the Hutterites: The Witness and Thought of the Communal Moravian Anabaptists during the Walpot Era, 1565–1578* (Scottsdale, Pa.: Herald, 1980).

172. Guggisberg, H.R., *Basel in the Sixteenth Century: Aspects of the City Republic Before, During and After the Reformation* (St Louis: Center for Reformation Research, 1982).

173. Guggisberg, H.R., 'The Defence of Religious Toleration and Religious Liberty in Early Modern Europe: Arguments, Pressures, and Some Consequences', *HEI*, **4**:1 (1983) pp. 35–50.

174. Haile, H.G., *Luther, An Experiment in Biography* (Garden City, N.J.: Doubleday, 1980).

175. Haile, H.G., *Luther and Learning* (Cranbury, N.J.: Susquehanna University Press, 1985).

176. Hall, B., 'From Biblical Humanism to Calvinist Orthodoxy', in *JEH*, **31**:3 (1980) pp. 331–43.

177. Hamilton, A., 'The Apocryphal Apocalypse: 2 Esdras and the Anabaptist Movement', *NAK*, **68**:1 (1988) pp. 1–16.

178. Hamilton, D., 'Pedagogical Juggernaut', *British Journal of Educational Studies*, **35**:1 (1987) pp. 18–29.

179. Hardel, L., *The Sources of Swiss Anabaptism: The Grebel Letters and Related Documents* (Scottsdale, Pa.: Herald, 1985).

180. Hardin, R.F., 'The Literary Conventions of Erasmus' Education of a Christian Prince: Advice and Aphorism', *RQ*, **35**:2 (1982) pp. 151–63.

181. Harding, R., 'Revolution and Reform in the Holy League: Angers, Rennes, Nantes', *JMH*, **53**:3 (1981) pp. 379–416.

182. Harran, M.J., *Luther on Conversion: The Early Years* (Ithaca, N.Y.: Cornell University Press, 1983).

183. Harrison, W., 'The Role of Women in Anabaptist Thought and Practice: The Hutterite Experience of the Sixteenth and Seventeenth Centuries', *SCJ*, **23**:1 (1992) pp. 49–69.

184. Hayden, J.M., 'States, Estates and Orders: the *Qualité* of Female Clergy in Early Modern France', *FH*, **8**:1 (1994) pp. 51–76.

185. Heffner, D., 'Regnum vs. Sacerdotum in a Reformation Pamphlet', *SCJ*, **20**:4 (1989) pp. 617–30.

186. Heller, H., *The Conquest of Poverty: The Calvinist Revolt in Sixteenth-century France* (Leiden: Brill, 1986).

187. Hendrix, S. H., *Luther and the Papacy: Stages in a Reformation Conflict* (Philadelphia, Pa.: Fortress, 1981).

188. Hendrix, S. H., 'Loyalty, Piety, or Opportunism: German Princes in the Reformation', *JIH*, **25**:2 (1994) pp. 211–24.

189. Hendrix, S. H., 'Luther's Impact on the Sixteenth Century', *SCJ*, **16**:1 (1985) pp. 3–14.

190. Hendrix, S. H., 'Toleration of Jews in the German Reformation: Urbanus Rhegius and Braunschweig (1535–1540)', *ARG*, **81** (1990) pp. 189–215.

191. Herman, A.L., 'Protestant Churches in a Catholic Kingdom: Political Assemblies in the Thought of Philippe Duplessis-Mornay', *SCJ*, **21**:4 (1990) pp. 543–57.

192. Heyer, H., *Guillaume Farel: An Introduction to His Theology* (Lampeter: E. Mullin, 1990).

193. Higgins, B., *God's Faithful Goose: John Hus* (Lookout Mountain, Tenn.: Grey Pilgrim, 1994).

194. Higman, F., *Censorship and the Sorbonne* (Geneva: Droz, 1979).

195. Hillerbrand, H.H. (ed.), *Erasmus and His Age: Selected Letters of Desiderius Erasmus* (London: Harper & Row, 1970).

196. Hinlicky, P.R., 'Luther Against the Contempt of Women', *LQ*, **2**:4 (1988) pp. 515–30.

197. Hoffman, P.T., 'Wills and Statistics: Tobit Analysis and the Counter-Reformation in Lyon', *JIH*, **14**:4 (1984) pp. 813–34.

198. Hoffmann, M., *Rhetoric and Theology: The Hermeneutic of Erasmus* (London: University of Toronto Press, 1994).

199. Hoffmann, M., 'Faith and Piety in Erasmus' Thought', *SCJ*, **20**:2 (1989) pp. 241–58.

200. Holt, M.P., *The French Wars of Religion* (Cambridge: Cambridge University Press, 1995).

201. Holt, M.P., 'Wine, Community and Reformation in Sixteenth-century Burgundy', *P&P*, **138** (1993) pp. 58–93.

202. Höpfl, H., *The Christian Polity of John Calvin* (Cambridge: Cambridge University Press, 1982).

203. Hsia, R. Po-Chia., 'Civic Wills as Sources for the Study of Piety in Muenster, 1530–1618', *SCJ*, **14**:3 (1983) pp. 321–48.

204. Hsia, R. Po-Chia., 'The Myth of the Commune: Recent Historiography on City and Reformation in Germany', *CEH*, **20**:3–4 (1987) pp. 203–15.

205. Hudon, W.V., 'Papal, Episcopal and Secular Authority in the Work of Marcello Cervini', *Cristianesimo nella Storia*, **9**:3 (1988) pp. 493–521.

206. Hudson, E.K., 'The Protestant Struggle for Survival in Early Bourbon France: The Case of the Huguenot Schools', *ARG*, **76** (1985) pp. 271–95.

207. Hudson, E.K., 'Two Instructions to Preachers from the Tridentine Reformation', *SCJ*, **20**:3 (1989) pp. 457–70.

208. Hutten, U. von (ed.), *On the Eve of the Reformation. 'Letters of Obscure Men'*, trans. F.G. Stokes (London: Harper & Row, 1964).

209. Iserloh, E., 'Luther and the Council of Trent', *CHR*, **69**:4 (1983) pp. 563–76.

210. James, F.A., 'It was both "a Horrible Decree" and "Very Sweet Fruit": Calvin on Predestination', *CH*, **5**:4 (1986) pp. 24–6.

211. Jansma, L.G., 'Crime in the Netherlands in the Sixteenth-century: the Batenburg Bands after 1540', *MQR*, **62**:3 (1988) pp. 221–35.

212. Janz, D.R., *Luther and Late Medieval Thomism: A Study in Theological Anthropology* (Waterloo, Ontario: Wilfrid Laurier University Press, 1983).

213. Janz, D.R., *Luther on Thomas Aquinas: The Angelic Doctor in the Thought of the Reformer* (Stuttgart: F. Steiner, 1989).

214. Jensen, K., 'Protestant Rivalry – Metaphysics and Rhetoric Germany *c.* 1590–1620', *JEH*, **41**:1 (1990) pp. 24–43.

215. Johnson, S.M., 'Luther's Reformation and (un)holy Matrimony', *Journal of Family History*, **17**:3 (1992) pp. 271–88.

216. Johnson-Burn, L.T., 'The Politics of Conversion: John Calvin and the Bishop of Troyes', *SCJ*, **25**:4 (1994) pp. 809–22.

217. Jónsson, M., 'Incest and the Word of God: Early Sixteenth-century Protestant Disputes', *ARG*, **85** (1994) pp. 96–118.

218. Kaplan, B.J., 'Dutch Particularism and the Calvinist Quest for "Holy Uniformity"', *ARG*, **82** (1991) pp. 239–56.

219. Kaplan, B.J., '"Remnants of the Papal Yoke": Apathy and Opposition in the Dutch Reformation', *SCJ*, **25**:3 (1994) pp. 653–69.

220. Karant-Nunn, S.C., 'The Transmission of Luther's Teaching on Women and Matrimony: The Case of Zwickau', *ARG*, **77** (1986) pp. 31–46.

221. Keen, R. (ed. and trans.), *A Melanchthon Reader* (Zürich: P. Lang, 1988).

222. Kelly. H.A., 'Inquisition and the Prosecution of Heresy: Misconceptions and Abuses', *CH*, **58**:4 (1989) pp. 439–541.

223. Kiermayr, R., 'On the Education of the Pre-Reformation Clergy', *CH*, **53**:1 (1984) pp. 7–16.

224. Kiermayr, R., 'How Much Money was Actually in the Indulgence Chest?', *SCJ*, **17**:3 (1986) pp. 303–18.

225. Kiermayr, R., 'The Reformation in Duderstadt, 1524–1576, and the Declaratio Ferdinandea', *ARG*, **75** (1984) pp. 234–55.

226. Kingdon, R.M., *Adultery and Divorce in Calvin's Geneva* (Cambridge, Mass.: Harvard University Press, 1994).

227. Kingdon, R.M., *Myths about the St Bartholomew's Day Massacre, 1572–1576* (Cambridge, Mass.: Harvard University Press, 1988).

228. Kingdon, R.M., *The Political Thought of Peter Martyr Vermigli: Selected Texts and Commentary* (Geneva: Droz, 1980).

229. Kingdon, R.M., 'Calvin and the Establishment of Consistory Discipline in Geneva: The Institution and the Men who Directed It', *NAK*, **70**:2 (1990) pp. 158–72.

230. Klaasen, W., 'Anabaptism: Neither Catholic nor Protestant', *CH*, **4**:1 (1985) pp. 10–12, 34–5.

231. Klucas, J.A., 'Erasmus and Erasmians on the Jews in Sixteenth-century Portugal', *Luso-Brazilian Review*, **17**:2 (1980) pp. 153–70.

232. Knecht, R.J., *Francis I* (Cambridge: Cambridge University Press, 1982).

233. Knecht, R.J., *Renaissance Warrior and Patron: The Reign of Francis I* (Cambridge: Cambridge University Press, 1994).

234. Kolb, R.A., 'Augsburg 1530: German Lutheran Interpretations of the Diet of Augsburg to 1577', *SCJ*, **11**:3 (1980) pp. 47–61.

235. Kolb, R.A., 'Festivals of the Saints in Late Reformation Lutheran Preaching', *Historian*, **52**:4 (1990) pp. 613–26.

236. Kolb, R.A., '"Good Works are Detrimental to Salvation": Amsdorf's Use of Luther's Words in Controversy', *R & R*, **4**:2 (1980) pp. 136–51.

237. Kolb, R.A., 'Teaching the Text: The Commonplace Method in Sixteenth-century Lutheran Biblical Commentary', *BHR*, **49**:3 (1987) pp. 571–85.

238. Konnert, M., 'Provincial Governors and their Regimes during the French Wars of Religion: The Duc de Guise and the City Council of Châlons-sur-Marne', *SCJ*, **25**:4 (1994) pp. 823–40.

239. Konnert, M., 'Urban Values versus Religious Passion: Chalons-sur-Marne During the Wars of Religion', *SCJ*, **20**:3 (1989) pp. 387–405.

240. Korrick, L., 'Instrumental Music in the Early Sixteenth-century Mass: New Evidence', *Early Music*, **18**:3 (1990) pp. 359–70.

241. Kossmann, E.H. and Mellink, A.F. (eds), *Texts Concerning the Revolt of the Netherlands* (Cambridge: Cambridge University Press, 1974).

242. Krahn, C., *Dutch Anabaptism* (Scottsdale, Pa.: Herald, 1981).

243. Kümin, B. (ed.), *Reformations Old and New: Essays on the Socio-Economic Impact of Religious Change, c. 1470–1630* (London: Scholar, 1996).

244. Labalme, P.H. (ed.), *Beyond Their Sex: Learned Women of the European Past* (New York: N.Y. University Press, 1980).

245. Ladurie, E. le Roy, *The Royal French State: Louis XI–Henri IV, 1460–1610* (Oxford: Blackwell, 1994).

246. Laube, A., 'Social Arguments in Early Reformation Pamphlets, and their Significance for the German Peasants' War', *SH*, **12**:3 (1987) pp. 361–78.

247. Lehmann, H. and Roth, G., *Weber's Protestant Ethic: Origins, Evidence, Contexts* (Washington, D. C.: German History Institute, 1993).

248. LeRoux, N., 'The Catholic Nobility and Political Choice During the League, 1585–1594: The Case of Claude de La Châtre', *FH*, **8**:1 (1994) pp. 34–50.

249. Letham, R., '*The Foedus Operum*: Some Factors Accounting for its Development', *SCJ*, **14**:4 (1983) pp. 457–67.

250. Lessnoff, M. F., *The Spirit of Capitalism and the Protestant Ethic: An Enquiry into the Weber Thesis* (Aldershot: E. Elgar, 1994).

251. Liechty, D., *Early Anabaptist Spirituality: Selected Writings* (New York: Paulist, 1994).

252. Lindberg, C., *Beyond Charity: Reformation Initiatives for the Poor* (Minneapolis, Minn.: Fortress, 1993).

253. Lindberg, C., 'Luther on the Use of Money', *CH*, **6**:2 (1987) pp. 17–19, 34.

254. Linder, R.D., 'Allies of Enemies? Luther's Rocky Relationship with his Fellow Reformers', *CH*, **12**:3 (1993) pp. 40–4.

255. Loades, D.M., 'The Netherlands and the Anglo-Papal Reconciliation of 1554', *NAK*, **60**:1 (1980) pp. 39–55.

256. Locker, G.W., *Zwingli's Thought: New Perspectives* (Leiden: Brill, 1981).

257. Lohse, B., *Martin Luther: An Introduction to his Life and Work* (Philadelphia, Pa.: Fortress, 1986).

258. Lotz, D.W., 'Albrecht Ritschl and the Unfinished Reformation', *HTR*, **73**:3–4 (1980) pp. 337–72.

259. Luther, M., *Three Treatises*, trans. C. M. Jacobs, A. Steinhaeuser, and W. Lambert (Philadelphia, Pa.: Muhlenberg, 1943).

260. McCue, J.F., 'Luther and the Problem of Popular Preaching', *SCJ*, **16**:1 (1985) pp. 33–43.

261. McGinness, F.J., 'Roma Sancta and the Saint: Eucharist, Chastity, and the Logic of Catholic Reform', *HR*, **15**:1 (1988) pp. 99–116.

262. McGrath, A.E., *A Life of John Calvin: A Study in the Shaping of Western Culture* (Oxford: Blackwell, 1990).

263. McGrath, A.E., *Luther's Theology of the Cross: Martin Luther's Theological Breakthrough* (Oxford: Blackwell, 1985).

264. McGrath, A.E., 'Humanist Elements in the Early Reformed Doctrine of Justification', *ARG*, **73** (1982) pp. 5–20.

265. McGrath, A.E., 'John Calvin and Late Medieval Thought: A Study in Late Medieval Influences upon Calvin's Theological Development', *ARG*, **77** (1986) pp. 58–78.

266. Makkai, L., 'Peer Melius, the Hungarian Reformer', *Études historiques hongroises*, **2** (1985) pp. 1–19.

267. Mansfield, B., *Phoenix of His Age: Interpretations of Erasmus, c. 1550–1750* (Buffalo, N.Y.: University of Toronto Press, 1979).

268. Markish, S., *Erasmus and the Jews* (Chicago, Ill.: University of Chicago Press, 1986).

269. Martin, A.L., *The Jesuit Mind. The Mentality of an Élite in Early Modern France* (Ithaca, N.Y.: Cornell University Press, 1988).

270. Martin, A.L., 'Jesuit Encounters in Rural France in the Sixteenth-century', *Australian Journal of French Studies*, **18**:3 (1981) pp. 202–11.

271. Martin, A.L., 'Jesuits and their Families, the Experience in Sixteenth-century France', *SCJ*, **13**:1 (1982) pp. 3–23.

272. Martin, A.L., 'Vocational Crises and the Crisis in Vocations among Jesuits in France during the Sixteenth-Century', *CHR*, **72**:2 (1986) pp. 201–21.

273. Mathers, C.J., 'Early Spanish Qualms about Loyola and the Society of Jesus', *Historian*, **53**:4 (1991) pp. 679–90.

274. Matheson, P., 'Martyrdom or Mission? A Protestant Debate', *ARG*, **80** (1989) pp. 154–72.

275. Maxcey, C.E., 'Why Do Good? Dietenberger's Reply to Luther', *ARG*, **75** (1984) pp. 93–112.

276. Mehl, J.V., 'Ortwin Gratius, Conciliarism, and the Call for Church Reform', *ARG*, **76** (1985) pp. 169–94.

277. Mellink, A.F., 'The Beginnings of Dutch Anabaptism in the Light of Recent Research', *MQR*, **62**:3 (1988) pp. 211–20.

278. Mentzer, R.A. (ed.), *Sin and the Calvinists. Morals Control and the Consistory in the Reformed Tradition* (Kirksville, Mo.: Sixteenth-century Essays and Studies, 1994).

279. Mentzer, R.A., '*Disciplina Nervus Ecclesiae*: The Calvinist Reform of Morals at Nîmes', *SCJ*, **18**:1 (1987) pp. 89–115.

280. Methuen, C., 'Securing the Reformation Through Education: The Duke's Scholarship System of Sixteenth-century Württemberg', *SCJ*, **25**:4 (1994) pp. 841–52

281. Michael, R., 'Luther, Luther Scholars, and the Jews', *Encounter*, **46**:4 (1985) pp. 339–56.

282. Miles, M.B., 'Theology, Anthropology, and the Human Body in Calvin's Institutes of the Christian Religion', *HTR*, **74**:3 (1981) pp. 303–23.

283. Miller, J., 'The Origins of Polish Arianism', *SCJ*, **16**:2 (1985) pp. 229–56.

284. Miller, T., 'A Guide to the Literature on the Hutterites', *Communal Societies*, **10** (1990) pp. 68–86.

285. Minnich, N.H., *The Catholic Reformation: Council, Churchmen, Controversies* (Aldershot: Variorum, 1995).

286. Minnich, N.H., *The Fifth Lateran Council (1512–17): Studies on its Membership, Diplomacy and Proposals for Reform* (Aldershot: Variorum, 1995).

287. Mitchell, D., *The Jesuits: A History* (New York: Watts, 1981).

288. Mitchell, J., *Not by Reason Alone: Religion, History, and Identity in Early Modern Political Thought* (Chicago, Ill.: University of Chicago Press, 1993).

289. Mitchell, J., 'Protestant Thought and Republican Spirit: How Luther Enchanted the World', *American Political Science Review*, **86**:3 (1992) pp. 688–95.

290. Monfasani, J., *Byzantine Scholars in Renaissance Italy: Cardinal Bessarion and other Emigrés* (Aldershot: Variorum, 1995).

291. Monheit, M.L., '"The Ambition for an Illustrious Name": Humanism, Patronage, and Calvin's Doctrine of the Calling', *SCJ*, **23**:2 (1992) pp. 267–87.

292. Monter, E.W., 'Women in Calvinist Geneva (1550–1800)', *Signs*, **6**:2 (1980) pp. 189–209.

293. Moore, W.L., 'Catholic Teacher and Anabaptist Pupil: The Relationship between John Eck and Balthasar Hubmaier', *ARG*, **72** (1981) pp. 68–97.

294. Naphy, W.G., *Calvin and the Consolidation of the Genevan Reformation* (Manchester: Manchester University Press, 1994).

295. Naphy, W.G., 'Baptisms, Church Riots, and Social Unrest in Calvin's Geneva', *SCJ* (April 1995).

296. Naphy, W.G., 'The Usefulness of Calvin's Letters for the Study of Genevan History', *ARG* (1995).

297. Naphy, W.G. and Roberts, P. (eds), *Fear in Early Modern Society* (Manchester: Manchester University Press, 1997).

298. Nelson, R., 'Erasmus and Grotius on Just War Theory', *Canadian Journal of Netherlandic Studies*, **6**:1 (1985) pp. 40–60.

299. Neumann, H.B., 'The Impact of the Counter-Reformation on the Styrian Estates, 1578–1628', *Austrian Historical Yearly*, 15–16 (1979–80) pp. 47–59.

300. Neuser, W.H., *Calvinus Sacrae Scripturae Professor* (Grand Rapids, Mich.: Eerdmans, 1994).

301. Ngien, D., *The Suffering of God According to Martin Luther's Theologia Crucis* (Zürich: P. Lang, 1995).

302. Nicholls, D.J., 'The Nature of Popular Heresy in France, 1520–1542', *Historical Journal*, **26**:2 (1983) pp. 261–75.

303. Nicholls, D.J., 'Protestants, Catholics and Magistrates in Tours, 1562–1572: The Making of a Catholic City During the Religious Wars', *FH*, **8**:1 (1994) pp. 14–33.

304. Nienkirchen, C., 'Reviewing the Case for a Non-Separatist Ecclesiology in Early Swiss Anabaptism', *MQR*, **56**:3 (1982) pp. 227–41.

305. Nischan, B., *Prince, People, and Confession: The Second Reformation in Brandenburg* (Philadelphia: University of Pennsylvania. Press, 1994).

306. Nischan, B., 'The Exorcism Controversy and Baptism in the Late Reformation', *SCJ*, **18**:1 (1987) pp. 31–51.

307. Nischan, B., 'The Second Reformation in Brandenburg: Aims and Goals', *SCJ*, **14**:2 (1983) pp. 173–87.

308. Oberman, H.A., *Anticlericalism in Late Medieval and Early Modern Europe* (Leiden: Brill, 1992).

309. Oberman, H.A., *The Dawn of Reformation: Essays in Late Medieval and Early Reformation Thought* (Edinburgh, T&T, 1986).

310. Oberman, H.A., *Luther* (New York: Doubleday & Co., 1992).

311. Oberman, H.A., *Luther: Man between God and the Devil* (New Haven, Conn.: Yale University Press, 1990).

312. Oberman, H.A., *Masters of the Reformation: The Emergence of a New Intellectual Climate of Europe* (Cambridge: Cambridge University Press, 1981).

313. Oberman, H.A., *The Reformation: Roots and Ramifications* (Edinburgh: T&T, 1994).

314. Oberman, H.A., *The Roots of Anti-Semitism in the Age of Renaissance and Reformation* (Philadelphia: Fortress, 1984).

315. Oberman, H.A., 'Europa Afflicta: The Reformation of the Refugees', *ARG*, **83** (1992) pp. 91–111.

316. Oberman, H.A., 'Teufelsdreck: Eschatology and Scatology in the "Old" Luther', *SCJ*, **19**:3 (1988) pp. 435–50.

317. Olin, J.C., *Catholic Reform: From Cardinal Ximenes to the Council of Trent* (New York: Fordham University. Press, 1990).

318. Olin, J.C., *Essays on Erasmus: The Outreach of Humanism* (New York: Fordham University Press, 1994).

319. Olson, J.E., *Calvin and Social Welfare: Deacons and the Bourse Française* (Selingsgrove, Penn.: Susquehanna University Press, 1989).

320. Olson, J.E., 'Reformation and Revolution in Calvin's Geneva', *Halcyon*, 7 (1985) pp. 93–103.

321. Olson, O.K., 'The Rise and Fall of the Antwerp Martinists', *LQ*, **1**:1 (1987) pp. 98–119.

322. O'Malley, J.W., *Religious Culture in the Sixteenth-Century* (Aldershot: Variorum, 1995).

323. O'Malley, J.W., *Rome and the Renaissance* (Aldershot: Variorum, 1995).

324. O'Malley, J.W., 'Was Ignatius Loyola a Church Reformer? How to Look at Early Modern Catholicism', *CHR*, **77**:2 (1991) pp. 177–93.

325. O'Reilley, J., *From Ignatius to John of the Cross: Spirituality and Literature in Sixteenth-Century Spain* (Aldershot: Variorum, 1995).

326. Oyer, J.S., 'Luther and the Anabaptists', *BQ*, **30**:4 (1983) pp. 162–72.

327. Oyer, J.S., 'Sticks and Stones Broke their Bones, and Vicious Names did Hurt Them! Sixteenth-century Responses to the Anabaptists', *CH* **4**:1 (1985) pp. 17–19.

328. Ozment, S., 'Re-Inventing Family Life', *CH*, **12**:3 (1993) pp. 22–6.

329. Packull, W.O., 'Anna Jansz of Rotterdam, a Historical Investigation of an Early Anabaptist Heroine', *ARG*, **78** (1987) pp. 147–73.

330. Packull, W.O., 'The Beginnings of Anabaptism in Southern Tyrol', *SCJ*, **22**:4 (1991) pp. 717–26.

331. Packull, W.O., 'Luther and Medieval Mysticism in the Context of Recent Historiography', *R&R*, **6**:2 (1982) pp. 79–93.

332. Packull, W.O., 'In Search of the "Common Man" in Early German Anabaptist Ideology', *SCJ*, **17**:1 (1986) pp. 51–67.

333. Parker, G., 'Success and Failure During the First Century of the Reformation', *P&P*, **136** (1992) pp. 43–82.

334. Parker, C.H., 'French Calvinists as the Children of Israel: An Old Testament Self-consciousness in Jean Crespin's *Histoire des Martyrs* before the Wars of Religion', *SCJ*, **24**:2 (1993) pp. 227–48.

335. Parker, T.H.L., 'The Life and Times of John Calvin', *CH*, **5**:4 (1986): 7–11, 35

336. Partner, P., *The Pope's Men: The Papal Civil Service in the Renaissance* (Oxford: Oxford University Press, 1990).

337. Partner, P., 'Papal Financial Policy in the Renaissance and Counter-Reformation', *P&P*, **88** (1980) pp. 17–62.

338. Partree, C., 'Calvin's Central Dogma Again', *SCJ*, **18**:2 (1987) pp. 191–9.

339. Pater, C.A., 'Westerburg: The Father of Anabaptism. Author and Content of the *Dyalogus* of 1527', *ARG*, **85** (1994) pp. 138–62.

340. Pearl, J.L., '"A School for the Rebel Soul": Politics and Demonic Possession in France', *HR*, **16**:2–3 (1989) pp. 286–306.

341. Perry, D., '"Catholicum Opus Imperiale Regiminis Mundi". An Early Sixteenth-century Restatement of Empire', *History of Political Thought*, **2**:2 (1981) pp. 227–52.

342. Peterson, W.J., 'Idelette: Calvin's Search for the Right Wife', *CH* **5**:4 (1986) pp. 12–15.

343. Pettegree, A.D.M., *Emden and the Dutch Revolt: Exile and Development of Reformed Protestantism* (Oxford: Oxford University Press, 1992).

344. Pettegree, A.D.M., *Foreign Protestant Communities in Sixteenth-century London* (Oxford: Oxford University Press, 1987).

345. Pettegree, A.D.M., 'The Exile Churches and the Churches "Under the Cross": Antwerp and Emden during the Dutch revolt', *JEH*, **38**:2 (1987) pp. 187–209.

346. Pettegree, A.D.M., 'Reformation Essays', *German History*, 7:3 (1989) pp. 365-75.

347. Pettegree, A.D.M., 'The Struggle for an Orthodox Church: Calvinists and Anabaptists in E. Friesland, 1554–1578', *Bulletin of the John Rylands University Library of Manchester*, **70**:3 (1988) pp. 45–59.

348. Pettegree, A.D.M. (ed.), *The Early Reformation in Europe* (Cambridge: Cambridge University Press, 1992).

349. Pettegree, A.D.M. (ed.), *The Reformation of the Parishes: The Ministry and the Reformation in Town and Country* (Manchester: Manchester University Press, 1993).

350. Pettegree, A.D.M., Lewis, G. and Duke, A. (eds), *Calvinism in Europe, 1540–1620* (Cambridge: Cambridge University Press, 1994).

351. Pipkin, H.W. and Yoder, J.H., *Balthasar Hubmaier: Theologian of Anabaptism* (Scottsdale, Penn.: Herald, 1989).

352. Polverini-Fosi, I., 'Justice and its Image: Political Propaganda and Judicial Reality in the Pontificate of Sixtus V', *SCJ*, **24**:1 (1993) pp. 75–95.

353. Poole, S., 'Church Law on the Ordination of Indians and Castas in New Spain', *Hispanic American Historical Review*, **61**:4 (1981) pp. 637–50.

354. Porter, J.M., 'Luther and Political Millenarianism: The Case of the Peasants' War', *JHI*, **42**:3 (1981) pp. 389–406.

355. Potter, M., 'Gender Equality and Gender Hierarchy in Calvin's Thought', *Signs*, **11**:4 (1986) pp. 725–39.

356. Power, D.N., *The Sacrifice We Offer: The Tridentine Dogma and its Reinterpretation* (New York: Crossroad, 1987).

357. Powis, J., 'Gallican Liberties and the Politics of Later Sixteenth-century France', *SCJ*, **26**:3 (1983) pp. 515–30.

358. Prestwich, M. (ed.), *International Calvinism* (New York: Clarendon Press, 1985).

359. Priestly, T.M.S., 'Slovene Protestants in Carinthia', *Slovene Studies*, **6**:1–2 (1984) pp. 177–89.

360. Prodi, P., *The Papal Prince, One Body and Two Souls: The Papal Monarchy in Early Modern Europe* (Oxford: Oxford University Press, 1988).

361. Quinn, P. A., 'Ignatius Loyola and Gian Pietro Carofa: Catholic Reformers at Odds', *CHR*, **67**:3 (1981) pp. 386–400.

362. Rabikauskas, P., *The Foundation of the University of Vilnius (1579): Royal and Papal Grants* (Rome: Pontifical Georgian University, 1979).

363. Reid, W.S., 'The Four Monarchies of Daniel in Reformation Historiography', *HR*, **8**:1 (1981) pp. 115–23.

364. Reid, W.S., 'John Calvin: One of the Fathers of Democracy', *CH*, **5**:4 (1986) pp. 27–30.

365. Remer, G., 'Rhetoric and the Erasmian Defence of Religious Toleration', *History of Political Thought*, **10**:3 (1989) pp. 377–403.

366. Rice, E.F. and Grafton, A., *The Foundation of Early Modern Europe, 1460–1559* (New York: W.W. Norton & Co., 1994).

367. Rix, H.D., *Martin Luther: The Man and the Image* (N.Y.: Irvington, 1983).

368. Roberts, P., *A City in Conflict: Troyes during the Wars of Religion* (Manchester: Manchester University Press, 1996).

369. Roberts, P., 'Marlowe's *The Massacre at Paris*: An Historical Perspective', *Renaissance Studies* (1995).

370. Roberts, P., 'Religious Conflict and the Urban Setting: Troyes During the French Wars of Religion', *FH*, **6** (1992) pp. 259–78.

371. Rogers, E.F. (ed.), *St Thomas More: Selected Letters* (London: Yale University Press, 1961).

372. Rowan, S., 'Luther, Bucer, and Eck on the Jews', *SCJ*, **16**:1 (1985) pp. 79–90.

373. Rowland, I.D., 'Revenge of the Regensburg Humanists, 1493', *SCJ*, **25**:2 (1994) pp. 307–22.

374. Roynesdal, O., 'Luther's Polemics', *LQ*, **6**:3 (1992) pp. 235–55.

375. Rublack, H.C., 'Martin Luther and the Urban Social Experience', *SCJ*, **16**:1 (1985) pp. 15–32.

376. Rummel, E., *Erasmus and His Catholic Critics (1515–1536)* (Nieuwkoop: DeGraaf, 1990) 2 volumes.

377. Rummel, E., *Erasmus as a Translator of the Classics* (Buffalo: University of Toronto Press, 1985).

378. Rummel, E., 'Erasmus and the Louvain Theologians: A Strategy of Defense', *NAK*, **70**:1 (1990) pp. 2–12.

379. Rummel, E., 'Manifesta Mendacia: Erasmus' Reply to "Toxander"', *RQ*, **43**:4 (1990) pp. 731–43.

380. Runzo, J., 'Hutterite Communal Discipline, 1529–1565', *ARG*, **71** (1980) pp. 160–79.

381. Russell, W.R., 'Martin Luther's Understanding of the Pope as the Antichrist', *ARG*, **85** (1994) pp. 32–44.

382. Sawyer, E.A., 'The Waldensian Influence on the Moravian Church', *Transactions of the Moravian Historical Society*, **25** (1988) pp. 47–61.

383. Schantz, D.H., *Crautwald and Erasmus: A Study in Humanism and Radical Reform in Sixteenth-century Silesia* (Baden-Baden: Koerner, 1992).

384. Schilling, H., *Civic Calvinism in Northeastern Germany and the Netherlands: Sixteenth to Nineteenth Centuries* (Kirksville, Mo.: Sixteenth-century Essays and Studies, 1991).

385. Schilling, H. (ed.), *Religion, Political Culture and the Emergence of Early Modern Society: Essays in German and Dutch History* (Leiden: Brill, 1992).

386. Schilling, H., 'Innovation through Migration: The Settlements of Calvinistic Netherlanders in Sixteenth- and Seventeenth-century Central and Western Europe', *SH*, **16**:31 (1983) pp. 7–33.

387. Schilling, H., 'The Reformation in the Hanseatic Cities', *SCJ*, **14**:4 (1983) pp. 443–56.

388. Schneider, R.A. 'Mortification on Parade: Penitential Processions in Sixteenth- and Seventeenth-century France', *R&R*, **10**:1 (1986) pp. 123–46.

389. Schrader, W.C., 'The Catholic Revival in Osnabrück and Minden, 1591–1651', *CHR*, **78**:1 (1992) pp. 35–50.

390. Schulte-Herbrüggen, H., 'A Hundred New Humanists' Letters: More, Erasmus, Vives, Cranvelt, Geldenhouwer and other Dutch Humanists', *BHR*, **52**:1 (1990) pp. 65–76.

391. Schurhammer, G., *Francis Xavier: His Life, His Time* (Rome: Jesuit Historical Institute, 1980) 3 volumes.

392. Schwartz, P.H., 'The Maternal Christ as Redeemer: Speech and Gender in the Thought of Martin Luther', *Journal of Psychohistory*, **12**:4 (1985) pp. 465–85.

393. Schwartz, R., 'Luther's Inalienable Inheritance of Monastic Theology', *American Benedictine Review*, **39**:4 (1988) pp. 430–50.

394. Schreech, M., *Ecstasy and the Praise of Folly* (London: Duckworth, 1980).

395. Scribner, R.W., *The German Reformation* (London: Macmillan, 1986).

396. Scribner, R.W., *For the Sake of Simple Folk: Popular Propaganda for the German Reformation* (Cambridge: Cambridge University Press, 1981).

397. Scribner, R.W., *Popular Culture and Popular Movements in Reformation Germany* (London: Mambledon, 1988).

398. Scribner, R.W., 'Incombustible Luther: The Image of the Reformer in Early Modern Germany', *P&P*, **110** (1986) pp. 36–68.

399. Scribner, R.W., 'Oral Culture and the Diffusion of Reformation Ideas', *HEI*, **5**:3 (1984) pp. 237–56.

400. Scribner, R.W., 'The Reformation, Popular Magic, and the "Disenchantment of the World"', *JIH*, **23**:3 (1993) pp. 475–94.

401. Scribner, R.W., 'Ritual and Popular Religion in Catholic Germany at the Time of the Reformation', *JEH*, **35**:1 (1984) pp. 47–77.

402. Seed, P., 'The Church and the Patriarchal Family: Marriage Conflicts in Sixteenth- and Seventeenth-century New Spain', *Journal of Family History*, **10**:3 (1985) pp. 284–93.

403. Selinger, S., *Calvin Against Himself: An Inquiry in Intellectual History* (Hamden, Conn.: Archon, 1984).

404. Shaw, C., *Julius II: The Warrior Pope* (Oxford: Blackwell, 1993).

405. Siggins, I., *Luther and His Mother* (Philadelphia.: Fortress, 1981).

406. Sloan, G., 'The Transformation of Religious Conversion from the Renaissance to the Counter-Reformation: Petrarch and Caravaggio', *Historical Reflections*, **15**:1 (1988) pp. 131–49.

407. Smith, M.C., 'Early French Advocates of Religious Reform', *SCJ*, **25**:1 (1994) pp. 29–52.

408. Smith, R.F. *Luther, Ministry, and Ordination Rites in the Early Reformation Church* (Zürich: P. Lang, 1995).

409. Smoller, L.A., 'Playing Cards and Popular Culture in Sixteenth-century Nuremberg', *SCJ*, **17**:2 (1986) pp. 183–214.

410. Snyder, A., 'Michael Sattler, Benedictine: Dennis Martin's Objections Reconsidered', *MQR*, **61**:3 (1987) pp. 262–79.

411. Snyder, A., 'Orality, Literacy, and the Study of Anabaptism', *MQR*, **65**:4 (1991) pp. 371–92.

412. Snyder, A., 'Word and Power in Reformation Zürich', *ARG* **81** (1990) pp. 263–85.

413. Soergal, P.M., 'The Image of Saints in the Bavarian Counter-Reformation', *Historian*, **53**:2 (1991) pp. 223–40.

414. Soergal, P.M., 'From Legends to Lies: Protestant Attacks on Catholic Miracles in Later Reformation Germany', *Fides et Historia*, **21**:2 (1989) pp. 21–9.

415. Soergal, P.M., 'Spiritual Medicine for Heretical Poison: The Propagandistic Uses of Legends in Counter-Reformation Bavaria', *HR*, **17**:2 (1991) pp. 125–49.

416. Solovyov, E., 'Martin Luther, Leader of the German Burgher Reformation', *Social Sciences*, **16**:1 (1985) pp. 106–26.

417. Sowards, J.K., 'Erasmus and the Education of Women', *SCJ*, **13**:4 (1982) pp. 77–89.

418. Spitz, L.W., *Luther and German Humanism* (Aldershot: Variorum, 1995).

419. Spitz, L.W. (ed.), *The Protestant Reformation* (Englewood Cliffs, N.J.: Prentice-Hall, 1969).

420. Stackhouse, M.L., 'Protestantism and Poverty', *This World*, **17** (1987) pp. 18–42.

421. Stadtwald, K., 'Pope Alexander III's Humiliation of Emperor Frederick Barbarossa as an Episode in Sixteenth-century German History', *SCJ*, **23**:4 (1992) pp. 755–68.

422. Stayer, J.M., 'Anabaptists and Future Anabaptists in the Peasants' War', *MQR*, **62**:2 (1988) pp. 99–139.

423. Stayer, J.M., 'Saxon Radicalism and Swiss Anabaptism: The Return of the Repressed', *MQR*, **67**:1 (1993) pp. 5–30.

424. Stayer, J.M., '"The Separatist Church of the Majority" – A Response to Charles Nienkirchen', *MQR*, **57**:1 (1983) pp. 151–55.

425. Stayer, J.M., 'Zwingli before Zürich: Humanist Reformer and Papal Partisan', *ARG*, **72** (1981) pp. 55–68.

426. Steinmetz, D.C., *Luther and Staupitz: An Essay in the Intellectual Origins of the Protestant Reformation* (Durham: Duke University Press, 1980).

427. Steinmetz, D.C., *Luther in Context* (Bloomington, Ind.: Indiana University Press, 1986).

428. Steinmetz, D.C., 'Calvin and the Absolute Power of God', *JMRS*, **18**:1 (1988) pp. 65–79.

429. Steinmetz, D.C., 'Hermeneutic and Old Testament Interpretation in Staupitz and the Young Martin Luther', *ARG*, **70** (1979) pp. 24–58.

430. Stephens, W.P., *The Theology of Huldrych Zwingli* (Oxford: Oxford University Press, 1986).

431. Steven, O., 'Luther and the Family', *Harvard Library Bulletin*, **32**: 1 (1984) pp. 36–53.

432. Stow, K.R., 'The Papacy and the Jews: Catholic Reformation and Beyond', *Jewish History*, **6**:1-2 (1992) pp. 257–79.

433. Stow, K.P., *Taxation, Community and State: The Jews and Fiscal Foundations of the Early Modern Papal State* (Stuttgart: Hiersemann, 1982).

434. Strauss, G., *Enacting the Reformation in Germany. Essays on Institution and Reception* (Aldershot: Variorum, 1995).

435. Strauss, G. (ed.), *Manifestations of Discontent in Germany on the Eve of the Reformation* (Bloomington, Ind.: Indiana University Press, 1971).

436. Strehle, S., 'Fides et Foedus: Wittenberg and Zürich in Conflict over the Gospel', *SCJ*, **23**:1 (1992) pp. 3–20.

437. Sutherland, N.M., 'The Assassination of François Duc de Guise, Feb. 1563', *Historical Journal*, **24**:2 (1981) pp. 279–95.

438. Sutherland, N.M., 'William of Orange and the Revolt of the Netherlands: A Missing Dimension', *ARG*, **74** (1983) pp. 201–31.

439. Thompson, B., *Renaissance and Reformation* (Grand Rapids, Mich.: Eerdmans, 1994).

440. Thompson, J.L., 'Patriarchs, Polygamy, and Private Resistance: John Calvin and Others on Breaking God's Rules', *SCJ*, **25**:1 (1994) pp. 3–28.

441. Thompson, W.D.J.G., *The Political Thought of Martin Luther* (N.Y.: Barnes and Noble, 1984).

442. Thomson, J.A.F., *Popes and Princes, 1417–1517: Politics and Policy in the Late Medieval Church* (Winchester, Mass.: Allen & Unwin, 1980).

443. Tilmans, K., *Historiography and Humanism in Holland in the Age of Erasmus: Aurelius and the Divisiekroniek of 1517* (Nieuwkoop: DeGraaf, 1992).

444. Tinsley, B.S., *History and Polemics in the French Reformation: Florimond de Raemond, Defender of the Church* (Cranbury, N.J.: Susquehanna University Press, 1992).

445. Tinsley, B.S., 'Pope Joan Polemic in Early Modern France: The Use and Disabuse of Myth', *SCJ*, **18**:3 (1987) pp. 381–97.

446. Todd, J.M., *Luther: A Life* (New York: Crossroad Books, 1982).

447. Tolley, B., *Pastors and Parishioners in Württemberg During the Late Reform, 1581–1621* (Stanford: Stanford University Press, 1994).

448. Tourn, G., *You Are My Witnesses* (New York: Friendship, 1989).

449. Tracy, J.D., 'Heresy Law and Centralization under Mary of Hungary: Conflict Between the Council of Holland and the Central Government over the Enforcement of Charles V's Placards', *ARG*, **73** (1982) pp. 284–308.

450. Tracy, J.D., 'A Premature Counter-Reformation: The Dirkist Government of Amsterdam, 1538–1578', *JRH*, **13**:2 (1984) pp. 150–67.

451. Tracy, J.D., 'Two Erasmuses, Two Luthers: Erasmus' Strategy in Defense of *De Libero Arbitrio*', *ARG*, **78** (1987) pp. 37–60.

452. Treesh, S. K., 'The Waldensian Recourse to Violence, 1350–1550', *CH*, **55**:3 (1986) pp. 294–306.

453. Trueman, C.R., *Luther's Legacy: Salvation and English Reformers, 1525–1556* (Oxford: Oxford University Press, 1994).

454. Tyson, J.R., 'A Protestant City Handbook from the Mid-sixteenth Century', *SCJ*, **24**:1 (1993) pp. 3–20.

455. Valone, J.S., *Huguenot Politics, 1601–1622* (Lampeter: E. Mellin, 1994).

456. Veen, H.T., van, 'Erasmus on the "Carmelite Taboo"', *BHR*, **43**:2 (1981) pp. 335–39.

457. Venema, C.P., 'Heinrich Bullinger's Correspondence on Calvin's Doctrine of Predestination 1551–1553', *SCJ*, **17**:4 (1986) pp. 435–50.

458. Waite, G.K., *David Joris and Dutch Anabaptism, 1524–1543* (Waterloo, Canada: Wilfrid Laurier University Press, 1990).

459. Waite, G.K., 'From Apocalyptic Crusaders to Anabaptist Terrorists: Anabaptist Radicalism after Münster, 1535–1544', *ARG*, **80** (1989) pp. 173–93.

460. Waite, G.K., 'The Dutch Nobility and Anabaptism, 1535–1545', *SCJ*, **23**:3 (1992) pp. 458–85.

461. Waite, G.K., 'Popular Drama and Radical Religion: The Chambers of Rhetoric and Anabaptism in the Netherlands', *MQR*, **65**:3 (1991) pp. 227–55.

462. Wandel, L.P., *Always Among Us: Images of the Poor in Zwingli's Zürich* (Cambridge: Cambridge University Press, 1990).

463. Wandel, L.P., 'Brothers and Neighbours: The Language of Community in Zwingli's Preaching', *Zwingliana*, **17**:5 (1988) pp. 361–74.

464. Wandel, L.P., 'Envisioning God: Image and Liturgy in Reformation Zürich', *SCJ*, **24**:1 (1993) pp. 21–40

465. Wandel, L.P., 'The Reform of Images: New Visualization of the Christian Community', *ARG*, **80** (1989) pp. 10–24.

466. Watanabe, M., 'Martin Luther's Relations with Italian Humanism', *Lutherjahrbuch*, **54** (1987) pp. 23–47.

467. Watt, J.R., 'Women and the Consistory in Calvin's Geneva', *SCJ*, **24**:2 (1993) pp. 429–39.

468. Wawrykow, J., 'John Calvin and Condign Merit', *ARG*, **83** (1992) pp. 73–90.

469. Wayne, J.W., 'Church, State, and Dissent: The Crisis of the Swiss Reformation, 1531–1536', *CH*, **57**:2 (1988) pp. 135–52.

470. Weiss, J.M., 'Hagiography by German Humanists, 1483–1516', *JMRS*, **15**:2 (1985) pp. 299–316.

471. Wells, B.J., 'Folly in the Heptameron of Marguerite of Navarre', *BHR*, **46**:1 (1984) pp. 71–82.
472. Wesseling, A., 'Dutch Proverbs and Ancient Sources in Erasmus' *Praise of Folly*', *RQ*, **47**:2 (1994) pp. 351–78.
473. White, R., 'Women and the Teaching Office according to Calvin', *Scottish Journal of Theology*, **47**:4 (1994) pp. 489–510.
474. Wicks, J., 'Roman Reactions to Luther: The First Year (1518)', *CHR*, **69**:4 (1983) pp. 521–63.
475. Wilcox, P., '"The Restoration of the Church" in Calvin's "Commentaries in Isaiah the Prophet"', *ARG*, **85** (1994) pp. 68–95.
476. Williams, G.H., 'Radicalization of the Reformed Church in Poland, 1547–1574: A Regional Variant of Sixteenth-century Anabaptism', *MQR*, **65**:1 (1991) pp. 54–68.
477. Wandel, L.P. (ed. and trans.), *The History of the Polish Reformation: Stanislaw Lubieniecki and Nine Related Documents* (Minneapolis, Minn.: Fortress, 1994).
478. Williams, R.L., 'Martin Cellarius and the Reformation in Strasbourg', *JEH*, **32**:4 (1981) pp. 477–97.
479. Wilson, B., 'Music and Merchants: The Laudesi Companies in Early Renaissance Florence', *R&R*, **13**:1 (1989) pp. 151–71.
480. Winkler, M.G., 'A Divided Heart: Idolatry and the Portraiture of Hans Asper', *SCJ*, **18**:2 (1987) pp. 213–30.
481. Wood, C.S., 'In Defense of Images: Two Local Rejoinders to the Zwinglian Iconoclasm', *SCJ*, **19**:1 (1988) pp. 25–44.
482. Wood, D. (ed.), 'Martyrs and Martyrologies', *Studies in Church History*, **30** (1993).
483. Wright, A.D., *The Counter-Reformation: Catholic Europe and the Non-Christian World* (Manchester: Manchester University Press, 1982).
484. Wright, D.F., *Martin Bucer: Reforming Church and Community* (Cambridge: Cambridge University Press, 1994).
485. Wright, W.J., 'Mainz versus Rome: Two Responses to Luther in the 1520s', *ARG*, **82** (1991) pp. 83–105.
486. Wright, W.J., 'Personality Profiles of Four Leaders of the German Lutheran Reformation', *Psychohistory Review*, **14**:1 (1985) pp. 12–22.
487. Xavier, F., *The Letters and Instructions of Francis Xavier*, trans. M.J. Costelloe (Buffalo, N.Y.: University of Toronto Press, 1979).
488. Ziegler, D. J. (ed.), *Great Debates of the Reformation* (New York: Random House, 1969).

Index